A-level Study Guide

Modern History

Hermione Baines

Richard Davies

Andrew Hall

Philip Nichols

Mark Seymour

Revision Express

Series Consultants: Geoff Black and Stuart Wall

Project Manager: Geoff Black

Pearson Education Limited

Edinburgh Gate, Harlow

Essex CM20 2JE, England

and Associated Companies throughout the world

www.pearsoned.co.uk

British Library Cataloguing in Publication Data

A catalogue entry for this title is available from the British Library.

ISBN 1-405-82363-1

First published 2000

10 9 8 7 6 5 4 3 2 1

09 08 07 06 05

Set by 35 in Univers, Cheltenham

Printed by Ashford Colour Press, Gosport, Hants

British history 1783–1868

This period of English history is remarkable for the developments that took place, politically, socially and economically. Alongside the development of Britain into a predominantly industrial society, there was movement towards a parliamentary democracy run by firmly established political parties. This section will also trace the growing influence of the working classes in society as well as looking at the role of leading personalities of the time.

Exam themes

→ Development of the political parties.

→ Reconstruction of England as a major power at home and abroad.

→ Demand for, and successes in, extending the right to vote.

→ Changing social and economic circumstances and government reaction to these.

→ The impact of individuals on the politics of their times: Pitt, Liverpool and Peel.

Topic checklist

○ AS ● A2

	AQA	EDEXCEL	OCR	WJEC
Pitt the Younger in peace and war		○	○	
Lord Liverpool and the Tories 1	○	○	○	○
Lord Liverpool and the Tories 2	○	●	○	○
The Great Reform Act 1832	○	○		○
Whig reforms 1833–1841	○	○	○●	○
Peel and the Conservative Party	○●	●	○	○
The Chartists	●	●	○	○
The economy, railways and free trade	●	○	○	
Social conditions and reforms 1	○	○●	●	○
Social conditions and reforms 2	●	○		○
Foreign policy 1815–1865	○	●	○●	○

Pitt the Younger in peace and war

"A mincepie ministry led by a schoolboy"

Charles James Fox

Pitt's time as prime minister (1783–1801 and 1804–1806) saw the beginning of a 'national revival' after the disastrous American War of Independence, the emergence of a cabinet-style government and a protracted war with France. The fact that Britain was able to sustain itself in this war was due in no small measure to Pitt's earlier handling of the British economy. During his first ministry Pitt also had to deal with the problem of Ireland, with which he had mixed success.

Pitt's rise to power ●●●

In 1783, King George III effectively dismissed the coalition government of **Charles Fox** and Lord North. He chose William Pitt, then only 23, to lead a new government. Pitt had the confidence of the King because:

→ He had expressed views on the constitution that matched the King's.
→ He was seen as a 'patriot'.
→ He was the son of a previous prime minister, Lord Chatham, who had governed well for George previously.

In order to administer the country effectively Pitt also had to gain the approval of Parliament. This would prove, initially, to be difficult as many MPs resented the way he had been appointed. He managed it by:

→ Using **government patronage** to buy support in the Commons.
→ Gaining the support of backbenchers because of his policies.
→ Financial support from the East India Company.
→ Mistakes by Fox leading to an unfavourable contrast between him and Pitt.

By the elections of 1784, Pitt was in a strong position. The results of the election showed that public opinion was on his side as well.

Pitt and the 'national revival' ●●●

When Pitt took over the country was in a bad way. The war with America and the inefficiency of previous governments had left Britain with a national debt of £239 million. Annual revenue was only £18 million, while interest payments were £9 million and normal annual expenditure was £20 million. Yet in 1793 Britain was in a position to finance wars against the French. Pitt improved national finances by:

→ Reducing government expenses through reorganization of the administration.
→ Reforming the collection of taxes and introducing the **Consolidated Fund**.
→ Improving the revenue from customs and excise and reducing smuggling.
→ Introducing ingenious new taxes such as a window tax.
→ A trade treaty with France to increase the national wealth.
→ Introducing a sinking fund to pay off the national debt (it had to be abandoned when war came).

The jargon

A *patriot* is someone who is seen to govern for the benefit of the country as a whole rather than for the benefit of a particular group or party.

Checkpoint 1

Why was it so important for Pitt to have the confidence of both the King and Parliament?

Checkpoint 2

How was Pitt able to reduce government spending?

Threats to Pitt's position

For Pitt to govern effectively he needed to retain the confidence of both the King and Parliament. There were occasions where he was in danger of losing this:

→ **The regency crisis 1788–1789**. In 1788, the King had a breakdown and was incapable of ruling. It was proposed that the Prince of Wales, a friend of Fox, act as Regent. Pitt's position was threatened. Pitt solved the problem by making the Queen the guardian of the King's interests.

→ **The question of reform.** Pitt faced demands from the Commons for parliamentary reform and the ending of slavery. Both of these threatened his relationship with the King. In 1785 Pitt introduced proposals for some minor changes. Faced with opposition, he backed down, not wishing to lose the King's confidence. In the same way, although personally in favour of ending slavery, he was not prepared to disrupt his political system by actively working for it.

Pitt and the French wars

After the French Revolution of 1789 the fear that it could spread to Britain led Pitt to introduce a number of repressive measures to curb the emergence of radicalism.

In 1793, the execution of the French king and the French invasion of the Austrian Netherlands, threatening British trade, forced Pitt to go to war. His original aim was to fight a traditional colonial war against France while supporting the anti-revolutionary movements within France. This proved to be unsuccessful.

The poor state of Britain's army after 1783 meant that Britain was restricted to a naval war. What Pitt could do was to finance coalitions of other countries to fight the land war. He paid for these by introducing **income tax** for the first time.

Pitt and Ireland

The problem of Ireland was brought into focus during the French wars. In 1798, rebellion by the Irish and an attempted French invasion of Ireland convinced Pitt to bring Ireland into the British system with the Act of Union 1800 ending the separate Irish parliament. This was only partially successful as the King refused to allow Catholic emancipation.

Exam questions   answers: pages 26–7

1   Why was Pitt the Younger able to retain power for so long? (45 min)

2   How far was Pitt responsible for the national revival after 1783? (45 min)

3   How successfully did Pitt deal with the threat posed by the French Revolution? (45 min)

Check the net

You'll find a brief biography of Pitt and links to associated subjects at www.spartacus.schoolnet.co.uk/Britain.html

Checkpoint 3

Why was Pitt unwilling to press for reforms during his ministry?

"For personal purity, disinterestedness and love of his country, I have never known his equal"

William Wilberforce

Checkpoint 4

How successful was Pitt in fighting the French?

Test yourself

When you have finished reading these pages, take a blank sheet of paper and make a list in two columns of Pitt's successes and his failures. Try to think why each could be considered a success or failure.

Examiner's secrets

The examiner is looking for you to show that you understand the measure of Pitt's success. You must evaluate this.

Lord Liverpool
and the Tories 1

> *"This breach within the nation was allowed to develop and widen because the ruling classes had been taught by the economists that the pursuit of self-interest was the key to national well-being"*
>
> Arthur Bryant

The period from 1815 to 1822 was marked by social and economic unrest, caused in part by the policies of the Tory government. The fear that this unrest could develop into a repeat of the French Revolution led the government to adopt a number of repressive measures.

Reasons for unrest in Britain

Economic problems

These had started before the end of the war with the emergence of **Luddism** from 1812 but reached a peak after the end of the French wars. They were caused by:

→ The ending of government contracts for arms and uniforms, causing high unemployment in manufacturing areas.
→ The introduction of new machinery as part of the ongoing Industrial Revolution. This also led to unemployment, particularly among certain craft groups such as the handloom weavers.
→ The sudden demobilization of thousands of soldiers and sailors, who flooded the labour market.

Government economic policies

Now that the war was over the Tory government wanted a return to the *laissez-faire* style of government. This resulted in:

→ A return to cash payments in 1819. During the war paper currency had been used. This was called in, resulting in a cash shortage and leading to a fall in prices and wages.
→ Income tax was scrapped and replaced by taxes on goods. While many of the poor had been exempt from paying income tax they now had to bear the burden of taxes on spending.
→ The Corn Laws 1815. During the war, when imports of corn from Europe had stopped, the price of corn rose, allowing landowners to charge high rents. They wanted to keep these 'war rents'. The Corn Laws were introduced, stopping the import of corn until it reached a very high price.

The radicals

The social and economic distress led to calls for changes to be made. Radical groups emerged, calling for parliamentary reform in the belief that a more representative parliament would bring in other reforms. The radicals were not a united group. They differed in their demands and opinions as to what actions to take. They ranged from the 'socialist' Spenceans to the moderate William Cobbett. They were also spread across the country. This lack of unity weakened them. They were easily infiltrated by Sidmouth's (home secretary) spies and *agents provocateurs*. This was in marked contrast to the strength and unity of purpose of the Tory government, which was determined to clamp down on unrest.

The jargon

Laissez-faire is the idea that the state should play as small a role as possible in the lives of the people.

Checkpoint 1

Why was there so much discontent in Britain in 1815?

The jargon

An *agent provocateur* is a police spy who deliberately incites trouble so that members of a group will be arrested.

Checkpoint 2

Why were the radicals unlikely to succeed in their aims?

Incidents of unrest

Included:

→ Machine breaking by the Luddites. In Nottingham the stocking knitters, in Yorkshire the wool croppers and in Lancashire the handloom weavers smashed the machines that were putting them out of work.
→ Spa Field riot 1816. A mass meeting of the Spenceans, infiltrated by an *agent provocateur*, attempted to storm the Tower of London and the Bank of England.
→ March of the blanketeers 1817. Handloom weavers attempted to march from Lancashire to present a petition to the Prince Regent. They were stopped by troops at Stockport.
→ Derbyshire rising 1817. An attempt to stir up Derbyshire and then march on London. It failed because the plotters had been infiltrated by a government spy.
→ Peterloo massacre 1819. A peaceful mass meeting in St Peter's Field, Manchester, addressed by **Henry 'Orator' Hunt** was broken up with a great deal of violence by the local magistrates and yeomanry. Eleven people were killed and 400 injured.
→ Cato Street conspiracy 1820. A plot by Arthur Thistlewood to murder the entire Cabinet. The plot failed when it was revealed by a government spy, and the leaders were hanged.

Government reaction

The government was determined not to allow the discontent to escalate into a revolution, so it passed a number of repressive measures in reaction to the incidents:

→ Made machine breaking punishable by transportation.
→ *Habeas corpus* temporarily suspended 1817. Allowed arrest and imprisonment without trial.
→ **Seditious Meetings Act 1817.** Outlawed meetings of over 50 people unless permission granted by a magistrate.
→ **The Six Acts 1819.** Gave magistrates powers to seize arms, outlawed most public meetings, accelerated the prosecution process, clamped down on newspapers evading stamp duty, allowed the seizure of seditious literature and banned paramilitary training.

As the economy picked up after 1819 the radical movement died down.

Exam questions
answers: page 27

1 How was Liverpool able to survive the radical challenges of 1815–1822? (45 min)

2 How did the Tory government respond to domestic problems between 1815 and 1822? (45 min)

3 How far was the Tory government's repressive reaction to the problem of the radicals between 1812 and 1822 justified? (45 min)

Check the net

You'll find plenty of information about this topic at www.spartacus.schoolnet.co.uk/Britain.html

Test yourself

After you have finished reading these pages, take a blank sheet of paper and make a list of the incidents and then link the government reaction to each of them.

Checkpoint 3

How many of these incidents really posed a threat to the government?

Checkpoint 4

What effect would these measures have had on the radicals?

"I defy you to agitate a fellow with a full stomach"

Richard Cobbett

Examiner's secrets

The examiner will be impressed if you can demonstrate background reading on this subject and an awareness of the different interpretations there have been regarding the events.

Lord Liverpool
and the Tories 2

From 1822 the nature of Liverpool's government changed. The decline of the radical movement as the economy improved allowed the government to make some reforms. The personnel of the government changed. Although Liverpool was to remain as prime minister until 1827, his government was made up of younger men, more open to new ideas. However, historians have discussed whether 1822 really marked a turning point in British politics or whether repression was being eased before 1822.

Changes in the Cabinet

The changes began after Castlereagh's suicide. Canning replaced him as leader of the House of Commons. Although Canning was a strict Tory, he was enough of a realist to know that if radicalism was not to resurface then some reforms had to be made in order to remove grievances. This marked a change from the old style of Toryism, where all reform was looked on with suspicion. He was supported in his ideas by Liverpool and by new members of the Cabinet: **Huskisson** at the Board of Trade, Robinson as chancellor of the exchequer and **Peel** at the Home Office. To an extent his idea worked. There was a temporary decline in interest in parliamentary reform. However, it should be noted that some of the 'Ultras' remained and the government was kept together only by the skill and persuasiveness of Liverpool, who avoided reforms to the Constitution. After Liverpool went the Tories soon split.

The jargon

Ultras were the right-wing Tories, who believed the system was perfect and so did not need to change.

'Liberal Tory' reforms

Free trade

Huskisson believed in free trade. He was influenced by the merchants and industrialists who argued that tariffs on imports encouraged other countries to put tariffs on British exports. As Britain was superior in manufacturing this worked to its disadvantage. Tariffs could not be scrapped completely as the government relied on them for revenue, especially since the ending of income tax, but they could be reduced.

→ 1822 Relaxation of the Navigation Acts.
→ 1823 Reciprocity of Duties Act. Duties on goods from certain countries would be reduced in return for similar concessions for British exports.
→ 1824 Duties on a number of articles were reduced.
→ 1825 Duties on an even wider range of goods were reduced considerably. Duties on all other goods fell from 50% to 20%.

All of this benefited British trade and reduced the cost of living for many people.

Checkpoint 1

What was the effect of these changes on the British economy?

Trade unions

Trade unions had been essentially illegal since the introduction of the Combination Acts in 1799. Workers had no protection.

In the period 1815–1822 the government seemed to have justification for this measure. The change of tone in the government coupled with the improving economy led to a feeling that the Combination Acts were actually harming industrial relations. Francis Place manipulated a parliamentary committee into reporting that the Acts should be scrapped, which they were in 1824. A wave of strikes almost saw them reinstated, but a compromise was reached in 1825 with certain restrictions placed on strikes. Trade unions were now legal.

Peel at the Home Office

A combination of pressure from humanitarians such as Elizabeth Fry and John Howard and the need for a more efficient system of law and order led Peel to make reforms:

→ 1823 The death penalty was abolished for the majority of crimes. This encouraged juries to convict more often.
→ 1823 Gaols Act. Gaolers to be paid salaries. Separate gaols for women. Some education for prisoners. Gaols to be inspected.
→ 1829 Metropolitan Police Force created. This drastically reduced crime in London and was soon copied by other cities.

The Tories after Liverpool

Liverpool resigned due to ill health in 1827. Canning became PM but died shortly afterwards. The post was filled temporarily by Goderich, but he resigned in 1828. In the end Wellington took over as he saw it was his duty to do so. His ministry was not particularly successful. The party split into the progressives, led by Huskisson, and the 'Ultras'. Wellington did not have Liverpool's skill in keeping the party united.

During this time there were two notable pieces of legislation:

→ Modification of the Corn Laws. Duties to be on a sliding scale.
→ Repeal of the Test and Corporation Acts. **Dissenters** were allowed to hold office and become MPs.

Catholic emancipation

Daniel O'Connell, backed by the Catholic Association, won an election in Clare. As a Catholic, he was not allowed to take his seat. If the situation were to be repeated across Ireland there would be chaos. Wellington realized that the time had come for Catholic emancipation. Reluctantly aided by Peel, he managed to get the Bill through Parliament. In doing so he split the Tory Party even more. The Ultras left the ministry, and a weakened Tory Party did badly in the 1830 election, having to give way to the Whigs.

Exam questions   answers: page 28

1   '1822 was a turning point in British politics'. Discuss. (45 min)

2   How liberal were the 'Liberal Tories'? (45 min)

3   Did Liverpool deserve the description 'arch mediocrity'? (45 min)

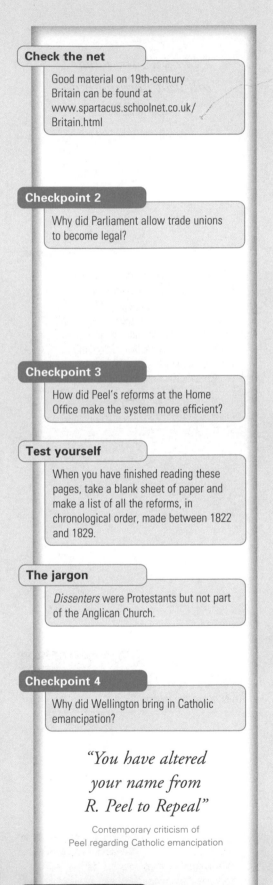

Check the net

Good material on 19th-century Britain can be found at www.spartacus.schoolnet.co.uk/Britain.html

Checkpoint 2

Why did Parliament allow trade unions to become legal?

Checkpoint 3

How did Peel's reforms at the Home Office make the system more efficient?

Test yourself

When you have finished reading these pages, take a blank sheet of paper and make a list of all the reforms, in chronological order, made between 1822 and 1829.

The jargon

Dissenters were Protestants but not part of the Anglican Church.

Checkpoint 4

Why did Wellington bring in Catholic emancipation?

"You have altered your name from R. Peel to Repeal"

Contemporary criticism of Peel regarding Catholic emancipation

Examiner's secrets

The examiner will be looking for you to show that you are aware of the scope of the reforms.

The Great Reform Act 1832

The Whig government that took power in 1830 realized that some parliamentary reform was badly needed to take into account the changes that had happened in Britain.

After a long fight with the Lords the Reform Act was passed. The actual changes were not as important as the fact that the principle of reform had been established.

The jargon

Rotten boroughs were those such as Old Sarum where there were few or no inhabitants but still elected MPs. *Pocket boroughs* were those where the voters were controlled by the landowner, who usually gave or sold the right to be MP. *Franchise* is the right to vote in elections.

The situation before 1830

The parliamentary system had developed in the Middle Ages and no longer reflected the true situation in Britain.

→ Each county elected two MPs and each borough, regardless of size, also elected two MPs. As these boroughs had been created hundreds of years ago, there was a situation where large, industrial towns such as Manchester had no MPs, while at the same time there were 'rotten' and 'pocket' boroughs. There was also a geographical imbalance. The south of England had 380 out of 588 seats and so landowners dominated Parliament.

→ The franchise was also full of anomalies. In the counties the vote went to owners of property worth £2 a year. In the boroughs there were a variety of qualifications: in some virtually all male householders could vote, in others hardly anyone was qualified to do so. This meant that most of the workers and some of the rising middle class had no vote.

Who was for and who was against reform?

The Whigs, led by **Earl Grey**, were for reform. They were supported by the industrialists and the emerging middle class. They realized that unless some reform was brought in from the top, Britain could face revolution from below. They had no intention of bringing in democracy. The franchise would be limited to 'responsible' (property-owning) members of society. Their arguments for change were:

Checkpoint 1

Why were the Whigs in favour of parliamentary reform?

→ An unreformed Parliament did not reflect the changed needs of the people.

→ An unreformed Parliament was open to corruption as MPs tried to recoup the expense of gaining a seat through patronage.

→ An unreformed Parliament would not act to make other vitally needed reforms.

The Tories were against reform. They saw it as an attack on the establishment that would ultimately destroy the institutions of the country. Their main spokesman was Peel, who argued:

Checkpoint 2

Why were the Tories against parliamentary reform?

→ The anomalies in the system actually made sure that all interests were represented somewhere.

→ Rotten and pocket boroughs were useful in allowing men of talent to enter Parliament.

→ Reform would make it difficult to carry out the government's business, as insufficient patronage would be available.

→ Once started, reform would be difficult to control.

How the Bill was passed ●●●

Grey instructed a committee to draw up a Bill that would satisfy demands for reform for good but would not go too far. In March 1831 **Russell** introduced the Bill. News had already leaked out and the government had already received hundreds of petitions demanding reform.

The details were:

→ Seats
  → 56 small boroughs lost both MPs. 30 others lost one MP.
  → 22 towns gained two MPs and 20 others gained one MP.
→ The franchise
  → In the counties the £2 qualification was retained, but tenants of property worth £50 a year could also vote.
  → In the boroughs the vote went to men who owned or rented property worth £10 a year. All the previous qualifications were abolished.
  → Voters now had to be registered.

The bill got through the Commons by one vote as the Tories had planned not to oppose the introduction but sabotage it at a later stage. This they did in the committee stage, delaying it. The King allowed the Whigs to hold a general election with reform as the main issue. The result was an overwhelming victory for the Whigs and reform. The Tories then blocked the Bill in the Lords. This led to riots and demonstrations throughout England. Finally, the threat by King William IV to create as many Whig peers as necessary forced the Lords to back down. In June 1832 the Bill became law.

The results of the Act ●●●

The Act increased the number of voters by about 50%, from about 440 000 to 652 000. However, the first elections after the Act saw a parliament similar to those before the Act. The south was still over-represented at the expense of the north.

Still only a fifth of the population could vote. There was still no secret ballot and still, except in the big towns, most elections were not contested. Parliament remained dominated by the land-owning classes.

Although the Great Reform Act had not brought in democracy it had paved the way for future reforms of Parliament. It did not, as Grey had hoped, end the demands for parliamentary reform. Too many people were disappointed with the provisions and it would not be long before workers demanded that they be allowed into the system.

Exam question   answer: pages 28–9

(a) Why was there a demand for parliamentary reform in 1830?

(b) How far did the government meet this demand? (1 hour)

Check the net

www.spartacus.schoolnet.co.uk/Britain.html is good for information on this topic.

Checkpoint 3

Why did the Tories leave it until the Bill reached the Lords to block it?

Test yourself

After you have read these pages, take a blank sheet of paper and write down the details of the Bill in one column and list the problems each part of the Bill was supposed to solve in another column.

"the most aristocratic measure that was ever proposed in Parliament"

Earl Grey, describing the Bill

Checkpoint 4

What changes were made to the electoral system by the Great Reform Act?

Examiner's secrets

This topic might well be a source-based question. You will impress the examiner if you can demonstrate a detailed knowledge of the leading personalities on both sides and their motives.

Whig reforms 1833–1841

The jargon

Evangelicals were a group, usually rich men, within the Church of England who thought it their duty to help the less well-off.
The *Benthamites* followed the writings of Jeremy Bentham. The best known Benthamite was Edwin Chadwick.

Checkpoint 1

Why was there such a need for change to the system of poor relief?

Checkpoint 2

How successful was the Act?

With their majority in the Commons, the Whigs could make reforms in other areas. They made use of **royal commissions**, which would investigate the problem thoroughly before legislation.

Reasons for reform

The Whigs as a party believed in religious and civil liberties and wanted to extend them. Groups such as the Nonconformists, Evangelicals, **Benthamites** and the middle classes, who wanted cheap and efficient government, also influenced the Whigs in their reforms. The theme of the main reforms was standardization and efficiency.

The Poor Law Amendment Act 1834

The problem:

➜ Poor relief was chaotic. Throughout the country there were various schemes for dealing with the poor. 10% of the population were classed as paupers, and poor relief was costing the country £7 million a year, equivalent to 10 shillings per head.
➜ The **Speenhamland system** was no longer working efficiently and was criticized for creating a dependency culture and depressing rural wages.

The Act:

➜ The royal commission, led by **Edwin Chadwick**, wanted to standardize the system and make it cheaper, as well as provide a free market for labour.
➜ The new system had two guiding principles: the workhouse test, where the able-bodied had to go into the workhouse or receive no relief at all, and 'less eligibility', where the conditions were made as miserable as possible to deter people from entering the workhouse.
➜ Poor Law Commission created. Outdoor relief was abolished. Parishes were grouped into unions to build workhouses (573) to be run by an elected board of guardians and managed by salaried officials.

Criticisms of the Act:

➜ It was more suited to agricultural areas, rather than northern industrial areas, where unemployment was cyclical. It proved impossible to abolish outdoor relief completely because of fierce resistance.
➜ Tories opposed it as it went against the concept of *laissez-faire*.
➜ Radicals said that it treated the symptoms of poverty but not the causes.

Results of the Act:

➜ There was no overnight revolution. It took time to change tradition and build workhouses. By 1854, 12% of the population were paupers. Only a quarter of those were in workhouses.
➜ The annual cost was cut by 1854 to £5.25 million or 6 shillings per head.

Municipal Corporations Act 1835

The problem:

→ Local government in the 170 chartered towns was chaotic. They were run by corporations, which tended to be undemocratic, self-perpetuating and with no public accountability. The corporations often neglected their duties. They were also notoriously corrupt.

A royal commission recommended changes in line with the Great Reform Act.

The Act:

→ The corporations were replaced by 179 municipal boroughs elected by all the ratepayers.
→ Borough accounts were to be audited.

Results of the Act:
Administrative rather than radical reform. Powers granted to new councils were too few, being supplemented by later Acts. Some new, large towns such as Manchester and Birmingham were not included as they were not incorporated. The middle class was still in power, so there were few moves to improve conditions.

Other reforms

Factory Act 1833:
After pressure from Evangelicals and radicals, a royal commission led by **Lord Shaftesbury** looked into the question of child labour.

→ The Act set a minimum age of 9 for child labour and limited the hours worked. Factory inspectors were appointed to police this.
→ The Act only applied to textile factories. There were only four inspectors. Until the registration of births the Act was not effective.

Abolition of Slavery Act 1833:
Pressure from **William Wilberforce** and religious groups led to Parliament abolishing slavery throughout the British Empire.
The Church:
The Whigs merely made a few changes to please the Nonconformists. The 1836 Marriage Act allowed them to marry in their own churches and legalized civil marriages as well as the registration of births and deaths. The Nonconformists were disappointed.

Why did the Whigs decline?

In 1832 the Whigs had a massive majority, but in 1841 the Conservatives won the general election easily because of:

→ Lack of reform after 1835 and weak control of national finances.
→ The Whigs' failure to deal successfully with Ireland.
→ Peel's Conservatives emerging as a real alternative to the Whigs.

Exam questions   answers: pages 29–30

1 How far were the Whig reforms after 1832 the result of pressure from influential groups? (45 min)

2 How radical were the Whig reforms after 1832? (45 min)

3 Did the people of England benefit from the Whig reforms after 1832? (45 min)

Check the net

You can find brief biographies of the Whig prime ministers at www.britannia.com/history

Checkpoint 3

Why did the Whigs want reform of local government?

Test yourself

When you have read these pages, take a blank sheet of paper and list the Whig reforms.
Try to remember as many details of the Acts as you can.

"The first great piece of legislation based upon scientific or economical principles"

Edwin Chadwick on the new Poor Law

The jargon

Nonconformists, previously known as Dissenters, were Protestants other than Anglicans.

Checkpoint 4

Why were the Nonconformists so disappointed with the Whig reforms?

Examiner's secrets

It is important for you to show that you not only know the details of the reforms but also the situation before and after.

13

Peel and the Conservative Party

Action point

Make your own notes on the words shown in bold in the text.

Checkpoint 1

What were the differences between the Tories and the Conservatives?

The jargon

Manchester School was a name given to a group of northern industrialists who were supporters of free trade.

Check the net

Excellent material on Britain from Peel onwards can be found at http://landow.stg.brown.edu/victorian/

Between 1834 and 1846 Robert Peel created and, according to some, destroyed a new party, the Conservatives. In that time he changed the emphasis of the old Tory Party and introduced far-reaching economic changes. Broadly speaking, Peel followed Pitt in placing the emphasis on good government rather than party gain. His legislation was determined by the needs of the situation rather than by party ideology. He was finally brought down by forces within the party who disliked the changes he had made, suggesting that some of the old Tory elements had survived.

Formation of the Conservatives

In an 1834 election address, the '**Tamworth Manifesto**', Peel, now leader of the Tories, stated that the party accepted the terms of the Great Reform Act and would not try to change them. He also stated that while the party would maintain (conserve) the existing institutions of the country, it would also review the situation and make changes as necessary. This acceptance of what had gone before, and the acceptance that reform might be needed over particular issues in future, gathered support from more than the traditional Tory supporters. In 1841 the Conservative Party, as it was then known, soundly defeated the Whigs.

Peel and the economy 1841–1846

The work of Peel's ministry was mainly to do with finance and the economy. Peel was influenced by the **Manchester School.** He believed that free trade was necessary for the economy to flourish and wanted to cut import duties. This would help the country, which was undergoing a slump in the economy. However, these duties were the government's chief source of income (80%). To add to his problem, the Whig government had been in deficit for the previous five years. Peel decided to cut duties to encourage consumption, which would, in the long run, increase government revenue. In the 1842 budget he:

→ Cut the duties on 300 articles, mainly raw materials.
→ Reintroduced income tax at 7d in the £ as a temporary measure to cover the fall in government revenue.
→ In his 1845 budget he persuaded Parliament to continue with income tax for a further three years.
→ Abolished completely the duties on 600 articles and reduced duties on many others.

His plan worked. There was a revival of the economy and a fall in unemployment. The '**Hungry Forties**' were over. Also, by 1844, the government was back in surplus. In that year, a rapid increase in the number of small banks able to issue paper money had led to an increase in speculation and a tendency for the smaller banks to collapse, making the currency unsound. A Bank Charter Act was introduced, which limited the banks that could issue notes and placed restrictions on them. Also, the Bank of England had to cover its note issue with reserves of gold. These measures succeeded in stabilizing the currency. Other Acts included:

→ Companies Act 1844 – this attempted to regulate the setting up of new companies in order to protect the investors.
→ Mines Act 1842 – forbade women, girls and boys under 15 working in the pits.
→ Factory Act 1844 – limited the hours to be worked by women and children in textile factories.

Opposition to Peel ●●●

Despite Peel's successes, he faced growing opposition from within his own party. This was led by '**Young England**,' who reacted against Peel's seemingly middle-class policies. They looked for an opportunity to get rid of him. One such opportunity was the **Maynooth Grant**. This was an attempt by Peel to relieve some of the troubles in Ireland by funding a Catholic training school. Although the measure got through Parliament with the support of the Whigs, many Conservatives voted against it, partly because they saw it as a betrayal of the Anglican Church, and partly as a reaction against Peel himself.

The repeal of the Corn Laws ●●●

The **Anti-Corn Law League**, founded in 1838 and led by **Cobden** and **Bright**, put forward convincing arguments for the ending of the Corn Laws. They argued that these laws were no longer needed for the protection of British agriculture and so had no justification. Ending them would reduce the cost of living and promote foreign trade to the benefit of Britain. The league was well organized and had the support of the majority of the country. The practical Peel became converted to the idea. The **Irish potato famine** of 1845 gave him the chance to do something to end the Corn Laws. In 1846, despite fierce opposition from many Conservatives, led by **Disraeli**, Peel, with the help of the Whigs, forced through a Bill that reduced duties on corn to a nominal one shilling. This was seen by the Conservatives as a complete betrayal of the party and, in voting against him on the next Bill he introduced, forced his resignation as PM. In doing so, they split the party between his supporters, the 'Peelites', and the rest. It would be over 20 years before the Conservatives would have a majority government again.

Checkpoint 2

How successful was Peel's economic policy?

The jargon

Young England was a small group of 'romantic Tories'. Mainly the sons of aristocrats, their chief spokesman was Disraeli.

Checkpoint 3

Why was there opposition to Peel from within his own party?

Test yourself

When you have finished reading these pages, take a blank sheet of paper and make a list, in chronological order, of the legislation during Peel's ministry. Then divide the legislation under the headings: economic, social and Ireland.

Checkpoint 4

Why did Peel become convinced of the need to end the Corn Laws?

"a Minister who thought more of the lives of the people than his own continuance in power"

Richard Cobden on Peel

Exam questions answers: pages 30–1

1 How far do you agree that Peel's reforms, 1841–1846, were more popular with the people than with his party? (45 min)

2 The creator of the Conservative Party or the destroyer of the Conservative Party – which better describes Peel? (45 min)

3 What was the importance of the financial and commercial policies of Robert Peel? (45 min)

Examiner's secrets

The examiner will be looking for you to show that you fully understand the changes made by Peel not only in the economy but also in the development of party politics.

The Chartists

The emergence of Chartism was an attempt to gain representation for the working man. The main period of Chartism was between 1836 and 1848. After that the movement declined. Historians have debated whether the movement was merely a 'knife-and-fork' issue or whether Chartism was a valid working-class movement.

Who were the Chartists and what did they want?

The jargon

A *knife-and-fork issue* was primarily about improving the living conditions of the workers.

The working classes were disappointed with the Great Reform Act. It had failed to give them parliamentary representation. It had also ended support from middle-class radicals. The workers were now on their own. In 1836 the **London Working Men's Association** was founded. In 1837 it drew up the People's Charter, designed to unite the radicals. It demanded:

→ Universal male suffrage – all men to have the vote.
→ Equal electoral districts – so all areas would be equally represented.
→ No property qualification for MPs – so workers could stand for Parliament.
→ Payment for MPs – so workers could support themselves if elected.
→ Secret ballot – to avoid bribery and intimidation during elections.
→ Annual parliaments – so bad governments would not last.

Checkpoint 1

Why did the radicals unite in support of this programme?

This programme proved very popular throughout Britain and over 150 Chartist Societies were formed. The prestigious Birmingham Political Union also joined in.

Chartist methods

Almost from the beginning there was a split in the Chartists. The London and Birmingham groups led by **William Lovett** and **Thomas Attwood** became known as 'moral-force' Chartists. They thought that moral persuasion was enough to get the charter accepted by Parliament.

The Chartists, mainly in the north, led by **Feargus O'Connor**, editor of the *Northern Star*, were known as 'physical-force' Chartists in that they were prepared to use violence to achieve their ends. Chartism can be seen to go in phases, often reflecting the state of the economy:

Checkpoint 2

Why was 'physical-force' Chartism stronger in the north of England?

Check the net

Good material on Chartism can be found at www.spartacus.schoolnet.co.uk/chartism.htm

→ In 1839, Attwood proposed that a petition be presented to Parliament asking for the terms of the charter to be adopted, and there should be a general strike (the 'Sacred Month') if the petition was rejected. A **National Chartist Convention** was set up to prepare the petition. It was here that the differences between the two brands of Chartism became apparent. Attwood and the Birmingham group walked out in protest at the views of the physical-force Chartists. The convention resolved to start a run on the banks, go on strike, boycott hostile newspapers and arm themselves. Both the Chartists and the authorities were preparing for conflict. The clash came in July 1839 at the Bull Ring in Birmingham. When Chartists defied a ban on meetings, the mayor brought in London police and troops to break up the meetings.

Parliament rejected the first petition (1.28 million signatures), saying that the charter amounted to a confiscation of private property. The reality of the situation hit the Chartists, and the Sacred Month was cancelled. 'Moral force' had proved to be useless.

→ The physical-force Chartists then organized the **Newport rising**, which proved to be a fiasco as the authorities were well prepared for the Chartists. Many leaders were gaoled.
→ 1840 to 1842 saw a dip in Chartist activities as many leaders were still in gaol and there was a revival in trade.
→ In 1842, a second convention met and drew up another petition (3.25 million signatures). Once again it was rejected overwhelmingly by Parliament and violence followed. There were serious riots in the industrial cities, and the 'plug plot' brought factories to a standstill.

Again there was a fall-off of support as Chartists were gaoled and there was a revival in trade.

→ 1847 saw another trade depression causing high unemployment. Encouraged by the revolution in France in 1848, the Chartists decided to try another petition. The authorities in London prepared to prevent any large rally presenting the petition, and the Chartists had to make do with a delegation of ten men. The petition, supposedly signed by 6 million, was shown to have a considerable number of forgeries and was rejected outright. Chartism faded away completely by 1852.

Why did Chartism fail? ●●●

To allow all of the points of the charter would have meant the establishment signing its own death warrant.

→ The split between the two branches weakened the movement. Physical-force Chartism alienated possible middle-class support.
→ The authorities were very well prepared. The new railways could move troops and police to where they were needed.
→ Very little support in Parliament.
→ Workers' support varied according to the state of the economy.
→ Chartist leaders became involved with other issues such as the **Chartist Land Scheme**, which diluted the impact of Chartism.

Exam questions   answers: pages 31–2

1   Was Chartism merely a 'knife-and-fork' issue or the first truly working-class movement? (45 min)

2   Account for the emergence and decline of Chartism. (45 min)

3   Why do historians differ in their views on Chartism? (45 min)

The jargon

Plug plot when strikers would knock the plugs out of factory boilers, so disabling the machinery.

Checkpoint 3

Why did the activities of the Chartists go in phases?

Test yourself

After you have read these pages, take a blank sheet of paper and draw a timeline from 1836 to 1848. Mark on it the main Chartist activities and the periods of trade revival.
Can you see any connection?

"They were united in the Charter itself but on little else"

Asa Briggs

Checkpoint 4

Why did Chartism decline after 1848?

Examiner's secrets

If the question is a document question, the examiner will be looking for your knowledge of the principal personalities involved and your knowledge of the different interpretations.

17

The economy, railways and free trade

Action point

Make your own notes on the words shown in bold in the text.

The jargon

The *domestic system* consisted of small-scale production, often done at home rather than in factories.

Checkpoint 1

Why did Britain have the first 'Industrial Revolution'?

Checkpoint 2

What were the driving forces behind the Industrial Revolution?

This period saw the culmination of the change from Britain being a predominantly agricultural country to Britain being an industrial country. This process was helped and accelerated by the rapid spread of the railway system and the moves towards free trade. The Great Exhibition of 1851 marked the high point of British industrial achievement.

The industrialization of Britain

By the 1780s the process of industrialization had already begun, particularly in the textile industry. A combination of factors had allowed this to happen:

→ A good supply of raw material, either within Britain – coal, iron, wool; or from the colonies – cotton.
→ A **growing population**, which provided not only an increased market for manufactured goods but a labour force as well.
→ Changes in agriculture, which allowed more people to live and work away from the land.
→ The **development of new machinery**, such as Crompton's mule, which changed the nature of production from the domestic system to the factory system, allowing a greater quantity of goods to be produced.
→ Improvements in iron production, which allowed the making of precision machinery.

In 1785 the first **Boulton and Watt** rotary steam engine was used in a factory. This was to revolutionize industrial production as factories no longer had to rely on water power. The French wars (1793–1815) stimulated production in industry, due to the demand for uniforms, blankets, arms and ammunition.

After the wars, textiles, particularly cotton, remained Britain's most important industry. By now the introduction of new machines such as the power loom had an impact on the workers. Skilled workers such as handloom weavers, wool croppers and stocking knitters lost their jobs, giving rise to an outbreak of machine breaking, or **Luddism.**

Improvements continued in all branches of industry. The Naysmith steam hammer improved the forging of iron. The Bessemer converter (1859) allowed high-quality steel to be produced in quantity. By 1851, Britain was the 'workshop of the world'. However, there would be an impact on working and living conditions.

The importance of the railways 1825–1868

In 1825, George Stephenson built the first modern railway, using locomotives between Stockton and Darlington. Although only built for carrying coal, it ushered in the age of the railways. Stephenson was appointed to build a railway from Liverpool to Manchester. It opened in December 1830 as a goods and passenger service, using Stephenson's *Rocket* as the locomotive. This proved very successful. By 1836–1837 there were 1 857 miles of railways. London was linked to most of the other major towns. 'Railway mania' began in earnest in 1846. The money to be made in building new railways was potentially very great. However, small railway companies did not last; they were swallowed up by the bigger companies, which controlled particular regions.

In the mid-1840s Parliament took a hand in the regulation of the railways. The 1844 Railway Act created the 'parliamentary train', which was an affordable regular service for workers, allowing them to live away from their place of work.

The effects of the railways were considerable:

→ Economically, they allowed the easier movement of both raw materials and finished goods. Branded goods could be sold anywhere in Britain, giving rise to the large national company.
→ Many new jobs were created by the railways, both directly – engine drivers, porters, etc., and indirectly – the building of the railways stimulated other industries such as iron and engineering. This added to the wealth of the country.
→ Socially, the effects were just as great. Railways brought the '**penny post**' and helped the spread of daily newspapers as opinion makers. Workers could now visit the seaside and resorts developed. They could also live in suburbs outside the cities.
→ Police and soldiers could be moved quickly around the country to put down disturbances such as Chartist demonstrations.

Free trade from Pitt to Gladstone ●●●

The idea behind free trade was that as Britain had an advantage over the rest of the world in producing manufactured goods, it would pay to allow in goods that it needed, food and raw materials, without tariffs and then sell British goods abroad. **Pitt** was the first PM to be convinced by the ideas of such as **Adam Smith** that free trade would benefit the country and lowered a number of duties to increase total consumption and therefore total government revenue. **Huskisson** at the Board of Trade after 1822 continued along the same lines, lowering duties on raw materials and negotiating trade agreements with other countries. **Peel** maintained this idea: working with **Gladstone**, he reduced or abolished duties on hundreds of articles in his budgets. The final end of 'protectionism' came in 1853 and 1860, when Gladstone, as chancellor of the exchequer, abolished virtually all duties. Britain remained a free-trade country until the early 20th century.

Examiner's secrets

Examiners are more concerned with the effects of the railways than with a description of their growth.

Test yourself

When you have finished reading these pages, take a blank sheet of paper and list the effects of the changes in the economy in two columns – positive and negative.

Checkpoint 3

What were the social results of the expansion of the railways?

Checkpoint 4

What were considered to be the benefits of free trade?

Examiner's secrets

This is a vast topic, and the examiner will be impressed if you can give factual examples to support each point you make.

Exam questions   answers: pages 32–3

1 (a) Why was Britain the first industrial nation?
   (b) What was the nature and scope of the changes in industrialization? (1 hour)

2 What was the economic and social impact of the spread of the railways between 1840 and 1868? (45 min)

3 Why did governments move towards a policy of free trade? (45 min)

Social conditions and reforms 1

The jargon

Laissez-faire is the idea that the government has little or no involvement in the way the economy is run, leaving it to individuals to manage their own affairs.

A combination of rapid economic changes and the government's attitude of *laissez-faire* meant that the industrialization process went ahead largely unregulated. This created problems as well as benefits for the people. Eventually and slowly the government was forced to take notice and bring in reforms.

The Luddites

Within the textile industry, certain trades were the province of highly skilled workers who could command high wages. These included the stocking knitters of Nottingham, the handloom weavers of Lancashire and the wool croppers of Yorkshire. Manufacturers introduced new machinery that could do these skilled jobs a lot more cheaply. The workers, as a result of the **Combination Acts**, had no legal way to protest against this so they retaliated by smashing the machines that were putting them out of work.

Machine breaking took place in 1811 in Nottingham and spread to Yorkshire in 1812. The workers grouped themselves into secret societies, supposedly under the leadership of a mythical General Ned Ludd. The government took these attacks seriously, making machine breaking punishable by transportation and sending 12 000 troops to the area. The violence escalated, culminating with the shooting of one wool master, William Horsefall.

A revival of trade in 1813 led to a fall in support for the Luddites. Many were arrested, and three were hanged for Horsefall's murder. The government had been forced to act because of the attacks on private property, though few lives had been lost.

Checkpoint 1

Why did the government act so severely against the Luddites?

The problem of poverty

Historians have long debated whether the condition of the people of England became worse or improved in the period up to 1841. Those who believe the former are known as 'pessimists'. The second group is known as 'optimists'.

The country went through **cycles of boom and depression** during this period. During times of depression there was widespread unemployment, particularly among unskilled workers. The economic changes also adversely affected particular groups of workers, as seen by the emergence of the Luddites.

The system of poor relief, which had evolved from the Elizabethan poor law, was not equipped to deal with this problem of cyclical unemployment. Nor was the system of **workhouse relief** introduced by the Whigs in 1834. The government's reluctance to become involved in the issue meant that Disraeli could talk of England being 'two nations'. It was not until the 1840s, when the government of the time, alarmed at the emergence of **Chartism**, began to take the matter of the condition of the people seriously. Until then it was considered that poverty was caused by the idleness of the poor.

Check the net

More information on these issues can be found at www.spartacus.schoolnet.co.uk/

Checkpoint 2

Why was the government reluctant to become involved in the problem of poverty?

Working conditions and reform

The change from domestic system to factory system had changed working conditions. Factory owners needed to gain the maximum amount of work from their employees if they were to compete successfully against other producers. This led to workers working long hours and cost cutting regarding safety. This was true for children as well as adult workers.

It was the **Evangelicals** who brought the matter to public attention and put pressure on governments to act. The reformers came up against fierce opposition:

➜ It was thought that regulation of industry went against the idea of *laissez-faire*. Owners were entitled to run factories as they saw fit.
➜ It was also thought that clear profit was made only in the last hour of work, so reducing hours would reduce profits.

There had been a couple of attempts to regulate the working conditions and hours for children earlier in the century. In 1802 'apprentices' (orphans) were given some protection, and in 1819 children working in cotton mills had their hours limited.

It was the publication in 1830 of the article 'Yorkshire Slavery' by the Evangelical **Richard Oastler,** in which he adversely compared the condition of child workers to that of plantation slaves, that really began the movement to improve factory conditions. Helped from within Parliament by **Sadler** and Lord Ashley (**Shaftesbury**), he pushed for reform, successfully initiating a series of Factory Acts:

➜ 1832 – a royal commission was set up to consider the problem. This led to the 1833 Factory Act – no children under 9 to work, between 9 and 13 maximum 8 hours a day, inspectorate created, limited to textile mills.
➜ 1842 Mines Act – no boys under 10 or females were to work underground, boys under 15 not to work machinery.
➜ 1844 Factory Act – reduced working day for children to 6½ hours, women not allowed to work nights, limited to textile mills.
➜ 1847 Factory Act – The 'Ten Hour Act' – restricted women and children under 18, in textiles, to a maximum of 10 hours.
➜ 1853 Factory Act – 10-hour day for all textile workers.
➜ 1867 Factory Act – extended provisions of Factory Acts to more than just the textile industry.

So by the end of the period the campaigners had beaten off the complaints of those in favour of *laissez-faire* and had established the right of the government to intervene in industry where necessary.

Checkpoint 3

What were the arguments both for and against factory regulation?

Test yourself

When you have finished these pages, take a blank sheet of paper and make a list, from memory, of the Factory Acts.

> *"Whilst the engine runs, the people must work – men, women and children are yoked together with iron and steam"*

J. P. Kay – a contemporary observer, 1832

Checkpoint 4

How did factory workers benefit from these Acts?

Examiner's secrets

The examiner will be impressed if you can show the views of at least two historians, one 'pessimist' and one 'optimist'.

Exam questions   answers: pages 33–4

1   Did the standard of living improve for workers between 1780 and 1867? (45 min)

2   What led to the regulation of children's working hours? Why was such a move opposed? (45 min)

Social conditions and reforms 2

Action point

Make your own notes on the words shown in bold in the text.

Checkpoint 1

Why did living conditions worsen in the 19th century?

The jargon

Death rate is the number of deaths per 1 000 of the population per year.

Checkpoint 2

Why did disease spread so rapidly?

Economic changes and population growth led to the rapid growth of large towns. The infrastructure of these was unable to cope with the demands of the population. The prevailing attitude of *laissez-faire* meant little was done about poor-quality water, sanitation and general living conditions. Only when the spread of disease threatened more than the poorest section of society was action taken.

Problems of public health

Housing
Many of the industrial towns were built rapidly. Housing for the workers tended to be near the factory. It was built either by the factory owner or by speculative builders. Either way costs were kept to the minimum. Houses were built back to back in terraces or in courts, where only 9 feet separated one row from the facing row. Ventilation was reduced and, near the factory chimneys, smog was common. The houses were usually just two rooms and normally very overcrowded. Kitchens were rare. Sanitary facilities were virtually non-existent. One privy would be shared by a number of households. A report in 1841 estimated that only half of Liverpool's working classes lived in acceptable accommodation. 22 000 of them lived in cellars, into which overflowing sewage from the privies often leaked.

Water supply
The two problems here were the lack of an adequate supply of water into the towns and the fact that the water was usually contaminated. Water was either supplied to the cities from wells, which could easily be contaminated by the overflowing sewage from the privies, or piped in from local rivers. The rivers themselves were contaminated, as it was into here that the sewage was drained. The water companies found it increasingly difficult to keep up with the growing demand for water, not only for domestic use but also for industrial use, let alone do anything about the quality. Generally, water was scarce for the working classes, so clothes were washed infrequently and baths taken rarely.

Disease
With the overcrowded and poor living conditions and the lack of clean water, disease was bound to spread. Water-borne diseases such as **cholera** and **typhoid** were common killers at this time. Other common diseases were diphtheria, **typhus** and scrofula (tuberculosis). These diseases spread rapidly among the poor. In some urban areas the death rate was 30, far higher than the national average. Poor living conditions provided ideal breeding grounds for bacteria to thrive. Cholera epidemics killed 50 000 in 1832 and 90 000 in 1848–1849. One problem facing those who wanted reform of public health was that the system of local government was inadequate to do anything about it.

Public health reforms ●●●

The driving force behind the reform of public health was **Edwin Chadwick.** His work with the Poor Law Commission had shown him the necessity of improving the conditions of the poor. He was helped in his work by the Whig **local government reforms**. The powers of the new councils allowed them to take action to improve the situation.

In 1842 he published a 'Report on the Sanitary Conditions of the Labouring Poor'. This showed a clear link between life expectancy and class and between poverty and disease. It was shown that disease was no respecter of class. Diseases started in the poverty-stricken areas could easily spread to the middle classes. Only government action and intervention could prevent this.

In 1844, following Chadwick's report, a Royal Commission on Health in the Towns was created. Its report confirmed Chadwick's views on the link between dirt, overcrowding and disease.

In 1848 The Public Health Act set up a General Board of Health with Chadwick and **Lord Ashley** as two of the commissioners. The board oversaw the setting up of local boards of health. These were compulsory in towns where the death rate was more than 23. Otherwise they were set up if 10% of ratepayers demanded it.

→ Despite the obvious need for reforms, the board was opposed by those who saw it as unnecessary government interference.

→ Chadwick himself was forced to resign in 1854. He had upset too many people and tried to impose too many new ideas.

In 1858 the General Board was wound up by the Local Government and Public Health Act. The initiative passed to local government. The weakness was that the legislation was permissive rather than compulsory. The amount of reform depended on the keenness of local ratepayers and how much they were prepared to spend. This varied considerably from town to town.

Other legislation:

→ 1832 Cholera Act – anti-cholera measures could be financed from rates.

→ 1840 Vaccination Act – free vaccination against smallpox, administered under the poor law system, but in 1853 compulsory vaccination against smallpox was rejected.

→ 1864 Contagious Diseases Act – designed to stop the spread of venereal disease among the armed forces.

→ 1866 Sanitary Act – increased powers for local government, and some element of uniformity and compulsion introduced.

Exam question answer: page 34

(a) Why was the problem of poor living conditions dealt with so slowly by governments in the period 1783–1868?

(b) How effectively did governments deal with the problem of poor living conditions in this period? (1 hour)

Check the net

For information on Chadwick see www.spartacus.schoolnet.co.uk/

Checkpoint 3

Why did public health reforms have to wait for the reform of local government?

Test yourself

When you have read these pages take a blank sheet of paper and list the public health reforms chronologically. Also mark on the dates of the main cholera epidemics. Can you see any connection?

Checkpoint 4

How effective were the public health reforms?

Examiner's secrets

Answer the question set. Avoid the temptation just to give a list of reforms or just to describe the dreadful conditions.

Foreign policy 1815–1865

> *"I called the new world into existence to redress the balance of the old"*
>
> Canning on the Monroe Doctrine

Checkpoint 1

What were British interests during this period?

Links

There is useful information on all of this in 'European history 1815–1894', pp. 77–97.

Checkpoint 2

Why did Britain withdraw from the congress system?

The jargon

The *Monroe doctrine* was a statement by the US president to the effect that the USA would not tolerate European attempts to gain colonies on the American continent.

Check the net

For Palmerston, look at http://landow.stg.brown.edu/victorian

During this period three men, Castlereagh, Canning and Palmerston, dominated British foreign policy. Despite having different styles, all three managed to safeguard British interests abroad.

Principles of British foreign policy

There were principles of policy common to all foreign secretaries, regardless of party:

→ Defence of Britain. As Britain was an island this meant controlling the seas and preventing any threat to its supremacy.
→ Defending trade routes and strategic areas. Britain's trade, particularly with India, was crucial to its prosperity. Certain strategic areas came under British control to ensure that the routes were protected.
→ Maintaining the balance of power in Europe. If one power dominated Europe, Britain's interests could be threatened and it might have to intervene directly.
→ Protection of British citizens and their interests abroad.
→ Liberal and national movements supported only if it suited Britain.

Castlereagh 1812–1822

Castlereagh's background as an aristocrat shaped his style as foreign secretary. He could talk with the nobility and monarchs of Europe, so preferred the personal diplomacy of the **congress system**.

→ At the **Congress of Vienna** in 1815, he advanced British interests by acquiring a number of strategic areas: Malta, the Cape of Good Hope, Trinidad and Mauritius. He also checked French expansion along the Channel coast by creating the kingdom of the Netherlands, an amalgamation of Holland and Belgium.
→ The congress system proved to be not always in the interests of Britain. The European monarchs wanted to use it for their own ends, crushing liberal and national movements. By the time of Castlereagh's death in 1822, Britain had left the system.

Canning 1822–1827

Canning had a different style to Castlereagh. Being a 'commoner', he would not have had the same success with personal diplomacy. He distrusted the congress system and kept Britain out of it.

→ He wanted to improve Britain's trade with South America. He prevented the former Spanish colonies being controlled by France by manoeuvring the USA into issuing the Monroe doctrine. Britain then recognized the independence of the former colonies.
→ He supported the new constitutional monarchy in Portugal by sending 4 000 troops to help against Spain.

He also maintained British interest in the 'Eastern question' by preventing Russia taking unilateral action to help the Greeks in their war of independence against the Turks. Canning worked with France and Russia to ensure Greece's independence from Russia.

Palmerston 1830–1841, 1846–1851 and 1856–1865

●●●

Palmerston claimed not to have any principles of foreign policy, but certain principles can be seen in his actions:

→ Working in concert with those powers that could be a threat and so limiting their actions.
→ Support for constitutional states as the natural allies of Britain.
→ Only intervening directly when naval power could be used.

With **Belgian independence** in 1830 he had to ensure that France did not dominate the new state. He did this by working with France against the Dutch and getting a guarantee of Belgian neutrality in 1839. He prevented French involvement in Spain by negotiating a quadruple alliance of Britain, Spain, Portugal and France.

→ The Straits Convention 1841 was another example of this diplomacy. By working with the major powers he prevented the collapse of Turkey and Russian domination of the eastern Mediterranean.
→ In the first Opium War, his 'gunboat diplomacy', bombarding Canton, gained Britain the island of Hong Kong.

Palmerston was less successful in his second term of office:

→ The Spanish marriages. He attempted to prevent the French King's son marrying a Spanish princess, fearing a possible union between the ruling houses of France and Spain. He failed.

Britain kept out of the revolutions that swept Europe in 1848, but Palmerston made it clear that he morally supported the liberal and national movements. This brought him into conflict with the Queen.

The Don Pacifico incident of 1850, where Palmerston used the navy to press the claims of a British citizen against the Greeks, won him a great deal of popularity with the British public. In 1851 he overstepped the mark by recognizing the new French government of Louis Napoleon without authority from the Queen or the Cabinet. He was forced to resign.

In his third term of office as PM, Palmerston successfully brought the **Crimean War** to an end with the Treaty of Paris (1856), forced China to open more ports to British trade and helped the cause of Italian unification in 1860. However, he was unsuccessful with Poland (1863) and Schleswig-Holstein (1864). Britain had to back down when it found itself isolated, but no major British interests were at stake.

Exam questions   answers: page 35

1   How effectively were British interests maintained in the period 1815–1841? (45 min)

2   What principles governed British foreign policy from 1830 to 1865? (45 min)

answers: page 35

The jargon

The *Eastern question* was Russia attempting to gain control over the Straits (entrance to the Black Sea) and have a way into the Mediterranean. Britain thought that this would be a threat to the route to India. *Gunboat diplomacy* was the use of force, usually naval, by Palmerston to chieve an objective.

Checkpoint 3

What issues were at stake with Belgium?

Test yourself

When you have finished reading these pages, take a blank sheet of paper and make a list of the main examples of policy in this period. Then link each one to one of the principles of foreign policy shown on the opposite page.

"Our interests are eternal, and those interests it is our duty to follow"

Palmerston

Checkpoint 4

Why was Palmerston unsuccessful with Poland and Schleswig-Holstein?

Examiner's secrets

The examiner is looking for you to define British interests and give examples of how they were dealt with. A long list is not needed!

Answers
British history 1783–1868

Checkpoints

1 At this time most MPs were independent; they were not part of a strict party organization as today. A government could not rely on getting legislation passed by reason of having a majority in the Commons. Legislation was passed or not according to its merits. If the MPs had confidence in the prime minister they were more likely to pass his legislation. In the same way the King's assent had to be given for a law to be passed. The King also had a great deal of influence and, as shown by the dismissal of the Fox–North ministry, could make or break an administration.

2 Pitt reduced government expenditure in a number of ways. He abolished sinecures (official jobs where the holder did no work but still received a fee). He reorganized the civil service and increased the workload of individuals, especially in the tax office. He also gradually changed the system of paying fees to officials to paying them salaries, which saved money in the long run.

3 As noted above, Pitt relied on the support of many independent MPs. Various items of reform appealed to only a minority of these MPs: most were against the reforms because they would adversely affect their own interests. Parliamentary reform they saw as an attack on property, likewise the abolition of slavery. In the same way the King, naturally conservative, was against reforms. Pitt saw his job as the administration of the country and if he lost the support of the King or the independents he would be unable to do his job. So, although in favour of reform personally, he was unwilling to press it at the expense of stability.

4 Initially, Pitt was not very successful. His strategy of fighting in the colonies did not, as he had expected, bring about the fall of France. His reliance on a naval strategy meant that Britain's trade routes were secure but it could not win the war. Half-hearted campaigns, such as Flanders, proved to be disastrous. During Pitt's time the bulk of the fighting was done by the continental allies, and they proved to be unreliable, constantly entering and leaving the coalitions when it suited them. It could be said that Pitt was partially successful as Britain was not defeated.

Exam questions

1 A useful start might be Fox's quote (see p.4), which implies that Pitt's ministry was not destined to last long. Then show that you understand that 15 years was a long time to be in power at that time. Show also that you realize that his ministry only came to an end in 1801 because he lost the support of the King over the question of Catholic emancipation.

Explain briefly how Pitt came to power and how a prime minister needed the confidence of both Parliament and the King to stay in power. Explain how and why Pitt had both for most of his ministry.

Explain what Pitt did to improve British finances and how this would have gained him support.

Go on to explain about the lack of any serious opposition to his ministry. Explain Fox's inability to muster enough support against Pitt. The Regency crisis could be looked at as an example of how Pitt managed to turn a potentially serious threat into something that gained him even more support.

Explain how Pitt dealt with contentious issues, such as parliamentary reform, in such a way as not to lose any major areas of support.

Conclusion. Pitt was able to retain power because of both the positive – the 'national revival' – and the negative – what he did not do – no unpopular legislation.

2 The question is asking you for an evaluation, so you must state this in your introduction. Briefly show that you understand that there was a 'national revival' by stating the position of the country in 1783 and then in 1793.

Explain what the problem was when Pitt came to power: loss of America, cost of the war to meet, government debt and other problems.

Explain what was done to remedy the problems. As you do, consider how much of the solution was due to Pitt himself and how much was due to other factors. For instance, some of the measures he took were already in the pipeline as a result of committees set up by previous administrations. You also need to consider the work of other individuals in Pitt's ministry.

Consider that government revenue would increase as the national wealth increased. This period saw increases in industrial output and trade due to the Industrial Revolution. Would the situation have improved anyway?

Conclusion. Again emphasize the difference in the situation between 1783 and 1793 and then state how much of the improvement was the result of Pitt's work.

3 Here you need to show that you understand that the threat from the French Revolution came in two forms. First was the threat that French radicalism might spread to Britain, causing revolution. Second, there was the threat of French expansion harming British trade or even Britain itself. The facts that Britain did not have a revolution nor was defeated by the French goes some way to answering the question.

Explain the threat in the domestic context. The growth of radicalism, shown by Tom Paine and the Corresponding Societies. Explain why they were considered a threat.

Explain what Pitt's government did to prevent the growth of radicalism: the repressive laws that were passed, such as the Treason and Sedition Acts and the Combination Acts.

Explain the threat posed to Britain by French expansion.

Explain how Pitt reacted to this threat. Here you will have to be more careful when you evaluate his success. You will need to be clear about his aims and how far they were achieved.

Conclusion. Pitt was perhaps more successful in dealing with the first part of the threat than the second part. Even so Britain was not invaded, nor was its trade seriously damaged during Pitt's ministry.

Lord Liverpool and the Tories 1

Checkpoints

1 The end of the wars with France brought an economic depression and high levels of unemployment. The fact that the Tory government acted just in its own interests by passing legislation such as the Corn Laws, which made matters worse, caused the discontent.

2 The radicals were split into so many different factions, all with different demands. Some were political, some merely economic. There was little in the way of cooperation or coordination between them. They had little support in Parliament. In contrast, the government had a unity of purpose and control of the military.

3 These incidents tended to be isolated. The march of the Blanketeers and Peterloo were peaceful and posed no threat at all. All of the incidents were easily dealt with by the military or the authorities.

4 The overall effect would have been to seriously limit the freedom of action by the radical groups. The measures were open to interpretation by the authorities and so could be used how they saw fit. It was difficult for the radicals to work around them and remain legal.

Exam questions

1 In your introduction, you need to assess the nature of the radical challenge. Was there really any challenge?

Explain the nature of radicalism after 1815; say what the groups wanted.

Explain the disadvantages faced by the radicals in achieving their aims.

Explain the advantages the government had over the radicals.

Give brief examples of incidents of unrest and show how the government dealt with these by introducing repressive measures.

Conclusion. The government held all the cards. The radical challenge was never really serious.

2 This is not just about the radical unrest. You must also show that you are aware of the economic problems as well.

Explain the economic problems after the end of the French wars: high unemployment and its causes.

Explain the government's economic policy of *laissez-faire* and go on to explain the measures it took: abolition of income tax, return to cash, the Corn Laws. Explain how these made matters worse for many people.

Explain the growth of radicalism as a reaction to the problems.

Explain the government's reaction to the radicals.

Conclusion. The Tory government reacted to the domestic problems in such a way as to protect what it saw to be the interests of those who generated the wealth and strength of the country, i.e. its own members.

3 This is an evaluation essay in two parts. You will need to consider whether the measures taken by the government really were repressive and then whether these measures were actually justified, given the circumstances.

Explain briefly the growth of radicalism and why the government was worried. Also evaluate just how serious the challenge actually was.

Explain in detail the government's measures to counter the radicals and then evaluate how repressive they actually were.

Conclusion. In reality, the challenge by the radicals was not serious, but the government thought it was, so it felt completely justified taking the measures it did.

Lord Liverpool and the Tories 2

Checkpoints

1 The effect was positive. Britain imported raw materials and other goods. By reducing the tariffs on these, British manufacturers could afford to reduce prices of their goods abroad and so sell more. Cheaper foreign goods were not in competition with British manufactured goods, so they were no threat at this time.

2 Parliament became convinced by the evidence that trade unions were not a revolutionary force, and indeed their existence would make it easier for employers to deal with the workers over questions such as pay.

3 With the death penalty not used so much, juries were more prepared to convict criminals, so making the prospect of crime less attractive, particularly now that the new police force was in existence.

4 Wellington saw it as his duty to bring in Catholic emancipation, against the wishes of his party, in order to avoid a possible civil war in Ireland. Without emancipation the Act of Union (1801) would have little strength.

Exam questions

1 It is important here to realize that the question is really asking for a value judgement. Traditionally, 1822 has been seen as a turning point because of the introduction of the 'Liberal Tories'. How true is this in reality?

It is easy to make a direct comparison between the government before 1822 and the government after 1822 and say that the first was reactionary and the second was liberal. Better answers will look at the different circumstances. Before 1822 the economic situation of Britain was not good, and this led to the radicals and the government's reaction to them. After 1822 the economy improved and the radicalism died down. The government did not need to be reactionary.

It is also important to look at the personnel in the government. Remember that Liverpool remained as PM until 1827. Also Peel, Wellington and even Canning were all true Tories.

Look at the reforms themselves and consider the motives behind them. Were they brought in to improve the condition of the people or were they brought in for more practical reasons? Note what was *not* reformed.

Conclude by deciding whether there were indeed enough changes to warrant the term 'turning point'.

2 This is very similar to the previous question but with a different emphasis. You should look more at the people involved and at what they did and conclude by examining the scope of the changes. You must make a value judgement. Were the changes in the way that the Tories governed really liberal or were they just practical solutions to practical problems? If you think that the changes were substantial and benefited the people of England, then you should say that they were 'liberal'. If you think that the changes merely served to improve the position of Tory supporters, then you need to say that they were not 'liberal'. Remember that there was no parliamentary reform during this period.

Examiner's secrets

Remember that in a question such as this, the examiner does not have any preconceived ideas. There is no absolute 'right' or 'wrong'. It is up to you to prove that you can justify whatever argument you put forward.

3 This question focuses on Liverpool as a personality. The key to answering this question is to demonstrate a thorough knowledge of the part played by Liverpool himself in the ministry from 1812 to 1827.

In your introduction, examine the phrase 'arch mediocrity'. State what you understand by the term. Then state whether you think that he deserves this description.

You should focus on his role as party leader. Remember that he had to keep together a fairly wide-ranging group of people to make the ministry work. At one extreme there were the 'Ultras', such as Sidmouth, while at the other extreme there were the 'Liberals', such as Canning and Huskisson.

Also look at his record as PM. He managed to steer Britain through the post-war problems and avoided revolution (even if the possibility did not really exist).

Also show that he was willing to be flexible. The changes to members of the government after 1822 show that.

Finally, state that he was PM for 15 years. Could he have been such an 'arch mediocrity' and held on to power for so long? He resigned through ill health. There were no serious challenges to his leadership. The Tory Party's troubles came after he resigned.

The Great Reform Act 1832

Checkpoints

1 The Whigs feared that unless some measure of reform was brought in then there could be revolution. Already they had seen revolutions in 1830 in France and Belgium. Closer to home the agricultural unrest known as the 'Swing Riots' had worried them. There was also the belief that if they gave the vote to the middle classes then they would vote Whig and keep them in office. They also had to appear different from the Tories.

2 The Tories really believed that the British Constitution was perfect and a model for all other countries. So any changes would be for the worse. They also saw reform as an attack on private property in that removing rotten and pocket boroughs was depriving the owners of an income.

3 The Tories feared a backlash of public opinion if they blocked the Bill too openly. They hoped to be more subtle and destroy it using parliamentary procedure and so not take the blame.

4 The changes were not as dramatic as the radicals had hoped for or the Tories had feared. The structure meant that the majority of men still could not vote and, without secret ballot, many were bribed or coerced into voting a particular way. The fact that landed interests still made up the bulk of the Commons shows that there was, in reality, little change.

Exam question

(a) To answer this part of the question you need to look at why parliamentary reform was needed and who wanted parliamentary reform.

You need to look at the system as it was before 1830 and highlight the problems. You need to explain that the system did not reflect the changes that had happened as a result of social and economic revolutions. Large industrial towns had no representation, while rotten and pocket boroughs did. Give some examples. The system favoured the south of England, while the population growth was highest in the north. You also need to show that there were a variety of voting qualifications in the boroughs, which meant that in some cases the rising middle classes were disenfranchised.

Having identified the problems, you now need to look at those areas of society that were looking for parliamentary reform. There were the Whigs themselves. Examine their motives. They wanted reform partly for idealistic motives and partly because it would gain support for their party. Remember also the fear of revolution. In 1830 there were revolutions in France and Belgium and also the Swing riots. There was a belief that if reform was not brought in then there would be an uncontrollable move towards revolution, which would damage the structure of society. The middle classes also wanted reform. They argued that it was they, particularly those in the northern industrial areas, who generated the real wealth of Britain. Yet they had little or no say in the running of the country, and the system as it stood favoured the landed interests, which were in decline. The workers also wanted reform. They had been convinced by the radicals that an unreformed Parliament would do nothing of any value to improve their conditions. Only a reformed Parliament would give them a real stake in society.

Sum up by showing that a cross-section of society wanted parliamentary reform. Demonstrate this by explaining the election results in favour of the Whigs and the riots in 1831 when it looked as if the Tories would block reform. Emphasize that the demand for reform was because it was long overdue and that various sections of society thought that they would benefit from reform.

(b) To start off this part of the question briefly examine what the Whigs wanted to do. Remember that they did not want to bring in democracy but merely extend the franchise to those they considered to be responsible. Think about their definition of 'responsible'.

Having looked at this, you can measure the changes brought about by the Great Reform Act against it and come to a conclusion as to whether or not the Whigs succeeded in their aims.

Then look at what the middle classes gained from the Act. Again measure this against what they had wanted. You should do the same for the workers. Did they gain what they wanted? You should attempt to put this in a wider context by looking at the reforms made by the Whigs after this.

Remember that the question asks for a value judgement as to how far the Whig government met the demands for reform. In your conclusion you need to look at the fact that shortly after the Act the Chartists were formed to fight for working-class representation. You also need to demonstrate that you understand that despite the Act being conceived of as final there were Reform Acts in 1867 and 1884 to rectify some of the deficiencies of the 1832 Act.

Whig reforms 1833–1841

Checkpoints

1 The system as it stood was inefficient. The Speenhamland system might have coped in agricultural areas but certainly did not in the cities. The last attempt at sorting out the situation had been the Elizabethan Poor Law, now completely out of date. The system around the country varied enormously and tended to be inefficient and costly. Also it was believed by some that a culture of dependence on poor relief was being created.

2 Certainly the Act was successful in cutting the cost of poor relief. However, the fact that it took so long to implement in northern areas and that its implementation was very patchy in Ireland leads to the conclusion that it was not completely successful.

3 The Whigs wanted the reform of local government for the following reasons. First, the existing system was considered too inefficient to deal with the pressing problems caused by social and economic changes. Second, there was a great deal of corruption in the corporations, and third, these corporations were traditional strongholds of the Tories. Reform should solve all three problems.

4 The Nonconformists had expected more from the Whigs, who had talked about extending civil and religious liberties. They had hoped for the disestablishment of the Anglican Church, which would have meant that the Anglican Church would no longer have been the official Church, putting their own branches of religion on an equal footing and ending the need to pay tithes to a Church that was not their own.

Exam questions

1 In your introduction you need to show that you understand that, apart from vague principles, the Whigs had no planned programme of reform after 1832.

Then look at the main reforms and consider which groups may have put pressure on the government to introduce them. The Poor Law Amendment Act came about as a result of demands from ratepayers, mainly the middle classes, for economy in government. The Municipal Corporations Act, again, can be linked to demands from the influential middle classes for cheap and efficient government at all levels. Factory reform and the abolition of slavery can be linked with the Evangelicals, while other Church reforms came about as a result of pressure from the Nonconformists.

Remember that, once again, this is an evaluation essay. You need to make up your own mind as to how many of the reforms came about because the Whigs had decided that change was needed and how many of the reforms happened because of pressure from various groups within society.

2 The key to this question is the term 'radical'. In your introduction you will need to define what you believe the term to mean. A good start is the idea of the reforms being far-reaching. You then need to state your estimate of how much change was brought about by the reforms.

In your answer, you need to show that you are aware of what was wanted from the reforms, what actually happened as a result of the reforms and the limitations of these reforms. An example of this might be the Factory Act of 1833. Consider what was wanted by the Evangelicals, what was actually done and the limitations of the Act: only applied to textile factories; only four factory inspectors; difficult to police. Do the same for the other reforms.

Conclude by measuring the situation in each case before the reforms against the situation after the reforms. How much real change had there been?

3 The idea behind this question is for you to demonstrate that you are aware that different groups in society benefited to different degrees as a result of the Whig reforms. In your introduction define what you mean by the 'people of England'. Show that the interests of the Whigs, the Nonconformists, the middle classes, the radicals, the workers and even the Tories were not always the same.

Then look at the major reforms after 1832 and, in each case, show which groups benefited from the reforms and which groups did not.

Conclude by deciding whether the majority of people were better-off as a result of the reforms or not.

Peel and the Conservative Party

Checkpoints

1 The Tories stood for maintaining the system as it was. They were against change, believing the system to be perfect. The Conservatives believed in conserving all that was good with the system but recognized that in order to save it they would need to address particular problems in the future and make changes where necessary.

2 Peel's policy was certainly successful in reviving trade and reducing unemployment considerably, incidentally causing the demise of Chartism. His commercial policy was slightly less successful: the Companies Act did not apply to railway companies, which were the worst offenders. The Bank Charter Act did stabilize the currency and led the way to the Bank of England becoming the chief note issuer for the country.

3 There was a growing feeling in the Conservative Party that Peel was putting the interests of the middle class industrialists before those of the party. The bulk of his legislation seemed to bear this out. The idea was reinforced by the fact that Peel was the son of a northern industrialist and spoke with a northern accent. Even before the repeal of the Corn Laws there were accusations of treason to the party.

4 Peel had already reduced tariffs and was swayed by the logical arguments of the Manchester School and the Anti-Corn Law League. These were that repeal would promote a two-way traffic with corn-producing countries and so would stimulate British exports, and that cheap food would relieve the poverty of the people of England. It would force British agriculture to become more efficient and would bring about better foreign relations through the mutual benefits of trade.

Exam questions

1 You could start your answer with Cobden's quote. Explain that Peel felt it necessary to put the interests of the country before the interests of the party and, at times, these interests clashed.

Start by looking at the interests of the Conservative Party. Essentially, it was still a party of landed interests. It was alarmed by the rise of the industrial middle classes. It was also solidly Anglican and feared Catholicism.

Now look at the situation that Peel faced when he assumed office. The government was in deficit, the economy was in a slump and there were problems in Ireland. Peel had to take action to remedy these problems. The measures he took were practical and did provide solutions. On the whole they brought benefits to the new industrialists and to the ordinary people of Britain. They seemed to be chipping away at the interests of the Conservatives. You will need to detail the steps he took, culminating in the repeal of the Corn Laws, and show how each affected the traditional interests of the Conservatives.

Conclude by showing how Peel's work improved the condition of the country but did not improve the interests of the Conservatives. Then you can agree with the statement.

2 Again you could begin with a quote: the one on p.14 would be a good place to start. Certainly, Peel has to bear some of the credit for changing the party from Tory to Conservative in 1834 and some of the blame for splitting it in 1846.

To answer this question properly you will need to do some reading about the organization of the party after 1832 in order to make a value judgement regarding the part played by Peel in the formation of the Conservatives. It is important that you show how, in the Tamworth Manifesto, he gave the party a new philosophy that was attractive to a wider section of society than the traditional Tory supporters, so perhaps allowing the Conservatives to assume power in 1841. However, many traditional Tories remained in the party and opposed Peel, even after the 1841 election victory.

You then need to consider how much of the blame for splitting the Party belongs to Peel. You will need to look at his actions as PM and how they alienated him from sections of the party. You should pay particular attention to the Maynooth grant and the repeal of the Corn Laws, the last straws as far as many of his party were concerned.

You should look at the growth of opposition within the party and decide whether it was justified or whether it was just a reaction against Peel's middle-class attitude and manner. You need to consider Disraeli and question his motives in opposing Peel.

Conclude by apportioning the credit for the formation of the Conservatives and then apportioning the blame for their destruction in 1846.

3 This is a more straightforward question than the previous two as it concentrates on Peel's policies rather than his position, though it still calls for a value judgement. You need to start the answer by looking at the state of British finances and the state of the economy when Peel assumed power in 1841. Remember that the first part of the decade has been labelled 'the Hungry Forties'. This should give you a place to start.

Look at the individual problems, such as government finances, unemployment, low level of exports, etc., then detail what Peel did about the problems. In each case try to evaluate the importance of these reforms in a wider context. For instance, the cutting of duties moved Britain towards complete free trade, while the Bank Charter Act led to the dominance of the Bank of England.

You then need to look at the success of each measure. Make a comparison between the state of the country in 1841 and the state of the country in 1846. Once again, put the overall success in a wider context by showing that Britain was financially and economically sound until the mid-1870s.

In your conclusion you must remember that the question asks about the importance of his policies, so do not just talk about his level of success but stress that his policies also led on to wider, far-reaching changes in the future. Give the example of Gladstone being inspired by Peel and continuing his economic policies.

The Chartists

Checkpoints

1 It was believed that only with working-class representation in Parliament could the grievances of the workers be dealt with. The charter was wide-ranging enough to cover the hopes of all the workers from skilled artisan to unemployed weaver.
2 It was in the north of England where economic slumps hit hardest. The workers in the north felt that any means was justified to gain a better standard of living. They were also influenced by the Leeds-based Feargus O'Connor and his newspaper, the *Northern Star*.
3 Intense Chartist activity tended to occur during periods of trade depressions. As these tended to be cyclical, so did Chartist activity.
4 After 1848 trade picked up, easing the situation. Also the reforms of Peel were beginning to work, further easing tension. Many of the workers now looked to the reviving trade union movement.

Exam questions

1 It is important in your introduction to define clearly the two terms and show that you understand that the question is asking whether you think that Chartism existed only because of the economic gains that the workers hoped to make or whether it was a real attempt to put the working class into Parliament.

The evidence for it being a 'knife-and-fork' issue is that Chartist activities and support for the Chartists tended to follow the economic cycles. In times of depression support was high, as seen by the first two petitions. When the economy improved support fell, as seen by the decline in Chartism after 1848. You could also show that some of the Chartists had economic aims, such as O'Connor with his land scheme.

The evidence for the second description is that the Chartists had virtually no middle-class support, unlike previous radicals. From this point of view, it was a truly working-class movement. The points of the charter were definitely political, designed to give workers a greater share in the government of the country. Chartism was also well organized at its peak. The conventions were funded by the movement itself. A network existed of Chartist reading rooms to help to educate the working class, so the Chartists can justifiably be called a movement.

In your conclusion you should come to a decision. Either you will decide that one of the descriptions is more realistic or you might decide that there is an element of truth in both of them. Consider the words of William

Cobbett talking about the earlier radicals: 'I defy you to agitate a man with a full stomach'.

2   This question again needs reference to the link between Chartism and the state of the economy.

You should start by explaining the disappointment of the workers with the terms of the Great Reform Act and their hatred of the new Poor Law. Also explain the belief that the workers' grievances would only be dealt with properly when there were workers in Parliament. Explain how the charter would bring this about. Then link the political with the economic. Explain the downturn of trade and the impact on the workers.

To account for the decline of Chartism you need to explain the reasons why the movement failed: wanting too much all at once, leadership split, authorities too powerful, no chance to influence Parliament, etc. Then show how disillusionment set in after the failure of the 1848 petition. Link this to the upturn in the economy and the effects of social reforms.

3   This is a question as much on historiography as the Chartists. In order to answer this you have to be aware of what historians have written about the Chartists.

First of all you need to explain that all historians have a particular point of view. In some cases they are openly political. For example, E. P. Thompson is left-wing in his attitude and will therefore have a different approach from other historians who are not as left-wing. He sees Chartism as a class movement, the working classes against the system, whereas J. M. Roberts sees Chartism as a temporary reaction to the economic problems of the times.

Historians will also differ in interpretations depending on when they are writing about Chartism. All historians are products of their own times. Thus Thompson was writing in the 1960s, when it was popular to take a socio-economic view of events, while more recent writers such as M. Falkus, writing in the 1980s, claim to take a more objective view and reject the idea of Chartism being 'socialist' or a working-class movement.

Historians will also differ according to whether they are economic or political historians. Economic historians will naturally look at the economic side of Chartism and stress the economic reasons for its emergence and decline. Political historians will emphasize the other side of the coin.

Differences will also occur depending on what aspect of Chartism is studied and from what perspective. What holds true for Chartism as a national movement does not necessarily hold true for Chartism as a local movement. For example, the handloom weavers in the north, who suffered continual poverty, were far more loyal to Chartism than the skilled artisans of the south, who suffered only in the depressions.

The economy, railways and free trade

Checkpoints

1   An accumulation of factors meant that Britain had the first Industrial Revolution. It had the resources and through its trade, the capital for investment. Its social system did not work against initiative, unlike on the continent. Its geographical position allowed it to trade all over the world.

2   The profit motive was the main driving force. There was money to be made from the expanding population if goods could be produced cheaply and quickly enough. The French wars acted as a further stimulus by accelerating the processes to help to fight the war.

3   At the time, railways were seen as a great leveller as both rich and poor could move around more. The country became 'smaller' with the use of the post, telegraph and the emergence of national newspapers.

4   It was believed that as Britain had no serious competition in industry it did not need a policy of protectionism. Once it became a net importer of food and raw materials it made sense for these products to come into the country cheaply. The standard of living would improve, while the balance of trade would remain in Britain's favour.

Exam questions

1   (a)   Start by explaining what was needed for the industrialization process and then show how Britain possessed these factors.

Capital came from the profits of Britain's trade, particularly with India, and the profits from the agricultural revolution. Markets came from the expanding population and the colonies. Britain had plenty of resources such as coal, iron, wool and cotton from the colonies. It had a system of navigable rivers, later, canals and, even later, railways to make internal transport easier. Its position as an island made international trade easy. The labour force was provided by the expanding population and by labourers dispossessed by the agricultural revolution. Management was often provided by Dissenters, who were by law barred from many other professions. The political climate was right as well: peace and stability and a social system that did not stifle enterprise.

Then make the point that other countries did not have all these factors together at the same time, and thus Britain was the first to become industrialized.

(b)   The nature of the changes was most importantly the change from the domestic system of small-scale production to the factory system of large-scale production. You should give an example of this: the textile industry is probably the best one. You should then look at the increasing interdependence of industries. The demand for machinery for textiles stimulated the iron industry and the engineering industry.

Discussing the scope of the changes requires a value judgement. Make a comparison of Britain at the beginning of the period in terms of output, location of industry, growth of towns, numbers employed in industry, etc., with the situation at the end of the period.

2 In your introduction, make a value judgement about the impact of the railways. You can then build on this in your answer.

Begin by looking at the economic effects. Speed of communication and ease of transport meant that raw materials and finished products could be moved easily, making the location of factories easier. Goods could be sold to a wider market. Agricultural produce could be sold to a wider market while it was still fresh, allowing specialization in different parts of the country. Businessmen could travel around more.

Look at the negative effects as well: the loss of jobs such as coachmen and others.

Social effects could include the growth of suburbs, the ease of communication with the penny post, the growth of newspapers as opinion formers, the idea of seaside excursions.

Again, look at the negative effects: police could be moved around easily to break up Chartist demonstrations; workers could be brought in by train to break strikes.

Conclude by making the same value judgement as in your introduction. If you have explained your points clearly this will hold true.

3 This is a fairly straightforward question but one that requires a detailed knowledge of the moves to free trade.

Begin by explaining the arguments of Adam Smith and later the Manchester School for free trade. Explain why governments were initially reluctant to abandon tariffs – source of revenue.

Then detail the actions taken by Pitt during his ministry, by Huskisson, by Peel and Gladstone and then finally by Gladstone. Put each into historical context. Show the circumstances under which each of them was able to move towards free trade.

Social conditions and reforms 1

Checkpoints

1 The government was alarmed by the Luddites for two reasons. First, their actions were an attack on private property, which was seen as sacred at the time. Second, the government feared that the ideas of the French Revolution would spread to Britain. As a result it treated the Luddites more harshly than was strictly necessary.

2 The government realized that any real solution to the problems of poverty would cost money. Governments were elected on the platform of *laissez-faire* and cheap government. Middle-class electors were unwilling to spend money on what they considered to be the idle poor, and the government reflected those views.

3 The arguments for regulation were that the government had a duty to protect its citizens even if it meant intervention. The conditions in which children worked were intolerable and had to be changed for humanitarian reasons. The employers would not do so, so the government would have to. The arguments against were that the factories were the private property of the owners and to intervene would go against the principle of *laissez-faire*.

4 Working hours were reduced gradually. By 1853, a 10-hour day was the norm. Less tired workers were less likely to injure themselves. Also machinery became guarded, again reducing the prospect of serious injury.

Exam questions

1 First define what you understand by the term 'standard of living'. Do you mean quality of life or the amount of goods that could be bought with wages?

You must also make it clear that you understand the distinction between long term and short term. In the short term the standard of living probably declined, particularly in the period 1815 to 1845, but in the long term, the period in the question, it probably improved.

Put one side of the argument first – the pessimists. These include E. Hobsbawm, who looked at the consumption of food and deduced that the standard of living fell during the period, and the Hammonds, who more emotively pointed out that the workers became 'slaves' to industrialization because of the new work discipline imposed on them.

Then put the case for the optimists such as R. Hartwell, who points out that workers may have spent less on food but they had a healthier diet. You can also point out that, certainly from the 1840s, the majority of workers also had a regular wage.

Bring in some evidence of your own – real wages rose faster than the cost of living, the death rate rose from 1800 but so did the birth rate, and total population grew rapidly. Unemployment was high during trade depressions and among the old crafts but was low after the 1840s, and most of the old crafts were no longer in existence.

Conclude by making up your own mind depending on how you defined the term 'standard of living' in your introduction

2 This question is really in two parts, and that is the way to deal with it after you have stated your case in the introduction.

First look at why regulation for children's working hours was introduced. You will need to look at early regulation such as the 1802 Act, which was in reaction to the treatment of orphans. Then look at the movements to regulate hours. Particularly look at Oastler and his 'Yorkshire Slavery', which brought the matter to the attention of the public. Also look at the evidence of the royal commission (even though it was rigged by Sadler). Also look at the '10 Hour Movement' and the idea that if the working hours of children were reduced this would naturally lead to a reduction in hours of adult workers.

Then finish off by detailing the provisions of the Acts that dealt with children's working hours.

To explain the opposition to regulation you need to look at different sectors. First, the factory owners, who claimed they could not run their factories without child labour. Children were useful for cleaning the machines and they were cheap to hire. The parents of the children themselves objected to regulation and often colluded with the factory owners to get around the regulations. Their children were an important source of income to the family, and shorter hours meant reduced income. Finally, a number of people, within Parliament, objected on the grounds that it was unnecessary government interference and a betrayal of the policy of *laissez-faire*. They argued that market forces would eventually solve the problem and that regulation was an artificial restriction on the competitiveness of British manufacturers.

Social conditions and reforms 2

Checkpoints

1 Living conditions worsened because of the rapid growth of urban areas. The new industrial cities could not provide adequate facilities quickly enough for their growing populations. Also, the lack of regulation meant that there was no check on what needed to be provided to ensure adequate living conditions.

2 Disease spread so rapidly because of the inadequate sewerage facilities and water supplies, which allowed cholera and typhoid to spread, and the overcrowding in the towns, which meant that other diseases spread rapidly. Also, the poor diet of the workers in the towns meant that they had little resistance to disease. Lack of medical knowledge aggravated the problem.

3 Before the 1835 Municipal Corporations Act, local governments were too corrupt or too inefficient to deal with the problem. After reform they at least represented the wishes of the ratepayers, and in some towns the ratepayers wanted positive action on public health and were prepared to pay for it.

4 The reforms were not as effective as they could have been. There was little in the way of compulsion and only some towns chose to make reforms. It tended to be the cholera scares that forced their hands. Further legislation in the 1870s was needed to deal with the problem.

Exam question

(a) Explain what the problems were: poor housing, over-crowding, poor water supplies, poor sewerage and the spread of disease.

Explain that the problems were seen very much as the province of local government and that until local government reform little could be done. Also explain the reluctance of the government to be seen as being too centralized and the opposition of the local authorities to what they saw as central government interference.

You must also show that the middle classes were more interested in cheap government than in public health.

You could then use the quote at the beginning of the spread to show why the situation began to change. Cholera was no respecter of class. The first cholera epidemic to hit England was in 1832, close to the time that the government began to take an interest in public health. Chadwick was convinced of the need for public health reforms. A combination of both slowly began to change attitudes. Even so it would be a slow process. Chadwick was forced to resign because it was felt by many that he was being too centralizing and too dictatorial in his actions at the General Board of Health. He was replaced by Dr Simon, who took things far more slowly in order to achieve reforms.

(b) This is an evaluation-type question, and you must say how effectively you think the government dealt with the problems.

Don't be tempted to list the problems again; you have already done that. Instead, make a comparison between the problems in 1830 and the problems in 1868. This will give you a good basis for your answer.

Look at what the government did in the period. Show that no real attention was paid to the problems until the 1830s and no real legislation was passed until the 1840s. Consider the motives of the government for each piece of legislation and then examine what it actually did. Explain that the last cholera epidemic hit Britain in 1865–1866 and link it to the legislation.

Make the point clearly that the bulk of the legislation was permissive rather than compulsory and that only some towns took full advantage of it.

Then sum up by saying what the government had achieved and what it had not achieved or even considered, such as housing. Make the point that it would be left to later governments to take further action to improve conditions.

Foreign policy 1815–1865

Checkpoints

1 Britain was mainly concerned with defence, trade and not becoming entangled in another war. So most of its interests concerned maritime issues and countries along its trade routes.

2 It was becoming increasingly obvious that the other major powers wanted to use the system as a means of crushing any liberal or national movement, as seen by the adoption of the Troppau Protocol. Matters that were of sole concern to the continental powers had no interest for Britain, and it did not want to become obliged to intervene to help the other powers.

3 Two issues were at stake here. If France gained influence or control over the new state of Belgium not only would it have an extended coastline from which to threaten Britain's defences but it might also open up the port of Antwerp as a rival to London as the centre of international trade.

4 He was unsuccessful in both cases as in neither could he bring British sea power to bear on the issue. Without a continental army he was unable to take effective action. In the case of Poland he was suspicious of the motives of France, the only ally. In the case of Schleswig-Holstein he was out-manoeuvred by Bismarck, the Prussian chancellor, and left without any continental allies.

Exam questions

1 This question covers the work of three foreign secretaries, Castlereagh, Canning and Palmerston. You need to show that you understand that there were differences in the style that they used but not necessarily in the way that they maintained the interests of Britain.

A possible approach is to look at Britain's fundamental interests and the basic principle of foreign policy and then give an example of how each of them was maintained.

For the defence of Britain you could explain Castlereagh at the Congress of Vienna preventing French expansion by creating the Kingdom of the Netherlands and Palmerston successfully dealing with the question of Belgium.

Defending trade routes could be dealt with by Castlereagh gaining valuable strategic areas at the Congress of Vienna, or Canning dealing with the Eastern question or Palmerston and the Straits Convention.

Maintaining the balance of power could be exemplified by Canning and the Monroe Doctrine and by Palmerston and the Quadruple Alliance.

The support of liberal and national movements is shown by Canning's support for the constitutional monarchy in Portugal.

Sum up by explaining that each of the foreign secretaries faced different problems and dealt with them in different ways, but they all put British interests first and managed to maintain them well. Britain in 1841 was just as powerful on the international scene as it had been at the end of the French wars in 1815.

2 Essentially this is a question about the foreign policy of Palmerston. Point out that for most of the period he dominated British foreign policy.

State that he himself claimed to have no principles regarding foreign policy, believing that each affair needed to be looked at individually. Also use the quote on p.25 and explain that Palmerston was bound by the fundamental principles of British foreign policy, as was any other foreign secretary. It is also useful to point out that certain 'principles', or at least similar ways of dealing with problems, can be discerned in his actions.

In the main part of your answer you need to show one of the principles of British foreign policy and how Palmerston dealt with it:

- Defence of Britain – Belgium.
- Trade routes – Straits Convention, Treaty of Paris.
- Balance of power in Europe – Quadruple Alliance; Spanish marriages (even though he was not totally successful it still shows adherence to a particular principle of policy).
- Looking after the interests of British citizens – First Opium War, the Don Pacifico incident and the Second Opium War.
- Support for liberal and national movements – the help given to Italian unification in 1860.

You also need to give examples of Palmerston's principle of working with potential enemies to neutralize them, or at least be able to control their actions. Examples would be working with France in the question of Belgium and working with Russia during the crisis that led up to the Straits Convention.

Although this is not a question on the success or otherwise of British foreign policy during the period, it would be useful to show how, with at least one instance, Palmerston maintained the principles of British foreign policy.

Examiner's secrets

The examiner is looking for an explanation of the principles rather than a list of everything Palmerston did. Pick one example for each principle and use it to support your answer.

This period of history saw the acceleration of the developments of the previous 90 years. Political parties developed into well-run machines. The Liberals rose and fell and the Labour Party became the second party in the country. Economically, Britain lost its place as 'workshop of the world' and went through a number of depressions from 1875 onwards. On the world stage, Britain gained and virtually lost an empire. However, it remained a world power despite going through two world wars.

Exam themes

→ Increasing difference between the political parties.

→ Changing focus of British foreign policy.

→ Social and political effects of the wars.

→ Extension of the franchise.

→ The question of Ireland.

→ The role of individuals on the politics of their times: Gladstone, Disraeli, Salisbury, Lloyd George, Chamberlain.

Topic checklist

○ AS ● A2

	AQA	EDEXCEL	OCR	WJEC
Gladstone 1868–1874	●	○	○●	○
Gladstone 1880–1893	●	○		○
Disraeli 1	●	○	○●	○
Disraeli 2	●	○	○	○
Parliamentary reform 1867–1918	●	○	●	●
Salisbury and the Conservatives	○	●	○	○●
Ireland 1868–1922	●	●	○●	○
The Liberals 1906–1914	○●	○	○	○
Votes for women	●	○	○	○●
Foreign policy 1902–1914	●	○	●	○
The rise of the Labour Party	●	●	○	●
Liberals in decline 1914–1922	○	●	○	○
Conservative inter-war domination	○	○	○	○●
Foreign policy in the 1930s	○	●	○●	○
The Labour government 1945–1951	●	●	○	●

Gladstone 1868–1874

The jargon

Nonconformists were Protestants who were not members of the Church of England.

Checkpoint 1

What was Gladstonian Liberalism?

Checkpoint 2

How did this legislation remove barriers to the progress of the individual?

Check the net

A good site for Gladstone is http://landow.stg.brown.edu/education

Gladstone was to dominate politics in the last quarter of the 19th century. He was to bring a new brand of politics to the country – Liberalism.

Gladstone's Liberal Party

The party that became known as the Liberals was not a single party but more a coalition of different groups. The one thing that united these groups was Gladstone. Within the party there were:

→ Whigs – the remains of the traditional aristocracy with their regard for individual freedoms.
→ Liberals – middle-class intellectuals who wanted religious and civil liberties but also well-run government.
→ Nonconformists – who wanted more religious liberties.
→ Radicals – who were on the left wing of the party and wanted to improve the condition of the working class.

Gladstone's high morality and his principles of removing barriers to advancement, efficient government and peace abroad united these groups. Without Gladstone and his 'crusades' they tended to fall apart.

Domestic policy 1868–1874

The Liberals, when they took power, had no specific policies apart from the disestablishment of the Church of Ireland. Their legislation came about as a result of particular problems:

→ Disestablishment of the Church of Ireland 1869 – the Anglican Church was no longer the official church in Ireland. Irish Catholics did not have to pay tithes to the Church. This was very successful in easing tension in Ireland.
→ Irish Land Act 1870 – provided a small degree of protection for Irish tenants and some review of rents. Not very successful.
→ **Forster's Education Act** 1870. Set up **Board Schools** to provide elementary education for all. The idea was to create an educated workforce and an educated electorate.
→ Civil Service reform 1870 – opened up entry to the Civil Service by competitive examinations rather than relying on patronage.
→ University Tests Act 1871 – non-Anglicans could be lecturers.
→ Trade Union Act 1871 – gave trade unions legal status and so protected their funds.
→ Criminal Law Amendment Act 1872 – removed the right of picketing.
→ Ballot Act 1872 – introduced secret ballot.
→ Army reforms 1870–1874 – ended purchase of commissions; officers were to be promoted on merit.
→ Licensing Act 1872 – magistrates to issue licences for pubs and limit opening hours.

The bulk of the legislation was completed by 1872, allowing Disraeli to describe the Liberals in 1874 as 'a range of exhausted volcanoes'.

Foreign policy

Gladstone wanted a moral foreign policy. This was a reaction against the aggressive policy of Palmerston. He wanted negotiation rather than force to be the way Britain conducted affairs.

→ He allowed the absorption of the Belgian railways by the French despite the fear that this might lead to French domination of Belgium.
→ Britain stayed neutral in the Franco-Prussian War of 1870.
→ Gladstone allowed Russia to cancel the **Black Sea clauses** of the Treaty of Paris and build naval bases in the Black Sea.
→ He agreed to go to arbitration over the **'Alabama' case** and to pay the USA £3¹/₄ million in compensation, describing the amount as 'dust in the balance' compared to the moral example Britain was setting.

The British public saw his policies as weak compared with Palmerston's, and he became very unpopular as a result.

Why did the Liberals lose the 1874 election?

Despite being elected with a huge majority in 1868, the Liberals lost resoundingly to the Conservatives in 1874. Gladstone's legislation had upset virtually every sector of the electorate.

→ The Irish Land Act upset the Whig landowners, who saw it as interference in private property.
→ The Education Act upset Nonconformists and the Anglicans by compromising on the position of Church-run schools.
→ The Civil Service reforms, the army reforms and the University Tests Act were seen as an attack on the establishment.
→ The Criminal Law Amendment Act was hated by the workers.
→ The Ballot Act was seen as an attack on the influence of the landowners.
→ The Licensing Act was hated by nearly all. Brewers and distillers transferred their allegiance and their money to the Conservatives.

Dissatisfaction with Gladstone's foreign policy was widespread. Gladstone had finished what he had set out to do, so took less interest in affairs, and after 1872 there was little legislation. The Liberals failed to address problems that still continued. The Conservative Party had been reorganized by **Gorst** at grass-roots level and was more efficient. Disraeli was making dynamic speeches in 1872 promising to build the British Empire and improve the 'condition of the people'.

Checkpoint 3

Why was Gladstone's foreign policy so unpopular?

Test yourself

When you have finished reading these pages, take a blank sheet of paper and make a list of the main legislation during the ministry. In a separate column, list which section of society would have been opposed to each piece of legislation.

"We have been borne down in a torrent of gin and beer"

Gladstone, 1874

Checkpoint 4

Why had the Liberals alienated so many people by 1874?

Exam questions   answers: page 68

1   How far do the domestic policies of Gladstone's first ministry (1868–1874) reflect the principles of Gladstonian Liberalism? (45 min)

2   Why, despite their majority in 1868, did the Liberals lose the 1874 election? (45 min)

Gladstone 1880–1893

The jargon

Beaconsfieldism was used to describe Disraeli's (Lord Beaconsfield) 'immoral and iniquitous' foreign and colonial policies.

Checkpoint 1

Why did the Liberals win the 1880 election?

Checkpoint 2

What was the importance of the 1884 Reform Act to the Liberals?

Gladstone's next ministries were not as successful as his first. He was forced into compromising his own principles of foreign policy, failed to solve the problem of Ireland, split his party and did little in the way of domestic reforms. However, he did pilot through some parliamentary reform.

The Midlothian campaign and the 1880 election

Gladstone considered that the special commission of the Liberals was foreign affairs. His political and moral zeal had been awakened by his disgust at Disraeli's foreign policy, which he termed 'Beaconsfieldism'. He resumed leadership of the Liberal Party and led a campaign against the Conservatives – the **Midlothian campaign.** He travelled widely around the country just before the election, putting the Liberal point of view. He was helped in the election campaign by the newly reorganized **Liberal Associations**. The old and ill Disraeli could not compete against him, and the Liberals were elected with a resounding majority.

Domestic policy and parliamentary reform

Gladstone had no positive programme for domestic reform, merely negative policies of retrenchment and low taxation. However, he had to deal with the radical wing of the party, led by **Joseph Chamberlain**, who were calling for various reforms. The only one of these reforms that the whole party would accept was parliamentary reform:

→ The 1884 Reform Bill would give the same rights of franchise to the counties as the 1867 Act had given to the towns. The electorate would rise from 3 million to 5 million. 60% of the adult male population could vote. This would break the power of the landowners.
→ The Bill passed through the Commons but was blocked by the Lords. The radicals stirred up the people in a 'peers against the people' campaign. 'Mend them or end them' was a popular slogan.

Gladstone and **Salisbury** negotiated the passage of the Bill and also redistributed a number of seats, effectively creating single-member constituencies. Small boroughs disappeared and cities were represented according to their importance.

Foreign and colonial affairs

Gladstone wanted to re-establish the idea of a concert of Europe, solving problems by negotiation. He failed, as **Bismarck** was determined to keep German political domination intact. Britain became increasingly isolated and lost influence in European affairs.

Despite his dislike of 'Beaconsfieldism', Gladstone followed a similar policy in colonial affairs. He had to deal with the problems left to him by Disraeli's government and had to protect British interests:

→ Afghanistan – he wanted to get Britain out of Afghanistan and break with Disraeli's 'forward policy'. He evacuated British troops in 1881, much to the disgust of the British public. When Russia threatened the border he was forced to threaten war, going against his principles.

→ Egypt – he had condemned Disraeli for buying Suez Canal shares, but the importance of the canal as a trade route meant that Britain was inextricably linked to Egypt. A nationalist revolt in 1881 threatened the canal and left Gladstone no choice but to occupy Egypt to protect British interests.

→ South Africa – the **Boer republics** wanted their independence back now the threat from the Zulus was gone. The First Boer War ended in British defeat in 1881, and Gladstone was forced to grant independence under British suzerainty. The 1884 London Convention saw more rights granted to the Boers. The public saw this as appeasement.

→ The Sudan – when Sudan came under attack from the Mahdi, Gladstone ordered **General Gordon** in to evacuate the Egyptians. Gordon disobeyed orders, tried to hold Khartoum and came under siege. By the time Gladstone agreed to send a relieving force it was too late. Gordon was dead. To compound his unpopularity, Gladstone withdrew all British troops in 1885.

Gladstone's policies had alienated the other European powers, alienated the public and gone against his own principles.

Gladstone and Ireland

In reaction to the obstructionist tactics of Parnell's Irish MPs, and the growing violence in Ireland, Gladstone passed the 1881 Irish Land Act, designed to improve on the 1870 Act and give Irish tenant farmers the Three Fs. It did not cover those in arrears, and Gladstone had to bring in a separate law (1882) after the 'Kilmainham Treaty' with **Parnell**.

The **Phoenix Park murders** alienated public opinion, ruining any chance of immediate progress. By 1886, Gladstone had become convinced of the need to give **Home Rule** to Ireland. His conversion was leaked and upset his own party. Chamberlain organized opposition to the Bill when it was introduced in April, and 93 Liberal Unionists joined the Conservatives to defeat it. A general election was held, with Home Rule the main issue. The Liberals were soundly defeated.

Gladstone's alliance with Parnell came to an end in 1889 as a result of the **O'Shea divorce case**. In 1893, during his fourth ministry, Gladstone introduced a second Home Rule Bill. After eight months it passed through the Commons but was rejected by the Lords. Gladstone resigned soon afterwards.

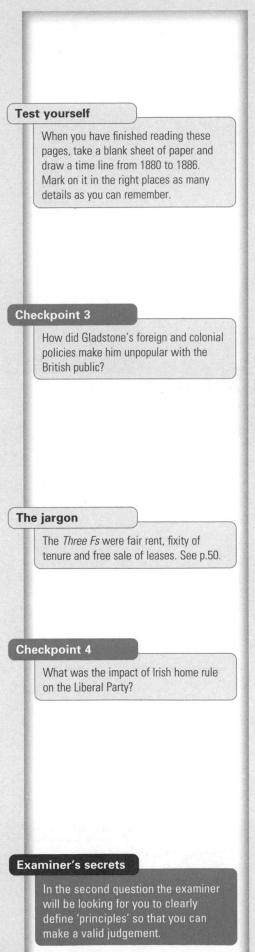

Test yourself

When you have finished reading these pages, take a blank sheet of paper and draw a time line from 1880 to 1886. Mark on it in the right places as many details as you can remember.

Checkpoint 3

How did Gladstone's foreign and colonial policies make him unpopular with the British public?

The jargon

The *Three Fs* were fair rent, fixity of tenure and free sale of leases. See p.50.

Checkpoint 4

What was the impact of Irish home rule on the Liberal Party?

Examiner's secrets

In the second question the examiner will be looking for you to clearly define 'principles' so that you can make a valid judgement.

Exam questions   answers: page 69

1   Why did Gladstone fail in his 'mission to pacify Ireland'? (45 min)

2   How far was Gladstone able to maintain the principles outlined in the Midlothian campaign during his second ministry? (45 min)

Disraeli 1

"I have climbed to the top of the greasy pole"

Disraeli, on becoming PM in 1868

After being involved in bringing down Peel in 1846, Disraeli had to reinvent the Conservative Party. He did this by accepting the policy of free trade and portraying the party as one-nation politicians. In his domestic policy he was to play to the working class and try to create the 'Tory working man'. Historians have seen him as either an unprincipled opportunist or a shrewd politician.

Disraeli's background 1832–1867

By the time that Disraeli attempted to enter Parliament in 1832 he was already a moderately successful novelist. Although a natural Tory, he stood as a radical to take advantage of the tide of opinion against the Tories. After three more attempts at being a radical, hoping for help from the Whigs, he stood as a Tory. It was not until 1837 that he was elected as a Tory. This chopping and changing gave him an early reputation for opportunism that he never quite lost.

Bitterly disappointed that **Peel** did not offer him a post in the 1841 government, he gravitated to Peel's opposition within the Conservatives and became the spokesman for '**Young England**'. As such he was instrumental in bringing an end to the ministry with his opposition to the Maynooth grant and the repeal of the **Corn Laws**.

→ With Peel gone, Disraeli became the driving force of the Conservatives in the Commons, formulating the philosophy that would later become policy.

→ In 1852 **Derby** formed a government with Disraeli as chancellor of the exchequer. His budget of 1852 was a collection of expedients with no coherence. It was successfully attacked by Gladstone, and the government was brought down. Disraeli, now in opposition again, began the convention of opposing anything promoted by the government of the day, regardless of its merits.

→ His second spell of office was in the minority Derby government of 1858, where he was given the responsibility of piloting a parliamentary Reform Bill through the Commons. A combination of radicals and Whigs defeated the bill, and Derby resigned.

The failure of Gladstone's Reform Bill of 1866 allowed the Conservatives back into office. Disraeli, under pressure from the Queen, introduced his own Reform Bill in 1867. Although he claimed that he had 'dished the Whigs' by doing this, in reality the Bill was much more radical than envisaged, due to Liberal amendments.

In February 1868 Derby resigned, and Disraeli became prime minister. His ministry lasted until the defeat of the Conservatives in December. In 1872, while in opposition, he made key speeches in Manchester and the Crystal Palace, promising social reform and to maintain Britain's imperial interests. These contributed to the Conservatives' election victory in 1874, when Disraeli once again became prime minister.

Action point

Make your own notes on the words shown in bold in the text.

Checkpoint 1

Why was Disraeli considered to be an opportunist?

Check the net

Information on Disraeli and links can be found at www.skittler.demon.co.uk/victorians/disraeli.htm

Checkpoint 2

Why were the speeches of 1872 so important?

Domestic policy 1874–1880 ●●●

Disraeli's justification for the social reforms carried out during his ministry was that he was implementing the 'aristocratic settlement'. In reality, despite the speeches of 1872, he can claim little personal credit for the reforms. Some of them were already in the pipeline from the previous government. Others were the work of his Cabinet, notably **Richard Cross**. It has been suggested that Disraeli was too concerned with his flamboyant foreign and imperial policy to concentrate on the mundane details needed for domestic legislation.

→ Public Health Act 1875 – this consolidated all previous complicated health legislation and introduced a measure of compulsion. It laid down a 'national sanitary minimum'. Medical officers and local authorities had responsibilities ranging from sewers and drainage to controlling cellar dwelling. The Act has been called 'the beginning of the modern code of public health law'.

→ Sale of Food and Drugs Act 1875 – stopped food adulteration.

→ Artisans Dwellings Act 1875 – this gave local authorities the power to demolish buildings thought unfit for habitation. There was no compulsion to do so and only a few authorities, notably Birmingham under **Joseph Chamberlain**'s leadership, did so.

→ Conspiracy and Protection of Property Act 1875 – made peaceful picketing by trade unions legal once again.

→ Employer and Workman Act 1876 – made employer and employee equal in law in matters of breach of contract.

→ Climbing Boys Act 1875 – illegal to send boys up chimneys to sweep them.

→ Merchant Shipping Act 1876 – after pressure from Samuel Plimsoll to reduce the loads on merchant ships to make them safer, the Plimsoll line was introduced to mark safe loads. Until 1890 ship owners could draw it where they liked.

→ Sandon's Education Act 1876 – school boards were given the power to compel attendance if they wished, but there was no compulsion to do so.

→ Factory Act 1878 – consolidated all previous legislation on factory conditions. It applied to all firms with over 20 workers.

The impact of all this legislation is not easy to assess. Much of it was permissive rather than compulsory, and it depended on the willingness of local authorities as to how effectively it was used. The desire for low taxation meant that little central government money was available.

The jargon

Aristocratic settlement was the idea that the aristocracy was best placed to look after the interests of the workers. As it already had power it had no need to legislate for more, unlike the middle classes, who were natural enemies of the workers.

Checkpoint 3

Why was the Public Health Act needed?

Test yourself

When you have finished reading these pages, take a blank sheet of paper and make a list of Disraeli's domestic legislation. Put the Acts in groups according to the problems they dealt with.

"The Conservative Party has done more for the working man in five years than the Liberals have done in fifty"

Trade Union Leader, 1879

Checkpoint 4

What did Disraeli do for the workers?

Examiner's secrets

First and foremost, the examiner is looking for an understanding of Disraeli's thinking about the issues that confronted him.

Exam questions

answers: pages 69–70

1 How and why did Disraeli change from a Tory to a Tory democrat? (45 min)

2 With reference to the domestic policies 1874–1880, define Disraelian Conservatism. (1 hour)

Disraeli 2

The jargon

The *Eastern question* was the fear that Russia would gain control of the entrance from the Black Sea to the Mediterranean and threaten the route to India.

Checkpoint 1

What had Disraeli gained at the Congress of Berlin?

Check the net

Good material for this topic can be found at www.spartacus.schoolnet.co.uk/Britain.html

Checkpoint 2

What were the benefits of half ownership of the Suez Canal?

Disraeli's main interest was the world stage. In foreign affairs he wanted Britain to be a major player in Europe. In colonial affairs he is credited with the revival of imperialism in Britain. His actions have been summed up as 'forward policy'. In fact, he was to leave many problems for Gladstone to deal with.

Foreign policy – the Eastern question

Disraeli wanted to reassert Britain's superiority in world affairs after Gladstone's disasters, to split the Eastern European powers and to build a friendship with France. Also, he would not underestimate **Bismarck**.

➡ His main foray into European affairs was the Eastern question. Turkey was decaying even faster, creating a power vacuum in the Balkans. In 1875 the peoples of the Balkans rebelled against the Turks. Disraeli feared that Russia would become involved and threaten British interests in the eastern Mediterranean.

➡ He offered full diplomatic help to the Turks. However, his freedom of action was limited by Gladstone, who published '**The Bulgarian Atrocities**' detailing the massacre of Bulgarians and turning public opinion against the Turks. Russia defeated the Turks and forced on them the Treaty of San Stefano 1878. An independent 'Big Bulgaria' was created with a Mediterranean coastline. Disraeli feared that Bulgaria would be a Russian satellite and that the coast would give Russia access to the Mediterranean, threatening British interests.

➡ Disraeli enlisted the aid of Austria and forced Russia, by threat of war, to agree to the **Congress of Berlin 1878**.

It was agreed that Bulgaria would be split into three and lose its Mediterranean coast. Britain received Cyprus in return for allowing Russia to extend its border a little way into Turkey.

As far as Disraeli was concerned the congress was a personal victory for him. He had returned from the congress bringing 'peace with honour'. In fact, all the details had been agreed before the congress.

Imperial policy

Disraeli's imperialism was affected by his view of Britain as a guardian of justice, peace and honour. He had no specific plans for pursuing imperialism but made the best use of opportunities as they arose.

➡ Suez Canal shares 1875. The **Suez Canal** had been built as a Franco-Egyptian project in 1869. It soon proved to be essential to British trade with India (80% of ships using the canal were British). The Egyptian ruler wanted to sell his shares. Disraeli did not want the canal to fall completely into French hands, so negotiated a loan of £4 million to buy them for Britain. Despite criticism from Gladstone, who claimed that Disraeli wanted to create a North African empire, the purchase proved to be very profitable and strategically important.

→ Royal Titles Act 1876. Queen Victoria was given the title of Empress of India. This was the start of the personal link between the British monarch and the colonies.

→ South Africa. Britain had recognized the independence of the Boer republics. However, the Transvaal was vital in protecting British South Africa from the advancing Zulus, but it was too weak financially to stand against them. Britain annexed the Transvaal and gave military aid. Disraeli had not sanctioned this move but realized that it enhanced British prestige. This prestige suffered a blow when the Zulus defeated the British in 1879. Disraeli had no choice but to send reinforcements to defeat them. He was out of office by the time the independence of the Boer republics became an issue again.

→ Afghanistan. British involvement came about because of the fear that Russia would use it as a route to invade India. In 1876 **Lord Lytton** was sent to bring the country into Britain's sphere of influence, offering subsidies and military aid against Russia. When the Afghan ruler refused, Lytton (without Disraeli's knowledge or approval) sent in troops, beginning the Second Afghan War. The Afghan ruler fled and the new ruler in 1879 agreed to British control of the passes into India and British control over Afghan foreign policy. As this seemed to be a major success, Disraeli accepted it. However, the British mission in Afghanistan was massacred and civil war broke out. The Third Afghan War began when British troops were sent in. Disraeli then fell from power, leaving the Liberals to sort it out.

Disraeli's policies, although they had revived the idea of a British Empire, gave Gladstone the motive to mount a campaign against him.

Why did the Conservatives lose the 1880 election? ●●●

Despite the exhilaration of the early part of the ministry Disraeli suffered a crushing defeat in 1880. The reasons for this were:

→ Growing resentment at the lack of social reform after 1876.
→ **Industrial slump** from 1875 caused high unemployment among the skilled artisans who had voted Conservative before.
→ An **agricultural depression** caused many bankruptcies among smaller farmers. Disraeli refused to put on tariffs to help them.
→ The organization of the party fell apart after Gorst resigned, whereas the Liberals mobilized support at grass-roots level.
→ The re-emergence of Gladstone as a dynamic leader mounting the Midlothian campaign against Disraeli's ambitious foreign and imperial policy, while Disraeli was too ill to campaign.

Checkpoint 3

What British interests were at stake in South Africa?

Test yourself

When you have read these pages, take a blank sheet of paper and make a list of Disraeli's actions in foreign and imperial policy. Explain what interests were involved in each case.

Checkpoint 4

What British interests were at stake in Afghanistan?

"immoral and iniquitous"

Gladstone's description of Disraeli's policy

Examiner's secrets

The examiner will be looking for you to show the principles of each as well as what they actually did.

Exam question   answer: page 70

Compare and contrast the foreign and imperial policy of Gladstone's first ministry and Disraeli's second ministry. (1 hour)

Parliamentary reform
1867–1918

46

The Great Reform Act (1832) had been designed to be the last parliamentary reform needed. However, by the 1860s, as circumstances changed, it was increasingly obvious that more was needed. It was not until 1918 that the goal of universal male suffrage was achieved.

1867 Reform Act

The Reform League was founded in 1865. The death of Palmerston opened the way for reform by **Lord John Russell** and Gladstone. Circumstances had changed. There had been a growth of a labour aristocracy with the trade revival. It was felt that these people were responsible enough to be given the vote.

Gladstone introduced a moderate Bill in 1866 that would have extended the electorate to 25%. Despite the moderation of the proposals, the Bill caused a storm of opposition. The Conservatives felt that any more reform would lead to 'total democracy'. The main criticism came from the right-wing Liberals led by **Robert Lowe**, who feared that the working class would end up ruling the country because of sheer weight of numbers. Working in conjunction with the Conservatives, he brought the government down.

The failure of the Bill led to agitation by the Reform League, culminating in the Hyde Park riots. A combination of pressure from below and from the Queen to settle the question led to Derby and Disraeli agreeing to take a 'leap in the dark' and bring in reform. In February 1867 Disraeli introduced a Bill based on household suffrage with safeguards. The Bill was so moderate that it was criticized severely. To ensure the passage of the Bill, Disraeli was forced to accept a number of amendments, including **Hodgkinson's Amendment**, making the Bill far more radical than he had originally intended. The vote, in the boroughs, was given to all rate-paying householders. An extra million men, one in three, could vote. In the counties there was little change. The £12 qualification increased the electorate by only 40%.

It may seem that the Act gave effective power to the working class. However, lack of payment for MPs, property qualifications for MPs and the lack of a secret ballot meant that real power stayed in the hands of the aristocracy and their middle-class allies.

The Ballot Act and after

The 1872 Ballot Act was designed to reduce the influence of the landowner or factory owner, who could dictate the outcome of the elections by bribery or intimidation. It also reduced the violence associated with open hustings.

The Corrupt Practices Act 1883 effectively stopped bribery by limiting the election expenses in each constituency.

"I venture to say that every man . . . is morally entitled to come within the pale of the constitution"

Gladstone, 1865

Checkpoint 1

What had been the changes in circumstances?

Checkpoint 2

What were Disraeli's motives for bringing reform?

"Political power has been transformed from a class to a nation"

Radical newspaper, 1867

· Check the net

Good resources for the period can be found at http://landow.stg.brown.edu/victorian/history/

The 1884 Reform Act ●●●

This was designed to correct the deficiency of the 1867 Act by giving the counties the same franchise qualifications as the boroughs. Chamberlain was the driving force behind the measures. He wanted to break the power of the (mainly Conservative) landowners. The Bill was not particularly controversial, extending the electorate from 3 million to 5 million, and passed through the Commons easily.

→ Then Salisbury used the Conservative majority in the Lords to block the Bill. He wanted a Redistribution Bill to offset the effects of the reform. By redistributing seats and creating single-member constituencies the Conservatives would benefit. They would pick up votes in the suburbs, the 'villa vote', while the Liberals would no longer be able to put up radical and Whig candidates in the same constituency to avoid splitting the vote.

→ A compromise was reached between Gladstone and Salisbury, and the 1884 Reform Act and the 1885 Redistribution of Seats Act were passed. Their effects were the fading away of the Whig element in the Liberal Party as they could not find enough support to be candidates in the single-member constituencies, and Salisbury was proved right, winning the next election. But over 40% of men and all women were still not eligible to vote.

1911 Parliament Act ●●●

The House of Lords had a traditional Conservative majority. The Lords had blocked parliamentary reform in 1832 and 1884. The conflict between the elected Commons and unelected Lords became a constitutional issue during the 1906 Liberal government.

→ The Lords tried to bring down the Liberals by blocking Bills. The last straw was when they rejected Lloyd George's 1909 Budget. The Liberals had to act or they could not govern. The election of 1910 was fought on this issue.

→ The Liberals won and introduced the 1911 Parliament Bill. The ability of the Lords to block Bills was severely reduced. They could only delay the passage for a limited amount of time, not stop them. The Bill only became law after threats by the King to create 249 Liberal peers to counter the Conservative majority.

→ Added to the Act was the payment of MPs for the first time.

1918 Representation of the People Act ●●●

This completed the process begun in 1832. The Act gave the vote to all men, and women over 30. Other women had to wait until 1928 before they received the vote.

Exam question answer: page 71

How and why did the size of the electorate increase during this period? (1 hour)

Test yourself

When you have finished reading these pages, take a blank sheet of paper and list the stages of parliamentary reform. List the main terms of each Act.

Checkpoint 3

What were the effects of the 1884 and 1885 Acts?

> *"The Lords are forcing a revolution. The Peers may decree a revolution but the People will direct it"*
>
> Lloyd George, 1909

Checkpoint 4

What were the effects of the Parliament Act?

Examiner's secrets

This is a question over time. Show that you understand that conditions changed during the period.

Salisbury and the Conservatives

> *"Whatever happens will be for the worse and therefore it is in our interest that as little as possible should happen"*
>
> Salisbury's view of foreign affairs, 1897

With the defeat of Gladstone's Home Rule Bill in 1886 the Conservatives under Salisbury took power. They were to remain in power, with a short Liberal interlude from 1892 to 1895, until 1905. For much of that time, Salisbury was prime minister and developed the foreign and defence policy that became known as 'splendid isolation'.

Domestic policy

Having dealt with the challenge of **Randolph Churchill**, Salisbury's government was not very radical in outlook. This is reflected in its domestic policy.

Local government reform 1888:

The Municipal Corporations Act had dealt only with the boroughs, and there were still too many unelected authorities dealing with various matters. After the 1884 Reform Act it seemed logical that local government be brought into line.

Checkpoint 1

What was the effect of local government reform?

→ 62 elected county councils and 60 county boroughs were created along with the London County Council.
→ The new authorities were given a number of administrative powers.
→ The Act was a success, and central government could add further powers as necessary.

Education:

→ 1888 – Cross Commission ended payment by results.
→ 1889 – Local authorities to deal with technical education.
→ 1891 – Fee Grant Act abolished fees for elementary education.

Colonial policy

Although Salisbury was not particularly keen on imperialism he bowed to pressure and allowed it to go ahead, particularly after **Joseph Chamberlain** became colonial secretary.

Chamberlain believed that with a strong empire Britain would be in a position where not only could it defend itself but it would also be economically strong enough to ride out any trade depressions. His radical Nonconformist background also caused him to believe that the colonies would benefit from British rule.

Checkpoint 2

What were the advantages for Britain of a large empire?

Salisbury's principal achievement was the peaceful partition of Africa. British, French, German and other countries' expansion meant the potential for conflict. Salisbury and **Bismarck** negotiated a series of agreements to stop this, each country recognizing each other's spheres of influence:

Check the net

Information on Salisbury and colonialism can be found at http://spartacus.schoolnet.co.uk/Britain.html

→ In **West Africa**, the defeat of the Ashantis in 1896 gave Britain effective control over most of the area.
→ The Sudan was recaptured in 1898 by **Kitchener** and became an Anglo-Egyptian administration.

South Africa was a more difficult problem. The growing power of the Boer republics, particularly after the discovery of gold, worried **Cecil Rhodes**, who wanted the whole of southern Africa under British rule.

The increasing independence shown by the Boers, as shown by their negotiations with Germany, was also seen as a threat to British interests. The failure of the **Jameson raid** (1895) and the Boers' harsh treatment of British citizens culminated in the outbreak of the **Boer War** in 1899.

'Splendid isolation' ●●●

The basic theme of Salisbury's foreign policy was not complete isolation. Instead, relationships were developed with other countries, stopping short of any binding alliance that might involve Britain in a war that was not in its interests. As an island, Britain could rely on its navy for defence and to protect its trade routes. It would adhere to the 'two-power standard'. A war on behalf of an ally would need a large army, built up at great cost to Britain.

Salisbury worked on the principle of avoiding or neutralizing any potential threats. He was prepared to make agreements, but only if they were limited in scope and to the benefit of Britain.

→ Balkan crisis 1886. Salisbury worked in cooperation with Austria and France to allow the union of Bulgaria, which he felt would be a more effective barrier to Russian expansion than the Bulgaria of the 1878 Congress of Berlin.
→ Mediterranean agreements 1887. Agreements between Britain, Italy and Austria to defend the Straits against Russian expansion. Salisbury agreed to this because the British navy could be used.

The dangers of splendid isolation ●●●

Certain incidents highlighted the dangers of an isolated Britain:

→ The Fashoda incident 1898 – the French laid claim to the Nile valley even though Britain had an interest in it. The situation was resolved to Britain's benefit by the Anglo-French Convention 1899, but only because France was equally isolated and had no support.
→ The Cleveland message 1897 – President Cleveland invoked the Monroe doctrine and forced Britain to go to arbitration over a border dispute between Venezuela and British Guiana. Salisbury had no choice but to agree, as he had no support elsewhere.
→ Greece and Turkey 1897–1898 – Salisbury failed to win support for a multilateral solution to problems between the two countries.
→ The Boer War 1899 – Britain's involvement in the war left it vulnerable to attack by other countries.

The problems were realized and a search began for an ally, culminating, after the resignation of Salisbury, in the Anglo-Japanese alliance 1902.

Checkpoint 3

How far did the British Empire expand under Salisbury?

The jargon

Two-power standard meant that Britain's navy would be equal in size to the next two largest navies combined. That way it could protect Britain even against two countries working in concert.

Test yourself

1 When you have finished reading these pages, take a blank sheet of paper and draw a timeline from 1885 to 1902. Above the line mark the events concerned with 'splendid isolation'; below the line mark on the progress of colonialism.
Can you see any links between the two?
2 Draw up a list of reasons why the Conservatives were able to dominate British politics between 1892 and 1905.

Checkpoint 4

Why did 'splendid isolation' end?

Exam question   answer: page 71

(a) Why was the policy of imperialism so popular up to 1902?

(b) How did the policy of imperialism contribute to the defence strategy of Britain? (1 hour)

Examiner's secrets

Look at the economic and strategic implications of imperialism to shape your answer. Also explain the role of personalities such as Chamberlain.

Ireland 1868–1922

During this period the 'Irish question' was to come to a head. Missed opportunities in not granting the Irish what they wanted until it was too late led to increased Irish radicalism and demands for complete independence.

The problem

Ireland was predominantly a land of Catholic tenant farmers where the land was owned for the most part by Protestant absentee landlords.

→ The Catholics resented paying tithes to the Protestant Church of Ireland. The tenants resented paying high rents and having little security. They wanted the 'Three Fs' – fair rent, fixity of tenure and free sale of leases.

→ Since Ireland had given up Home Rule with the Act of Union 1801 it had seemed to gain little from the English. There was a growing groundswell of opinion that only a separate Irish government could solve Irish problems. The English were not keen on this as they saw control over Ireland as an indispensable part of their defence policy. This conflict often resulted in violence, such as the **Fenian outrages 1867**.

The jargon

Home rule meant a separate Irish parliament, which would be able to deal with Irish affairs, while the Westminster government would keep control over foreign affairs, defence and trade.

Gladstone and Ireland

Gladstone was determined to solve the question of Ireland for both moral and practical reasons.

→ **1869 Disestablishment of the Irish Church** – this removed religion as a problem.

→ **1870 Irish Land Act** – courts were empowered to revise exorbitant rents. Not all that successful, as the courts were dominated by the landlords.

→ **1881 Irish Land Act** – a response to the formation of the Irish Land League led by Davitt and Parnell and designed to build on the 1870 Act. It granted the Three Fs, but this did not apply to those in arrears of rent.

→ 'Kilmainham Treaty' 1882 – violence led to the imprisonment of Parnell. Gladstone did a deal whereby he would pass an arrears Bill if Parnell stopped the violence.

→ **1886 Home Rule Bill** would have given the Irish a separate parliament, but it was destroyed by a combination of Conservatives and Liberal Unionists led by Chamberlain, who feared that this would start the disintegration of the empire.

→ 1893 Home Rule Bill – similar to the previous Bill, it was stopped by the Conservatives in the Lords.

Checkpoint 1

Why did the Irish want Home Rule?

Checkpoint 2

What were the arguments against Home Rule for Ireland?

Check the net

Plenty of material on aspects of this topic can be found at http://landow.stg.edu/victorian/

Parnell and Home Rule

Parnell was leader of the Irish MPs. He had followed a policy of 'obstructionism', forcing the other parties to take note of Ireland. The Kilmainham Treaty was recognition of the fact that England could not solve the question of Ireland without the cooperation of Irish leaders.

The failure of the Home Rule Bill led to a more radical attitude in Ireland. The Land League initiated the 'plan of campaign'. The Conservatives attempted to 'kill with kindness' the desire for home rule. Balfour brought in a Land Act 1887 but also a Crimes Act, leading to increased violence on both sides.

Parnell's position as leader of the Irish was undermined when, as a result of the O'Shea divorce case in 1889, Gladstone refused to work with him. The Irish faced a choice: Parnell or Liberal support. Backed by the Irish bishops, they chose the Liberals.

The Conservatives made some improvements with the Land Purchase Act 1891, helping tenants to buy their land, and the congested districts boards giving government money for improvements such as drainage.

The problem of Ulster

The question of home rule was revived after 1910. The Liberals were dependent on the support of John Redmond's Irish MPs. In Ulster the Protestants did not want home rule, which they felt would end their privileged position. Sir Edward Carson, leader of the Ulster Unionists, organized resistance to home rule. The Conservatives supported him.

→ In April 1912, the Home Rule Bill went through the Commons, but the Lords rejected it in 1913. Carson set up the Ulster Defence Volunteers ready to fight to maintain Ulster's position. The nationalists responded with Irish Nationalist Volunteers.

→ By 1914 both Unionists and Nationalists were well armed. The 'Curragh mutiny' (a threat by British army officers to refuse to obey orders to coerce Ulster) meant the government could not impose home rule by force. Civil war seemed inevitable, but a truce was called on the outbreak of the Great War. The delay in implementing home rule meant that the more radical Irish, e.g. **Sinn Fein**, wanted even more – *complete* independence. As shown by the **Easter Rising** 1916.

Lloyd George and Ireland

By 1918 Irish attitudes had hardened. In the 1918 election 73 Sinn Fein MPs were elected. They left Westminster and set up a rival government, the Dail, led by Eamonn de Valera. In 1919 the IRA, commanded by Michael Collins, began a guerrilla war against the British. Lloyd George responded initially by bringing in the 'Black and Tans' to fight the IRA. Violence escalated and Lloyd George had to negotiate a treaty giving Ireland, without Ulster, the same status as a dominion. In December 1922 the Irish Free State was formed, ending the Irish question.

Exam questions   answers: page 72

1   How effectively did British governments deal with the problem of Ireland during this period? (45 min)

2   Why did the Liberals fail in their attempts to bring in home rule before 1914? (45 min)

Checkpoint 3

How important was Parnell in Irish affairs?

Test yourself

When you have finished reading these pages, take a blank sheet of paper and write down in one column the attempts at home rule, and in another column attempts to solve the Irish question with other Acts of Parliament. Try to assess the success of these.

Checkpoint 4

How had the Irish question changed by 1914?

"Home Rule will be Rome rule"

Ulster Unionist slogan

Examiner's secrets

Do not just present a detailed list of the Acts that dealt with Ireland. Concentrate instead on evaluating the success of the policies.

The Liberals 1906–1914

*"This is a war budget.
It is for raising money
to wage implacable
warfare against
poverty and
squalidness"*

Lloyd George, April 1909

The Liberals regained power after a long absence. The party had changed and become more radical. In its time in power it was to introduce the concept of a welfare state and solve the problem of the House of Lords.

The emergence of 'New Liberalism'

New Liberalism involved more state intervention than the more *laissez-faire* approach of Gladstonian Liberalism. It developed as a result of:

→ Social surveys by **Rowntree** and **Booth** showing how much poverty there was in the country.
→ The work of Liberal thinkers Hobson and Hobhouse, who believed that the state should provide certain functions rather than leave them to individuals.
→ Pressure from the rising Labour Party in Parliament.
→ The poor state of health of the working class as revealed by recruitment during the Boer War.
→ Pressure from Nonconformist supporters, who saw New Liberalism as a moral crusade.
→ The main supporters of the new ideas were the young radical MPs such as **Lloyd George** and **Churchill**.

Checkpoint 1

What was 'New Liberalism'?

Social reform 1906–1914

The Liberals were elected in 1905 with a landslide victory. The election had been fought on a number of issues. Social reform was one of them – the Conservatives had ignored it for too long and as a consequence lost the workers' vote.

Action point

You should look up the other reasons why the Conservatives lost the election, particularly their ideas on tariff reform.

The idea behind the social reforms was to provide a safety net for the poorest elements of society and ensure a minimum standard of living:

Checkpoint 2

Why was social reform needed at this time?

→ 1906 Merchant Shipping Act. Regulated food and conditions.
→ 1906 – Local education authorities were empowered to provide school meals where necessary for those in need.
→ 1907 – School medical inspections began to try to catch medical problems early. Free medical treatment could be provided.
→ 1908 Children's Act (The 'Children's Charter'). This consolidated previous legislation and dealt with children's rights, including the creation of juvenile courts.
→ 1908 – Pensions introduced for those over 70 on low incomes.
→ 1908 Coal Mines Act set the maximum working day at 8 hours.
→ 1909 – Trade boards created to deal with the poor conditions and low pay in certain trades. The boards could fix minimum pay and maximum hours.
→ 1909 – Labour exchanges created to enable the unemployed to find work more easily.
→ 1911 National Insurance Act. The first part dealt with health insurance, a compulsory scheme for the low-paid whereby a weekly contribution would allow the worker to claim sick pay, receive some

Check the net

Short biographies of Balfour, Asquith and Lloyd George can be found at www.britannia.com/history

medical treatment and free medicine. The second part concerned unemployment insurance. It dealt with certain trades that were susceptible to high unemployment. For a weekly contribution, matched by the employer and the state, the unemployed would receive benefit for a limited time.

Much of this legislation was not new; it was copied from the Germans. Most of it was self-financing or funded from local rates. The importance of the legislation was that it provided a base from which a welfare state could later be developed.

Conflict with the House of Lords

Despite their huge losses in the election, the Conservatives under Balfour were determined not to give up power and instead exercised it through the Lords. On Balfour's instructions the Conservative peers would either reject Bills or wreck them with many amendments. They did this to an **Education Bill** in 1906 and again in 1908, to a **Plural Voting Bill** and a **Scottish Land Bill**.

The Liberals, now under **Asquith**, had to act or they would be seen as being unable to govern. They had already lost by-elections. Lloyd George's 'People's Budget' of 1909 was probably designed as much to provoke the Lords into taking action as it was to raise the money for social reform. By introducing supertax for the very rich and taxing increases in land values Lloyd George got the desired reaction. The Lords rejected the Budget, going against normal parliamentary tradition. In 1910 Asquith called two general elections on the issue of the unelected Lords blocking the will of the people. Although the Liberals lost seats the support of the Irish Nationalists and Labour was enough to enable them to attack the Lords.

The Parliament Bill of 1911 said that the Lords could not reject or amend a Money Bill and could only reject a Bill three times before it became law anyway. The Bill also reduced the maximum length of Parliament from seven to five years.

Naturally the Lords rejected the Bill, and Asquith had to get the King to threaten to swamp the Lords with newly created Liberal peers. Even then the Lords thought it was a bluff and it took Balfour, fearful of losing the Conservative majority in the Lords, to persuade them to finally accept the Bill. The 1911 Parliament Act can be seen as the highlight of the Liberal administration. It prevented the Lords completely rejecting Liberal Bills, but they could still block them, as they were to do with the Irish Home Rule Bill a couple of years later.

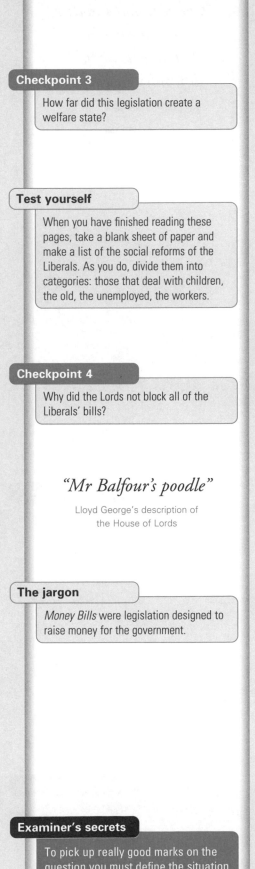

Checkpoint 3

How far did this legislation create a welfare state?

Test yourself

When you have finished reading these pages, take a blank sheet of paper and make a list of the social reforms of the Liberals. As you do, divide them into categories: those that deal with children, the old, the unemployed, the workers.

Checkpoint 4

Why did the Lords not block all of the Liberals' bills?

"Mr Balfour's poodle"

Lloyd George's description of the House of Lords

The jargon

Money Bills were legislation designed to raise money for the government.

Examiner's secrets

To pick up really good marks on the question you must define the situation and measure the success of the legislation, not just list it.

Exam question   answer: page 72

How far did the condition of the people improve under the Liberals between 1906 and 1914? (45 min)

Votes for women

In 1867 the first serious attempt to give women the right to vote was made as an amendment to the Reform Act. It took until 1918 for this to happen, and then only as the position of women in society underwent radical changes.

Changes in the position of women

Respectable women in mid-Victorian Britain did not work; they stayed at home with their fathers and then with their husbands. No professions were open to them, and as they had no claim in society they did not qualify for the vote – their fathers or husbands would represent their interests. Towards the end of the 19th century a number of changes occurred to alter this position. Women were to become more independent and so demand the right to vote.

→ The expansion of education after the **1870 Education Act** meant that not only were girls getting at least an elementary education but there was also a need for more teachers. Middle-class girls could now get a respectable job and support themselves.

→ The **1882 Married Women's Property Act** allowed women to keep their own property separate from their husbands. This allowed women to go into business if they wanted to.

→ The introduction of the typewriter into offices gave opportunities for women to work as they proved to be much faster than men. Once in the office they took on many duties previously done by men.

→ The introduction of labour-saving devices such as the vacuum cleaner and soap flakes meant less time was needed for running a home. Time could be spent organizing campaigns to get the vote.

By the beginning of the 20th century women believed that they now had just as much right to the vote as men of similar standing.

Checkpoint 1

How did the position of women change at the end of the 19th century?

Suffragists and suffragettes

In 1867 the London Society for Women's Suffrage was founded. In 1897 this had developed into the nationwide National Union of Women's Suffrage Societies (NUWSS) led by **Millicent Fawcett**. The group was dominated by well-educated middle-class women, who were determined to gain the vote by non-violent means of peaceful persuasion. They became known as the suffragists and achieved very little.

In 1903, **Emmeline Pankhurst** and her daughters began the Women's Suffrage and Political Union (WSPU). They were more militant than the suffragists and became known as the suffragettes.

→ To arouse public opinion and to keep the question of women's suffrage in the news the suffragettes carried out a policy of 'sensation mongering', seeking any sort of publicity for the cause.

→ There was hope that the Liberals were bound to win the next election and that they would be sympathetic to the cause of women's suffrage.

The jargon

Suffrage is the right to vote.

Checkpoint 2

What was 'sensation mongering'?

In fact the Liberals had too much to do and were not particularly interested in the subject.

→ In October 1905 Christabel Pankhurst and Annie Kenney were charged with disturbance and opted for prison. This gained the movement the publicity that they wanted. Other acts of violence followed, resulting in imprisonment. While there, the suffragettes went on hunger strike to gain even more publicity.

→ In 1907 the police attacked a demonstration. The government realized that this might damage its prestige and so allowed a Bill that would have given the vote to all over 21, men and women. The Conservatives blocked it.

→ In 1909, expecting another election, the suffragettes stepped up their campaign, resulting in more arrests and more hunger strikes. The government introduced the **forcible feeding** of the hunger strikers, a move that damaged its reputation.

The question of women's suffrage was overshadowed by the crisis with the Lords until 1911. Then Asquith promised a Bill and the suffragettes stopped their campaign, but, disappointed at the government's lack of speed, they began their campaign again in 1912. This was intensified when in 1913 the Bill was thrown out.

To avoid the suffragettes gaining a martyr, the government passed the '**Cat and Mouse Act**', allowing suffragettes on hunger strike to be released temporarily. The women gained their martyr, however, when Emily Davison threw herself under the King's horse at the 1913 Derby. In 1914 Asquith hinted that he was ready to bring in a Bill that would give women the vote. However, the Great War broke out and the suffragettes called a truce in order to help the war effort.

The effects of the war ●●●

Women played an important part in war work. Increasing demand for munitions meant that women went into the factories. They also took over many of the jobs of men who went into the army. Middle-class women volunteered as nurses, joined the Land Army or joined the auxiliary services to help the troops. The position of women had changed. They had proved themselves responsible members of society.

When, in 1918, the idea of enfranchising all males became an increasing necessity it was obvious that votes for women would have to come in as well. The huge loss of life in the war meant that women would be in the majority if given the votes on equal terms with men.

The **Representation of the People Act 1918** restricted the vote to about 8½ million women over 30. All women gained the vote in 1928.

Checkpoint 3

Why did the Conservatives block Bills designed to increase the electorate?

Test yourself

After you have finished reading these pages, take a blank sheet of paper and list the reasons why women did not get the vote by 1914.

"Woman are half the people and demand a voice in deciding the taxes"

WSPU poster

Checkpoint 4

What contribution did women make to the war effort?

Examiner's secrets

The examiner will be looking for a well-argued answer that reaches a balanced judgement, not just a chronological account of the issue.

Exam question answer: page 73

Which did more to gain women the vote – the actions of the suffragettes or the effects of the Great War? (45 min)

Foreign policy 1902–1914

*"We want eight and
we won't wait"*

Music hall slogan regarding
Dreadnoughts, 1909

The period from 1902 saw a marked change in British foreign policy. Britain moved away from 'isolation', searching for allies and becoming increasingly involved in European affairs. This was to culminate in it going to war in August 1914.

The end of 'splendid isolation'

By the end of the 19th century the dangers of the British policy of isolation had become only too apparent. Events such as the **Cleveland message** and the **Fashoda incident** had highlighted British vulnerability. If Britain had been attacked while involved in the Boer War it would have been in great danger. It needed allies.

→ The natural ally seemed to be Germany, which would be useful support against Britain's traditional enemies, France and Russia. In 1898 and 1899 such an alliance was offered and both times was rejected by the Kaiser as having no advantage for Germany.

→ Finally, Britain turned to Japan as a last resort. The **Anglo-Japanese Treaty of 1902** committed Britain to help if Japan was attacked by more than Russia. In return, Japan protected British interests in the North Pacific, allowing Britain to concentrate its navy nearer home.

Checkpoint 1

Why did Britain look for allies at the end of the 19th century?

The threat from Germany

Despite the agreements between Salisbury and Bismarck in 1890, the question of the colonies was always to be a possible area of conflict between Britain and Germany. German colonial expansion in Africa was limited by the existence of British and French colonies. This was highlighted by the '**Kruger telegram**', when the Kaiser congratulated the Boers after the failure of the **Jameson raid**.

→ The German Naval Laws 1898 also highlighted the potential threat from Germany. As a continental power, Germany had no real need of a large, powerful navy except to challenge the power of Britain and threaten its defence and trade routes.

→ Plans by Germany to build a Berlin–Baghdad railway could also be interpreted as a threat to British influence and interests in the Persian Gulf.

→ Britain's reaction to the threats was to modernise its army, creating the British Expeditionary Force, the Territorial Army and the Officer Training Corps. Also, the **Cawdor–Fisher naval reforms** led to the building of the *Dreadnought*, a new naval base at Rosyth and consolidation of the fleet into home waters.

Checkpoint 2

What was the threat to Britain from Germany?

Check the net

Information on this topic can be found at www.spartacus.schoolnet.co.uk/

Cooperation with France and Russia

Britain wanted an agreement with France to end any possible colonial difficulties between them. France wanted an agreement as a protection against Germany.

→ The Anglo-French Entente 1904 gave Britain a free hand in Egypt and France in Morocco. The entente did not commit Britain to help France against Germany.

→ The entente grew stronger as a result of the first Moroccan crisis 1905. The Kaiser challenged French influence in Morocco. He demanded an international conference to discuss the matter. Britain was just as worried about German intentions and at the Algeciras Conference 1906 stood by France, forcing Germany to back down. Joint military talks were held between the two countries.

→ The next step was for Britain to settle its differences with France's ally Russia. The Anglo-Russian Entente 1907, brokered by France, split Persia into two spheres of influence and agreed to keep Afghanistan neutral.

Cooperation between France and Britain increased further as a result of the second Moroccan crisis 1911. In a direct challenge to France the Kaiser sent a German gunboat to the port of Agadir. This was also a challenge to Britain; a German presence in Morocco would be a threat to trade routes.

In the **Mansion House speech**, Lloyd George made it clear that Britain would stand by France. Germany was once again forced to back down. British public opinion was now prepared to help France if it were to become a victim of a German attack.

Why Britain went to war ●●●

The crisis in the Balkans caused by the assassinations in Sarajevo did not concern the British. **Edward Grey** suggested a conference to solve the problem. Germany refused but tried to ensure British neutrality in the event of a war with France.

Britain refused, feeling that it had a moral obligation to France, especially after an agreement in 1912 that France would look after British interests in the Mediterranean. Britain promised France that it would not let the German fleet into the Channel.

→ Asquith found it easy to convince Parliament to help the French; the only opposition came from Labour. The War Council sat and Asquith agreed to the mobilization of the army.

→ The actual cause of Britain entering the war was the German invasion of Belgium as part of the **Schlieffen Plan**. As a guarantor of Belgian neutrality since 1839, Britain had no choice but to go to war.

The jargon

Entente is an understanding, not a formal alliance.

Test yourself

When you have finished reading these pages, take a blank sheet of paper and write down the process by which Britain became increasingly likely to go to war. Was this inevitable?

Checkpoint 3

Why did Britain draw closer to France in this period?

"The lamps are going out all over Europe; we shall not see them lit again in our lifetime"

Edward Grey, August 1914

Links

Pages 108–9 contain useful background information on this topic.

Checkpoint 4

What obligation did Britain have to Belgium?

Examiner's secrets

You should deal with this question thematically rather than just give a chronological account.

Exam question   answer: page 73

Why did Britain go to war in 1914? (45 min)

The rise of the Labour Party

In the 1880s there was a revival of the working-class desire for parliamentary representation. The Labour Party was the result of this. After the Great War the party became the second party of Britain and in 1924 became the government.

Socialism from the 1880s

The groups that eventually made up the Labour Party varied in their degree of socialism. However, all were convinced of the need for working-class representation in Parliament.

→ **H. M. Hyndman** had founded the Social Democratic Federation (SDF) in 1883. Originally, it had included left-wing Liberals, but as the SDF attacked Gladstone's policies they left, making it into a socialist organization. It stood for radical socialism and had strong links with the New Unions.

→ The Fabian Society (1884) consisted of middle-class intellectuals such as **G. B. Shaw** and the **Webbs**, who were moral socialists. They believed in 'gas and water socialism', the municipalization of local utilities.

→ **Keir Hardie** founded the Independent Labour Party (ILP) in 1892. It was a loose collection of Labour clubs believing in practical economic reform rather than revolutionary socialism.

→ The trade union movement had become more radical as employers attempted to maintain profits during the economic depression by cutting wages. In 1890 the radical new unions gained control of the Trades Union Congress (TUC).

The jargon

New unions were unions for the unskilled workers rather than for skilled workers. They tended to be more radical. *Municipalization* was the idea that utilities such as gas and water should be owned by the local authorities.

Checkpoint 1

Why did socialist groups emerge in the 1880s?

Check the net

Plenty of excellent material for this topic can be found at www.spartacus.schoolnet.co.uk/britain.html

Formation of the Labour Party

In the 1890s a number of legal decisions went against the unions. At the same time none of the Labour groups had done very well in parliamentary elections. The unions needed the Labour groups to represent their case; they could not rely on the Conservatives or the Liberals. The Labour groups needed the support and financial backing of the unions.

In 1900 the TUC created the Labour Representation Committee (LRC), under the leadership of Ramsay MacDonald, to run Labour candidates. It was a small group and only able to field 15 candidates in 1900.

The **Taff Vale** case led to an increase in membership to 800 000, and 180 unions were affiliated. With this new strength the LRC could do a deal with the Liberals whereby 30 Labour candidates would stand unopposed by the Liberals.

In the 1906 election the LRC fielded 50 candidates; 29 were elected. The Labour Party (as renamed) was now an effective force in politics.

Checkpoint 2

Why did the TUC agree to fund Labour candidates?

The Labour Party 1906–1918

The Labour Party's role between 1906 and 1914 was to act as a pressure group, persuading the Liberals to reverse the Taff Vale judgement and bring in social reform. It suffered a temporary set back as a result of the **Osborne judgement 1909**, when the unions were stopped from financing the party. This was rectified by the Trade Union Act of 1913.

The Great War was to have a positive effect on the development of the party. Labour joined the coalition government and supported Lloyd George in his bid to become PM.

→ When Labour left the coalition in 1917 after disagreements about war aims, **Henderson** reorganized the party along national lines, making it more efficient.

→ Sidney Webb gave it a new constitution and party programme, one to appeal to a broad spectrum of society by emphasizing social democracy and omitting radical socialism.

In the 1918 election, Labour was able to field 388 candidates and won 63 seats, more than Asquith's independent Liberals.

The first Labour government 1924

In the 1922 election Labour gained 142 seats and was now the official opposition party. This trend continued in 1923, when Labour won 191 seats.

In 1924 the Conservatives were brought down by a combination of Labour and Liberals, and MacDonald took over as PM in a minority government. Being dependent on the Liberals, MacDonald could do little to introduce socialism.

He decided on an election, but a combination of the Conservatives renouncing protectionism and the scare caused by the **Zinoviev letter** caused Labour to lose 40 seats. The government ended.

The second Labour government 1929

After the general election of 1929 MacDonald again became PM in a minority government but once again could do little to introduce a real socialist programme.

Labour also suffered from the difficulty of economic depression caused by the **Wall Street crash** in October 1929. Unemployment in Britain rose dramatically, causing problems for the chancellor, **Snowden**. Income from taxes was falling, while payment of unemployment benefits was rising. To balance the budget, cuts of 10% in benefits were needed. Half the Cabinet resigned over this and the Labour government came to an end.

Checkpoint 3

What was the importance of the Great War to the development of the Labour Party?

Test yourself

When you have finished reading these pages, take a blank sheet of paper and draw a timeline from 1900 to 1929. Mark on it events that contributed to the rise of the Labour Party. See if you can also mark on it the decline of the Liberal Party.

"To secure for the producers by hand or brain, the full fruits of their industry . . ."

Extract from the 1918 constitution of the Labour Party

Checkpoint 4

Why did Labour lose the 1924 election?

Action point

In 1926 the General Strike occurred. You should note how it affected the Labour Party. See page 63.

Examiner's secrets

Examiners will be looking for a good understanding of the issues regarding both the Labour challenge and the Liberal reaction.

Exam question   answer: pages 73–4

What was the nature and the impact of the Labour challenge to the Liberals from 1906 to 1929? (1 hour)

Liberals in decline
1914–1922

In the period 1906–1914 the Liberals had been at their peak, yet by 1922 they had become the third party in Britain. The decline of the Liberals was paralleled by the rise of Labour, which inherited the radical mantle from them.

The jargon

A *coalition government* is one made up from more than one political party.

Checkpoint 1

Why was Asquith's leadership challenged?

The effect of the Great War on the Liberals ●●●

Setbacks in the war, including the shortage of munitions and the failure of the **Dardenelles campaign**, forced Asquith to accept the advice of Lloyd George and the Conservative leader **Bonar Law** and form a coalition government. Asquith agreed to this in May 1915, and although it removed all overt opposition to the government it marked the first step in the decline of the Liberals.

The war still did not go well, and Asquith found himself attacked from all sides. The challenge to his position came from Law and Lloyd George. Asquith resigned in December 1916, hoping that no one else could form a government and he would come back on his own terms.

Lloyd George as prime minister ●●●

Asquith's bluff was called – Lloyd George formed what became a very successful government. This had the effect of splitting the Liberal Party into supporters of Asquith and supporters of Lloyd George.

→ Lloyd George proved to be an excellent war PM. He had already made a name for himself and good contacts with the unions and business while minister of munitions. He could now build on these contacts to increase the war effort.

→ His premiership was based on cooperation rather than coercion to get industry to work for the war. He was able to fix prices on a 'cost plus' basis, which satisfied both consumer and industrialist and stabilized the economy.

Checkpoint 2

How successful was Lloyd George in running the war?

→ In 1917, after Russia's February Revolution, Labour called for peace to be negotiated. This led to **Henderson** resigning from the Cabinet and the end of Labour in the coalition.

→ The rivalry between Lloyd George and Asquith came to a head in May 1918, when Asquith proposed setting up a select committee to look into claims that Lloyd George had lied to Parliament about the strength of the British army. Asquith was defeated. However, it meant an irreconcilable split between the two factions of the party, weakening it fatally in the light of the challenge from Labour.

The coalition government 1918–1922 ●●●

The war over, there was a pressing need to hold a general election. Lloyd George was quite prepared to carry on with the coalition as a government of national unity. The Labour Party and the Asquith Liberals were not. The Conservatives knew that they could win the election but realized that they still needed Lloyd George. He had great popular support as the man who had won the war.

Check the net

Material on this topic can be found at www.spartacus.schoolnet.uk/britain.html

In the 1918 election the Conservatives agreed not to oppose 150 'coalition Liberals' endorsed by Lloyd George. The Asquith Liberals fared badly: only 26 were elected. From here on the coalition would be dominated by the Conservatives.

→ Lloyd George had to deal with the problem of peace making. He negotiated the **Treaty of Versailles** but was criticized by many Conservatives for being too soft on Germany and by Labour for being too harsh.

→ British intervention in the **Russian Civil War** on the side of the anti-Bolsheviks also provoked criticism from Labour for being there and from backbench Conservatives for not doing enough to help the Whites.

After an initial post-war boom due to restocking, the British economy went into depression as Britain had lost most of its export markets during the war. **Unemployment** rose to 2 million. The government's reaction was to get rid of its economic responsibilities as quickly as possible. The railways and mines, nationalized during the war, were returned to their owners, who immediately brought in wage cuts. This finished working-class support for Lloyd George.

Lloyd George's promises to the returning soldiers seemed to be a sham. With **Addison's Housing Act 1919** government subsidies were given to builders who built houses for rent. Only 250 000 houses were built before the subsidies were drastically cut.

The fall of Lloyd George ●●●

Lloyd George's solution to the Irish question, granting Ireland virtual independence, did not find favour with many of the Conservatives. Also, coalition Liberals were losing support or leaving the coalition, feeling that Liberal principles were being sacrificed and still hoping for a reunification of the Liberal Party.

→ The Conservatives were becoming aware they no longer needed Lloyd George, who had lost much of his popular support. Right-wing opposition grew, fuelled by the existence of the '**Lloyd George fund**' whereby honours were sold to fund his group.

→ The final straw came in 1922, when Lloyd George wanted to go to war against Turkey over a matter where British interests were not really threatened. The Conservatives voted by a large majority to end the coalition and Lloyd George resigned as PM.

The Liberals were now a spent force. They had lost the middle classes to the Conservatives and the working classes to Labour.

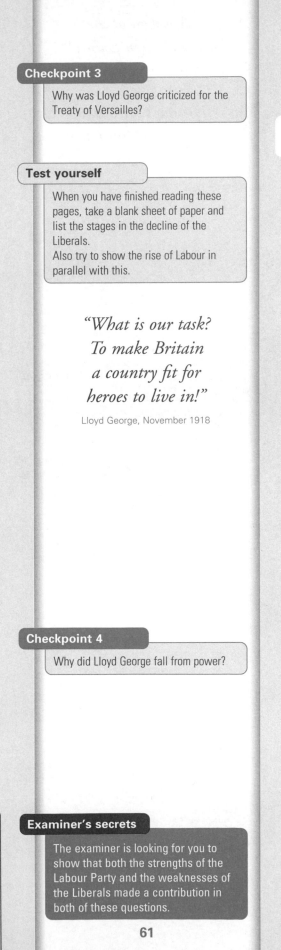

Checkpoint 3

Why was Lloyd George criticized for the Treaty of Versailles?

Test yourself

When you have finished reading these pages, take a blank sheet of paper and list the stages in the decline of the Liberals.
Also try to show the rise of Labour in parallel with this.

"What is our task? To make Britain a country fit for heroes to live in!"

Lloyd George, November 1918

Checkpoint 4

Why did Lloyd George fall from power?

Examiner's secrets

The examiner is looking for you to show that both the strengths of the Labour Party and the weaknesses of the Liberals made a contribution in both of these questions.

Exam questions   answers: page 74

1   Account for the changing fortunes of the Liberals between 1914 and 1929. (45 min)

2   How far can Lloyd George be held responsible for the decline of the Liberals after 1914? (45 min)

Conservative inter-war domination

From the fall of Lloyd George in 1922 to the outbreak of war in 1939 the Conservatives were to dominate politics except for two brief interludes when they allowed the Labour Party to take power. Even the National Government from 1931 was Conservative in all but name. Much of the credit for this domination goes to Stanley Baldwin, who reunited the Conservative Party.

Baldwin's ministries

After Lloyd George resigned, **Bonar Law** became PM, called a general election, which the Conservatives won, and then resigned through ill health. His surprise successor was Stanley Baldwin, the chancellor. Baldwin was essentially a moderate but, as a businessman himself, could win over both sides of the party. He cultivated the image of 'Honest Stan' with the public.

His first problem was that of the economic depression. In October 1923 he claimed that he could only deal with the problem if he had a free hand to end free trade. This was an important step. One of the reasons the Conservatives had lost the 1906 election had been their desire to bring in **tariff reform**. Other Conservative leaders, Balfour and Law, had ducked the issue. Baldwin called an election on the question and the Conservatives did badly, losing their majority and having to allow Labour to take office.

In June 1924 Baldwin publicly gave up the idea of protectionism just before the election. There was nothing to stop voters voting Conservative, and they were returned with a comfortable majority. The majority emphasized the Conservative domination of this period. Now free trade was no longer an issue the Liberals had no policies with which to oppose the Conservatives.

Although Baldwin's ministries are notable for their lack of radical legislation, there were some domestic reforms:

→ Chamberlain's Housing Act – Addison's scheme had come to an end. The Conservatives decided to give subsidies to builders of private houses for sale rather than rent. This benefited the middle classes.
→ Widows, Orphans and Old Age Pensions Act 1925 – extended the **National Insurance** scheme to cover these categories.
→ Unemployment Insurance Act 1927 – increased contributions and reduced benefits but increased the length of time benefits would be allowed.
→ Local Government Act 1929 – gave local authorities responsibility for poor relief. It also changed the system of rates and gave block grants from the government to cover certain functions.
→ The British Broadcasting Company was made into a corporation.
→ The Central Electricity Board was created to distribute electricity through the National Grid.

The jargon

Tariff reform was the idea of changing back from free trade to protectionism.

Checkpoint 1

What was the importance of Baldwin's renunciation of protectionism?

Check the net

A potted biography of Baldwin can be found at www.britannia.com/history

Checkpoint 2

What was the thinking behind these reforms?

The General Strike ●●●

The conflict between workers and employers during the depression in the 1920s was strongest in the coal industry. Britain had lost its export markets for coal and now faced competition from abroad. The mine owners wanted to maintain profits by lowering wages and increasing hours.

When the miners appealed for help from the **TUC** in 1925 they got it. The threat of a general strike forced the government to give subsidies and set up a commission to look into the matter. However, the government began to make plans for countering a general strike, creating volunteer organizations to help with the movement of supplies.

→ The Samuel Commission reported in March 1926, recommending an immediate reduction in wages. The miners were locked out when they refused to accept this and on 3 May the TUC sanctioned the General Strike.
→ The government was ready. Despite a very good response to the call, the TUC could not compete with a government that had had nine months to prepare, had its own newspaper, the *British Gazette*, and the use of the BBC.

On 12 May the TUC called off the strike. The government had won and to emphasize the fact passed an amendment to the **Trades Disputes Act** making it difficult for the unions to finance the Labour Party.

The National Government 1931–1939 ●●●

The collapse of the Labour Government led to the formation of a coalition National Government in August 1931 with MacDonald as PM until he retired in 1935, when Baldwin took over.

→ It immediately brought in the spending cuts initiated by Snowden, then called an election on the issue of protectionism, winning a resounding majority. The Conservatives were dominant within it.
→ The issue of free trade was dead; the public wanted tariff reform. The Abnormal Importations Act was passed as an emergency measure, followed by the Import Duties Act 1932, which introduced an immediate tariff of 10%. Further tariffs would be reviewed later.

The government had to deal with high unemployment:

→ Unemployment Act 1934 set up Unemployment Assistance, which was means-tested for the long-term unemployed.
→ Special Areas Act 1934 gave £2 million to particularly deprived areas to attract businesses to move there.

The real solution to the economic problems was rearmament.

Exam question

answer: page 74

Why were the Conservatives able to dominate so much of the inter-war period? (45 min)

Test yourself

When you have finished reading these pages, take a blank sheet of paper and make a list of reasons why the Conservatives dominated this period.

Checkpoint 3

Why did the government 'win' the General Strike?

Checkpoint 4

How successful was the government with its economic policies?

Examiner's secrets

The examiner is looking for a well-argued debate rather than a list of reasons.

Foreign policy in the 1930s

Action point

Make your own notes on the words shown in bold in the text.

The jargon

Aggressive nationalism is the idea that a country's economic problems can be solved by using force against other countries.

Checkpoint 1

Why was Britain unwilling to take action against aggressive nationalism?

Checkpoint 2

Why did Britain not stop Germany violating the Treaty of Versailles?

Check the net

You can find material on this topic at www.spartacus.schoolnet.co.uk/britain.html

---

In 1918 Britain had just fought the 'war to end all wars'. Hopes for peace were high and the 1920s were a period of optimism. In the 1930s this optimism seemed misplaced and in 1939 Britain was once again at war with Germany.

Post-war background

With the **Treaty of Versailles** negotiated, British foreign policy consisted of making agreements that would ensure the peace would last:

→ 1921 Washington Agreements – attempted to resolve potential problems in the Pacific between the USA, Britain and Japan.
→ 1922 Genoa Conference – an attempt by Lloyd George to bring about the economic reconstruction of Europe by involving Soviet Russia and Germany in European affairs.
→ 1924 Dawes Plan – designed to help Germany pay its **reparations**.
→ 1925 Locarno Treaties – Britain would act as guarantor, along with Italy, for Germany maintaining its post-war borders.
→ 1928 Kellogg–Briand Pact – Britain renounced the use of war.

After the Wall Street crash of 1929 Britain found itself unwilling to deal with the aggressive nationalism that emerged.

→ 1931 – as a member of the Council of the League of Nations it took no action to prevent the Japanese invasion of Manchuria.
→ 1935 – Britain failed to stop the Italian invasion of Abyssinia for fear of driving Italy towards Germany.
→ 1936 – Britain was neutral during the Spanish Civil War.

This lack of action sent a clear message to Hitler.

Relations with Germany 1933–1937

The prevailing mood in Britain in the early 1930s was one of pacifism. There was also a belief that Germany had been treated too harshly in the Treaty of Versailles and had legitimate grievances that could be settled without it being a threat to Europe. The threat from Soviet Russia seemed to be stronger than that from Germany. A strong Germany would prevent Soviet expansion.

Britain did not completely ignore the possibility of war. A White Paper in 1935 suggesting that Britain would have to rely on its own resources led to a programme of rearming and the formation of the Stresa Front with France and Italy. This was designed to stop German expansion after its failed attempt to take over Austria in 1934. However, it was believed that the best way to avoid war was to allow Germany to redress its legitimate grievances.

→ 1935 – Germany announced the reintroduction of conscription. Britain did nothing.
→ 1935 Anglo-German naval agreement – Britain allowed Germany to rebuild its navy up to 35% of Britain's in the belief that, by doing this, German rearmament could be controlled.

→ 1936 – when Germany remilitarized the Rhineland, Britain did nothing to stop it, stating that Germany had the right to station troops anywhere within its own country.

However, Britain did accelerate its rearming programme.

Chamberlain and appeasement ●●●

In 1937 Neville Chamberlain became PM. His policy was one of appeasement – avoiding war by giving into the demands of Germany. He realized that it would be difficult to stop Germany without going to war, a war that would last many years and tear Europe apart. He hoped Soviet Russia and Germany would keep each other in check and Britain would not have to intervene. He hoped that, once Hitler's claims were settled, Germany would settle down and become a responsible member of Europe. In practical terms, there was little Britain could do to stop Germany as the rearming programme was not yet complete.

→ March 1938 – German troops took over Austria. A plebiscite showed that the vast majority of Austrians were satisfied with this, and this gave Chamberlain the excuse for not reacting.
→ The Sudetenland – Hitler demanded that the German-speaking part of Czechoslovakia be handed over to Germany. Chamberlain was not too interested in the area, believing that a revision of the borders would secure peace. He decided to meet Hitler to resolve the matter.

He met Hitler twice, but each time Hitler increased his demands concerning the Sudetenland. It looked as if war could not be avoided, and preparations were made in Britain. The situation was saved by the **Munich Conference** in September 1938. It was agreed that Germany would have the Sudetenland but would make no other territorial demands. Appeasement seemed to have worked. Despite this, Britain began to rearm even faster.

The outbreak of war 1939 ●●●

Appeasement died in March 1939 when Germany invaded and partitioned Czechoslovakia. Hitler had proved that he could not be trusted, and Chamberlain had to change his policy. Britain guaranteed the integrity of Poland and Rumania.

When Germany invaded Poland in September 1939, Britain had no real choice but to go to war with Germany. At least the policy of appeasement had given Britain the time to rearm.

Exam questions   answers: page 75

1a Was the policy of appeasement justifiable in the 1930s?

1b Why did Britain go to war with Germany in 1939? (1 hour)

The Labour government 1945–1951

The Labour government lasted less than six years, yet in that time it was responsible for a great deal of change: the post-war economic construction of the country, a large amount of nationalization, the creation of the welfare state and granting independence to India.

The elections of 1945 and 1951 ●●●

The massive majority gained by Labour in **the 1945 election** came as a surprise. The reasons for the victory were:

➜ Labour had promised to support the Beveridge Report, bringing in social reform, while the Conservatives had not.
➜ Labour ministers had gained experience in the wartime coalition government and were trusted to do a good job.
➜ The voters remembered the Conservatives from before the war and the fact that they had done little to help the population during the Depression.
➜ Churchill was a good wartime PM but not necessarily the right man to lead peacetime reconstruction.

Checkpoint 1

Why did Labour win a landslide victory?

Clement Attlee was able to form a strong government with Cripps at the Board of Trade and then the Treasury, Bevin as foreign secretary, Bevan as minister of health. In 1951, Labour lost the election because:

➜ The country was tired of the policies of austerity and rationing.
➜ The party had split badly over the introduction of prescription charges.
➜ Economic reconstruction had not yet worked through the system.
➜ Aspects of Labour policy, particularly nationalization, aroused opposition.
➜ Liberal voters, seeing the Liberals as a spent force (only won 9 seats), voted Conservative rather than Labour.

Check the net

Plenty of resources for this topic can be found at
www.spartacus.schoolnet.co.uk/

The economy 1945–1951 ●●●

After the war the British economy needed urgent reconstruction. Clause 4 of the **1918 Party Constitution** committed Labour to nationalization. Now was the time to put it into practice. Nationalization would give the government control over essential industries so they could make a contribution to economic reconstruction.

Checkpoint 2

What were the reasons for such wide-scale nationalisation?

➜ 1946 Bank of England, civil aviation.
➜ 1947 National Coal Board created, Cable & Wireless.
➜ 1948 Public transport, electricity.
➜ 1949 Gas.
➜ 1950 Iron and steel.

The jargon

Austerity meant that the population would have to do without luxuries in order to help economic recovery.

20% of industry was nationalized, but they were ones needing massive government investment. The profitable industries stayed private. Cripps (Board of Trade) accepted £1 263 million of **Marshall aid** to help recovery. He began a programme of 'austerity', which included:

→ Continuation of rationing.

→ Rents, profits, interest rates and wages were strictly controlled.

→ Imports were restricted to raw materials and essential items.

→ Sterling was devalued to help exports.

The programme succeeded in helping Britain to recover: industrial production had risen by 33% by 1951, but the full effects were not felt in time for the 1951 election.

The welfare state ●●●

Labour acted on the **1942 Beveridge Report** in order to begin creating a 'cradle to grave' welfare state. In 1946 the National Health Service was created by **Bevan**, coming into operation in 1948. Essentially, it gave free medical care to everybody on a non-contributory basis. It established the principle of paying for health care out of taxation. Hospitals were nationalized in order to be part of the system. The party was to split in 1951 when Bevan and others resigned over the question of making charges for some of the services of the NHS.

→ National Insurance Act 1946 – this extended the **1911 National Insurance Act** to all adults.

→ National Assistance Act 1948 – this was designed to act as a safety net for those not covered by the insurance scheme. Financed by taxation, it provided assistance beyond the unemployment benefit.

→ New Towns Act 1946 – gave the government powers to build new towns in areas that were healthier than the old urban areas.

→ Housing Act 1949 – revitalized council house building, which was desperately needed due to damage during the war.

Foreign and colonial affairs ●●●

The Labour government found itself in the position of having to negotiate the post-war settlement at **Potsdam** and maintain occupation forces in Germany. Bevin decided carefully when to become involved in foreign affairs and when to stay out. Britain participated in the **Berlin airlift** in 1948–1949 and was a founder member of **NATO** in 1949. It also sent troops to fight in the Korean War in 1950. However, it did not want to become involved in the Schumann Plan, which developed into the European Coal and Steel Community, believing that its interests lay more with the Commonwealth and the USA. It also took no action when the Persians nationalized the Anglo-Persian Oil Company in 1951.

Britain granted independence to Jordan in 1946 and India in 1947, and also handed over its mandate in Palestine to the UN in 1948.

Checkpoint 3

What was so important about the Labour reforms?

> *"It treats the individual as a citizen, not as a 'pauper', an object of charity . . ."*
>
> *The Times*, July 1948, commenting on the social security system

Test yourself

When you have finished reading these pages, take a blank sheet of paper and list the legislation that created a welfare state.

Checkpoint 4

What was Britain's colonial policy at this time?

Exam questions   answers: page 75

1. What were the achievements of the Labour government 1945–1951? (45 min)

2. Why did Labour win the election in 1945 but lose the election in 1951? (45 min)

Examiner's secrets

Look at the questions thematically rather than just give a list of what was done.

Answers
British history 1868–1951

Gladstone 1868–1874

Checkpoints

1 Gladstonian Liberalism could be summed up as individual freedoms, cheap and efficient government, minimal government interference, free trade and a peaceful foreign policy.

2 The Education Act was designed to allow everyone to gain an elementary education, from which they could go on and better themselves. The university, Civil Service and army reforms would mean people gaining posts on merit only.

3 Gladstone suffered from comparison with Palmerston. Palmerston always seemed to promote British interests against foreigners; Gladstone always seemed to be giving in to the foreigners.

4 They did not set out to alienate most of the country. It was inevitable that all groups could find something to complain about among the mass of legislation.

Exam questions

1 You need to begin your answer by defining what you understand by the principles of Gladstonian Liberalism. The question specifies domestic legislation, so confine yourself to that. You would be as well to concentrate on the ideas of freedoms for the individual and cheap and efficient government.

Look at the major pieces of legislation and decide which principle they exemplify. In each case, state what Gladstone was trying to do and what he did, linking the legislation to the principles.

You should also show that much of the legislation came about after pressure from various groups. An example is the National Education League, which campaigned for a form of state education. The Education Act was Gladstone's response.

In your conclusion, you need to answer 'how far?' So you must make a value judgement. You should say that the legislation does not fully reflect his principles, as some of it was forced on him. Some of the legislation is open to interpretation. The Criminal Law Amendment Act can be said to have given individual workers the right to carry on working, but it can also be said that it took away the freedom of action for the workers as a whole.

2 Here it is necessary to look at both the negative side of Gladstone's legislation and the positive side of Disraeli and the Conservatives in 1874.

Start by looking at Gladstone's domestic legislation and, in each case, explain which groups would have been upset by it. An example might be Forster's Education Act; although brought in for positive reasons, the compromise on religious teaching alienated both the Anglicans and the Nonconformists. Many factory owners also resented it as a valuable source of cheap labour disappeared. Show how an accumulation of bad feeling built up as a result of the legislation and demonstrate how virtually every section of society could find something to complain about.

Explain how Gladstone's 'weak' foreign policy was disliked by many of the voters.

Contrast the dynamic Conservative organization under Gorst with the less than dynamic organization of the Liberals. It would be useful here to explain that the Liberals were a group of different persuasions held together by Gladstone. Once he had finished what he had set out to do he had lost interest and so the groups drifted apart.

Then refer to Disraeli and his speeches of 1872, which promised social reform and making Britain great again on the world stage. You could use the phrase 'a range of exhausted volcanoes'. It has been suggested that in the 1874 election many of the workers who were enfranchised by the 1867 Reform Act could vote for the first time, and they voted for Disraeli as a reward for the Act.

In your conclusion, use the quote by Gladstone and say that although there is an element of truth in it, it does not fully explain the Liberals' defeat.

Examiner's secrets

To help you prepare for any question concerning Gladstone's first ministry, make a list of his legislation and then link each Act to a particular principle and to a particular group that was upset by it.

Gladstone 1880–1893

Checkpoints

1 They won the 1880 election partly because of the failings of Disraeli's ministry and partly because in his crusade against 'Beaconsfieldism' Gladstone had reunited the Liberal Party and given it a dynamic image again.

2 On the positive side, it was important because it went some way to breaking the Conservatives' stranglehold in the counties. On the negative side, it meant that they could no longer run two candidates, Whig and radical in the same seat, so accelerating the move of the more right-wing Whigs away from the party. However, it did put parliamentary reform back into the hands of the Liberals after the 1867 Act.

3 Once again Gladstone suffered because of comparison, this time with Disraeli. Whereas Disraeli had stood up for British interests at the Congress of Berlin, and had expanded the Empire, Gladstone was seen as giving it all away with a policy of appeasement. At the other extreme, many of his own supporters disliked the British occupation of Egypt.

4 The impact of Irish home rule was to split the party badly, with 93 MPs leaving it. The right-wing Whigs were against it: many had land and other interests there and feared for their safety. Chamberlain and the Liberal Unionists were also against it, believing that it would be the first stage in breaking up the Empire.

Exam questions

1 This is a complicated question and needs to be answered carefully. In your introduction you should give a yardstick against which Gladstone's failure to bring in home rule in 1886 and 1893 can be measured. By then, only that would satisfy the Irish.

Explain the problem with Ireland, religion and land being paramount. Briefly explain how the disestablishment of the Irish Church removed the problem of religion. The land question was more difficult to deal with, as he had to balance the interests of Irish tenants against the interests of the landowners. Private property was still considered sacred. So the first Irish Land Act did not go far enough and aroused much resentment among the Irish, pushing them to the point where they felt that only home rule would solve their problems.

Show how Gladstone brought in the second Irish Land Act but still did not go far enough, being forced to cooperate with Parnell to stop the violence in Ireland.

Show Gladstone's conversion to home rule but explain how this was leaked before he had time to prepare his own party. Also explain the effect of the Phoenix Park murders. Explain the opposition to home rule within the party and within the country and use it to explain why home rule failed in 1886.

The next paragraph should deal with the end of cooperation between Gladstone and Parnell. The lack of links with the Irish leadership meant he could not stop increasing Irish unrest. Mention the failure of the 1893 Bill, blocked by the House of Lords.

Conclude that Gladstone acted too slowly at the beginning in not fully granting what the Irish wanted and too quickly later when he attempted to bring in home rule without fully preparing his party.

2 In your introduction explain that Gladstone had severely criticized Disraeli during the Midlothian campaign for his handling of foreign and imperial affairs, but when he came to power he ended up doing almost the same.

Your first major paragraph should explain Gladstone's criticisms of Disraeli. Emphasize Gladstone's disgust at all the actions that extended the Empire: the Suez Canal shares, the Royal Titles Bill, etc. Also how he criticized action in Afghanistan.

Say how he was forced by changing circumstances, and the need to protect British interests, to do almost the same. The British occupation of Egypt is a good example to use. Also the threat of war with Russia over Afghanistan went against his original principle.

Sum up by showing that Gladstone, when he was faced with the harsh reality of protecting British interests, could not maintain his original principles. However, do point out that many of his problems were a legacy of the previous government's actions.

Checkpoints

1 Obviously, his attempts to be elected first as a radical then as a Tory gave him a reputation as an opportunist. This was enhanced by the fact that he was an ardent admirer of Peel until 1841, when he joined the opposition to Peel, believing that it would gain him advancement within the party.

2 The Manchester Free Trade Hall speech and the Crystal Palace speech in 1872 were important as they gave the Conservatives a new identity. By promising social reform and to make Britain great again, the Conservatives could appeal to the whole spectrum of classes and win over Liberal voters.

3 Previous legislation on public health was piecemeal and not very coherent. The 1875 Act just made the system more standardized and efficient.

4 The answer to this would depend on where they lived. In some areas, local authorities took full advantage of the legislation and so workers' health and housing improved. In others, authorities did not want to spend money, and workers saw little improvement. They did get more rights in trade disputes though.

Exam questions

1 You first need to define what is meant by the two terms. A Tory could be defined as one who resists any change, as did the Tories for a while after the Napoleonic wars. A Tory democrat might be defined as one who wanted to preserve the institutions of the country but realized that some change would be needed to improve the position of the majority of people. You might even use the term 'one-nation Tory', here explaining that Disraeli portrayed himself and the Conservatives as the champions of the workers against the industrialists.

As to why he made the change, you might decide that it was opportunism, realizing after the Whig reforms of the 1830s that the Conservatives had no chance of being elected if they were not prepared to make concessions. Or you might decide that it was practical necessity that made him change. As the circumstances of Britain changed so the policies had to change to meet them. You may decide that it was a combination of both reasons. Whatever you decide, make it clear in the introduction and then prove it.

Start with him as a Tory, wanting little or no change in the 1830s, and then during Peel's ministry, where he joined the opposition to Peel within the Conservatives. Explain the issues on which he criticized Peel.

After the fall of Peel, he was in the position of giving the Conservatives a new policy. It was he who persuaded Derby to accept the principle of free trade. Without this the Conservatives would have been unlikely to have a majority government again.

A further move towards Tory democracy came with the 1867 Reform Act. Even though Disraeli's motives can be questioned, one of the impacts of the Act was to force political parties to take more notice of the grievances of their constituents. To win a majority after 1867 a party leader had to appeal to the workers. The speeches of 1872 and what they promised show the move towards Tory democracy.

Finally, show what he did in his second ministry to put his ideas into practice. Evaluate the legislation: did it show Disraeli as a Tory democrat, or was it merely window dressing?

2 This is a fairly straightforward question if you take care to keep within the limits set out. Begin by saying what you understand by Disraelian Conservatism and briefly explain how his legislation reflects that.

Look at the 1872 Free Trade Hall and Crystal Palace speeches, where he outlined what his future policies would be. Also consider what he had said before regarding his philosophy. As in the previous question bring in the concepts of the 'aristocratic settlement', one-nation Toryism and Tory democracy.

Now look at his legislation by themes: public health, the workers and education. Say what he did in each of these areas and what can be deduced from the legislation about Disraelian Conservatism.

Conclude with a short statement defining Disraelian Conservatism, reflecting your study of his policies.

Disraeli 2

Checkpoints

1 Disraeli felt that he had gained security for Britain's trade route to India by preventing the Russians having a base in the eastern Mediterranean. Also, Cyprus would be very useful strategically in that area.

2 Britain could now prevent the canal being shut to British traffic in the future. As a major shareholder, it was able to reduce tolls, making trade cheaper.

3 The British parts of South Africa, the Cape and Natal, were still seen as essential to protect trade routes. Also, diamonds had been found at Kimberley, bringing wealth to Britain.

4 Afghanistan was seen to be a buffer between Russian expansion and British India. If Afghanistan fell under Russian influence then, it was believed, there would be nothing to stop the Russians invading.

Exam question

This question can be divided into three separate sections: what each wanted to do; what each did; and the results of their actions.

Introduce your answer by briefly explaining that each had different principles and different degrees of success in achieving them. Each faced different challenges in protecting British interests.

Compare their principles. Gladstone's desire for a moral foreign policy and his more practical desire to avoid a costly war. Disraeli and his more flamboyant policy designed to maintain Britain's position as a major power, prepared to use force if necessary. Compare their views on the Empire: Gladstone criticizing Disraeli for the expansion of the Empire and criticizing the Royal Titles Bill; Disraeli openly stating that he intended to uphold the Empire.

Look at Gladstone's policies and explain how they could be seen as appeasement, particularly the 'Alabama' case. Compare with the more aggressive policies of Disraeli.

A good example where a direct comparison can be made is the Eastern question. Gladstone backed down and let Russia build naval bases on the Black Sea, while Disraeli threatened Russia and forced it to back down over the question of Big Bulgaria.

Explain, however, that in Gladstone's case he was diplomatically isolated so could not have done much more, whereas Disraeli had the support of Austria.

Conclude by showing how unpopular Gladstone's policy was with the British public and how popular was the policy of Disraeli but that each of them had tried to protect British interests as they saw them.

Parliamentary reform 1867–1918

Checkpoints

1 After Chartism, violence had died down. The workers had set up self-help organizations and were becoming increasingly literate. Skilled labour was showing other types of responsible behaviour. Gladstone was impressed by mill workers' attitude during the 'cotton famine'.

2 Disraeli had personal motives (revenge on the Whigs) and practical motives. He believed that the newly enfranchised working class would vote for Conservatives rather than Liberals, who were associated with the employers.

3 The Conservatives benefited most from the Acts. In some constituencies the Liberal vote was split and Conservatives got in. Constituency boundaries favoured Conservatives in the countryside, where their traditional support lay, and in the suburbs. Liberal votes tended to be concentrated in large urban areas.

4 The effects were not as great as might have been hoped. Although the Lords could not block Bills entirely they could delay them for quite a long time in the hope that the Liberal government would fall.

Exam question

This question is designed to look at change over a period of time. It is important that you demonstrate your understanding of the changing nature of Britain during the period to help you to explain your answer.

Although the question refers to the size of the electorate, it also needs explanation of the redistribution of seats, because even if qualified, a man could not vote unless there was a seat.

Begin your explanation by looking at the results of the Great Reform Act 1832: how they did not satisfy everybody, as shown by the Chartist movement. Show how the Reform League agitated for reform and why it was thought right and necessary by such as Gladstone that there should be reform.

Explain the reasons behind Gladstone's 1866 Bill. Then explain the reasoning behind Disraeli's 1867 Act. Show what the Act did to increase the size of the electorate in terms of reducing the qualifications and in the redistribution of seats. Look at what the Act did not do to explain the need for further reform.

Look next at the Acts of 1884 and 1885. Show why they were brought in and the impact they had on the size of the electorate. Look at what the Acts left undone regarding the poorest voters and women.

Next should come a brief explanation of the women's suffrage movement and the impact it had

A paragraph on the social impact of the Great War 1914–1918 should explain why the government felt it right to extend the franchise in 1918.

Explain the details of the 1918 Act, with particular emphasis on giving the vote to women.

Throughout the answer you need to look at the motives of those who brought in reform. Sometimes it was from a genuine belief that reform was necessary; at other times there were personal or political motives. Look also at the changes in the population of the country, both in terms of distribution and in terms of their share in the country's wealth creation.

Examiner's secrets

As the question specifies the size of the electorate, the examiner will expect you to have a detailed knowledge of the effect of the reform in respect to this.

Salisbury and the Conservatives

Checkpoints

1 The main effect was an increase in administrative efficiency in the new authorities. It also had the effect of reducing the power of county landowners.
2 A large empire would be advantageous for supplying raw materials and food at very good rates and also as a huge market for British goods. An empire could also provide manpower in the event of war.
3 During Salisbury's time the Empire expanded considerably, particularly in Africa. Parts of West Africa, British East Africa and Rhodesia were added.

4 It came to an end when the disadvantages outweighed the advantages. As the European nations moved into blocs it became increasingly dangerous to remain alone if Britain was to have any influence in world affairs. Its navy could defend Britain but not challenge the growing alliances.

Exam question

(a) Start by defining 'imperialism': deliberately seeking to acquire overseas land. Explain that it was not particularly popular with Salisbury, but he was driven by the need to protect British interests.

Look at the economic reasons behind imperialism. Money could be made by exploiting the natural resources. Also, according to Chamberlain, the Empire would provide both a source of raw materials and a market for British goods. Britain with an empire could ride out any economic depression. Britain had entered the 'Great Depression' in 1875, so this would be attractive to the population.

Look at the social aspect of imperialism. Many thought that the natives benefited from British rule as it brought civilization to them. In some cases this was true: Britain annexed Bechuanaland to protect the rights of missionaries and the natives. Mention the works of writers such as Kipling, who popularized the idea of 'the white man's burden'.

Finish off this part by also looking at the idea of pride in an empire, and 'patriotism'.

(b) There are two parts to this answer: positive and negative. On the positive side, the existence of the Empire provided a pool of manpower to create an army should Britain ever need one to fight a war on the continent. The Empire also provided Britain with a number of strategic bases from which it could defend its vital trade routes.

Then look at the negative aspect. Britain needed troops to protect the interests of citizens in the Empire. It was not until towards the end of the 19th century that some of the Empire was in a position to defend itself. The Empire provided a possible point of conflict with other countries, which might lead to war. An example was the Fashoda incident.

To defend the colonies, Britain needed to maintain a larger navy than it needed. As Britain's worries grew about the German Navy, it was hampered by the need to have ships all over the world.

Make a value judgement as to whether you think that the Empire made a positive or a negative contribution to Britain's defence strategy.

Examiner's secrets

For every point you make ensure that you have at least one actual example. For instance, for the point about having to maintain troops to protect British interests you could use the reconquest of the Sudan or the Boer War.

Ireland 1868–1922

Checkpoints

1 The Irish believed that the Westminster parliament had no interest and no desire to improve matters. Only when they had control over their own domestic affairs would their grievances be dealt with.

2 The Conservatives feared for the position of the Protestants in Ireland. The Whigs were often absentee landowners and were worried about their interests. The Liberal Unionists feared that home rule would be the first step to complete disintegration of the Empire. There was also a worry that Ireland under home rule might weaken Britain's defences.

3 Parnell was considered to be the 'uncrowned king of Ireland'. His ability and charisma meant that he had enormous influence over the Irish. Gladstone recognized this when he negotiated with Parnell in the 'Kilmainham Treaty'.

4 The question was no longer if the Irish would gain home rule but the terms of home rule. Would Ulster be included? The delays allowed extremists to emerge, and a sizeable section of the population would no longer be satisfied with just home rule; they wanted independence from Britain.

Exam questions

1 Identify the problems of Ireland during the period. These were religion, the land, the desire for home rule, the question of a separate Ulster and, running through the whole period, violence. You can argue that while British governments may have been able to deal with some of these problems effectively they did not deal with the problem as a whole very well or Ireland would not have become independent in 1922.

Deal with each of the problems separately. In each case say briefly what the problem was and how the governments attempted to deal with it (give examples of legislation).

Show how governments, whether Liberal or Conservative, tended to react rather than initiate. This often meant that by the time they gave the Irish what they wanted it was too late and the problem had escalated, with the Irish wanting more. An example of this is the number of Land Acts that were needed, as each one did not go far enough to solve the problem.

Conclude by evaluating the overall success of British policy towards solving Irish problems.

2 A simple statement that they faced too much opposition will do to introduce your answer. Then in the main part of your answer you can identify and explain the opposition to home rule.

Look at the three separate attempts by the Liberals to bring in Irish home rule: 1886, 1893 and 1912. You should make it clear that the nature of the opposition changed each time. In 1886 Gladstone failed to win over his own party to the idea, so the crucial opposition came from within the Liberals.

In 1893 the rest of the Liberals were lukewarm concerning Ireland and when the Lords rejected it were not prepared to put up a fight.

In 1912 it was the opposition of Ulster that caused the biggest problem. By the time that had been dealt with and the Lords had delayed the passage of the Bill it was too late. The Great War caused the suspension of the Act.

Sum up by explaining that the British public had little interest in home rule. There was little public opinion behind the idea, allowing the opposition to prevent it.

The Liberals 1906–1914

Checkpoints

1 This was a development from the collectivism of Gladstone. It was more interventionist, saying that the state had a right and a duty to intervene to ensure that there was a minimum standard of living for the poorest sections of the population.

2 It was needed because the social surveys and the condition of Boer War recruits showed the bad health of the poorest parts of the population. Childhood diseases and malnutrition were leading to unfit adults.

3 The legislation did not actually create a welfare state, nor was it meant to. It was restricted to only those who needed it rather than the population as a whole.

4 The Lords only blocked Bills concerning small sections of the community to avoid alienating the people. Some Bills (e.g. school meals) were let through to stop the Conservatives losing support.

Exam question

This is a fairly straightforward question as long as you remember that it calls for an evaluation.

First look at the condition of the people when the Liberals came to power. Explain the problems.

Briefly explain appropriate pieces of legislation, e.g. National Insurance Act or old age pensions. Look at the limitations of each Act. Who was covered by it?

Evaluate the effect of each Act in solving the particular problem and evaluate the effect of the legislation as a whole by looking at how many people benefited from the Liberal social reform.

Votes for women

Checkpoints

1 By the end of the 19th century, middle-class and upper-class women had more time and more status. They could enter a number of professions, run their own businesses and work in respectable jobs. They were more independent than before. The position of working-class women hardly changed at all.
2 This was the idea of gaining publicity for the cause. It started off mildly enough with leaflets and marches but developed into more violent actions, including breaking shop windows and disrupting the Derby.
3 They had no problem with giving certain women the vote but worried that enfranchising all over 21 would increase the number of Liberal and Labour voters as the poorest males were still disenfranchised.
4 Women played a valuable part in the war. Many munitions workers were women. They helped feed Britain by joining the Land Army. Their work in the Auxiliary Services freed up men to fight at the front.

Exam question

This is a question where the examiner is looking for debate rather than narrative.

Look at the actions taken by the suffragettes. Explain that before Mrs Pankhurst the government had taken little notice of the issue. Pankhurst's 'sensation mongering' (give some examples) prodded the government into taking some action.

Also show how the suffragettes' actions might have harmed their cause by making women seem extreme and not responsible enough to be given the vote.

Next look at the effects of the Great War, particularly the fact that women played such an important part in the war effort (give examples).

Explain that the government was going to extend the franchise in 1918 (one of the effects of the Great War), and giving the vote to women as well could be considered to be a reward for their war work.

However, consider that Asquith had hinted in 1914 that he was prepared to give the vote to women but then the Great War delayed this.

Sum up your answer. You might decide that the suffragettes brought the issue to the forefront, but the war finally decided the government.

Foreign policy 1902–1914

Checkpoints

1 The Cleveland message and the Fashoda incident showed how little influence Britain had without allies.

The Boer War had emphasized the danger. Britain would be stretched to defend itself and fight a war.
2 The main threat was Germany's colonial and naval ambitions. The British saw that Germany's growing navy could attack Britain or British trade routes.
3 They had a common interest in defending their empires and themselves against Germany.
4 Britain had guaranteed Belgian neutrality in 1839, and this had been reaffirmed by Gladstone in 1870.

Exam question

The simple answer to this question is: because the Germans invaded Belgium, and this was the excuse given. However, the causes are more complex.

Start by looking at the growing rivalry between Britain and Germany. Pay particular attention to colonial rivalry and naval rivalry. Give examples.

Explain how and why Britain became involved in the Anglo-French Entente and how this implied a moral, if not legal, commitment to help France.

Show how Britain both helped France and countered possible German threats to British interests in the two Moroccan crises, and explain the growing collaboration with France, as shown by joint military talks and naval agreements to the point where Britain would help France in the event of German attack.

Conclude that although it was the invasion of Belgium that caused Britain to go to war, it might have gone to war to support France. You could argue that Britain was already spoiling for a war with Germany, and Belgium's invasion gave the excuse.

The rise of the Labour Party

Checkpoints

1 Growing disillusionment with Gladstone's lack of reform, and the emergence of socialist thinkers such as Hyndman, helped the growth of socialist groups.
2 So many legal decisions had gone against the unions in the 1890s that the TUC realized the only way to protect itself was to have working-class MPs.
3 Participation in the coalition government gave the party some experience. Leaving it in 1917 emphasized the party's separateness from the Liberals.
4 Labour lost partly because of the fear of socialism caused by the Zinoviev letter and partly because once Baldwin had renounced protectionism, those in favour of free trade could now vote Conservative.

Exam question

The object of this question is to show how the rise of the Labour Party was paralleled by the decline of the Liberals. Was it cause and effect?

Begin by showing how socialist groups emerged as a reaction to the lack of real reform by the Liberals.

Explain that by 1906 the Labour Party was a real challenger to the Liberals for the working-class vote, so much so that they allowed a number of Labour candidates to stand unopposed in the 1906 election in return for Labour support of Liberal policies.

Show how the Labour MPs acted as a ginger group in the Liberal government contributing to social reform.

Look at how the Labour Party reinvented itself post-1918 to appeal to a wider spectrum of society. Mention that some Liberals defected to Labour.

Finish by showing the changing electoral fortune of the two parties after 1918. Use the fact that Labour was able to form governments in 1924 and 1929 as the second-largest party and come to an evaluation as to the impact of the Labour challenge.

Liberals in decline 1914–1922

Checkpoints

1 He was challenged partly because the war was not going well. Britain had failed to make a breakthrough, partly because of Lloyd George's ambition. He had already proved himself a competent politician and his work during the war had won him plenty of support.

2 Generally very successful in that he made sure the army was supplied with what it needed, built up good morale on the home front and forced the successful convoy system on the Admiralty. But he had little control over the generals in the actual fighting.

3 He was criticized by the Conservatives for not taking enough revenge on Germany. The Labour Party criticized him for accepting the German colonies. They had fought the war for ideals, not land.

4 He fell from power because the Conservatives no longer needed him, his popularity declined due to his failure after 1918 to tackle social problems. The Turkish affair was just an excuse.

Exam questions

1 You might possibly begin your answer with the quote from A. J. P. Taylor to explain how personal rivalries split the Liberals into two separate factions.

Explain how the election of 1918, when the Liberals fought as two groups, did great harm to the party.

Also show how the rise of the Labour Party took away a great deal of working-class support.

Explain how Baldwin's acceptance of free trade left the Liberals with no issues of their own with which to fight elections and so their parliamentary presence essentially declined.

2 You can use the same material as the previous question, but emphasize the role of Lloyd George.

Examine Lloyd George's challenge for the leadership of the party and the effect on the party. Look at his role in the 1918 election. Did he help or slow down the decline of the Liberals with his actions? Look at his lack of social reform after 1918. Did this change people's support for the Liberals?

Consider the other factors responsible. Asquith's actions and motives need to be mentioned. Also look at Labour's rise, taking away Liberal votes.

Sum up by saying how much of the responsibility for the decline of the Liberals should be Lloyd George's and how far their decline was due to other factors.

Conservative inter-war domination

Checkpoints

1 By giving up the idea of protection, Baldwin allowed those people who had voted Liberal or Labour in the previous election purely because they wanted to maintain free trade, to vote Conservative again.

2 The aim was to cut government expenditure by making the schemes efficient and as cheap as possible.

3 The government had nine months to prepare to counter the strike. In the same time the TUC had not prepared at all. The government had the power of the press and the BBC to put its case, unlike the TUC.

4 The government was successful in maintaining financial stability and keeping down government expenditure, but it did nothing about the root causes of distress. The situation was only resolved as a result of rearming prior to the war.

Exam question

Begin by explaining that the Conservatives were the real government of Britain for all but three of the years between the wars. In Lloyd George's coalition and later the National Government the Conservatives were the dominant partners. The Conservatives did not actually lose any elections between the wars.

Show how the Conservatives faced no real opposition during this time. Their acceptance of Lloyd George in 1918, while he was still a hero, guaranteed the coalition would win in 1918. From then on the Liberals were too split to be a viable opposition, and Labour was not yet developed enough.

Explain how Baldwin's acceptance of free trade gave Liberals nothing to oppose the Conservatives.

Explain why Labour was not re-elected in 1924.

Show how the Conservatives allowed the Labour government to take the unpopular decisions in 1931 before joining the National Government. Above all, emphasize the 'safety first' aspect of Baldwin's policies. He did nothing to upset the voters and so did not lose elections.

Foreign policy in the 1930s

Checkpoints

1 Britain was going through an economic depression of its own. It did not want the expense of taking action, especially as there was no guarantee that it would be supported by any other major power.

2 By the time Hitler came to power there was a growing belief that the Treaty was too harsh on Germany. While Germany remained within it own borders there seemed to be no compelling reason to stop it.

3 He had fought in the Great War and did not want a repeat. He wanted a strong Germany as a check on Soviet expansion. He believed that Germany had legitimate grievances. He realized Britain was not in a position to take military action against Germany.

4 It gave Britain a breathing space in which to complete rearming. The Conference and subsequent invasion of Czechoslovakia showed that Hitler could not be trusted and that appeasement would not work.

Exam questions

1a Begin by defining appeasement. Explain that although it is mostly linked with Chamberlain it was used by Britain throughout the 1930s.

The question asks 'Was the policy justifiable?', so you need to explain the situation of Britain in the 1930s. Suffering during the Depression, its resources were stretched. Its military strength had been run down after the Great War. To take an active role in world affairs it would need to rearm, at great cost. There was a mood of pacifism in the country. Few people wanted to get into another war so soon after the last.

Look at particular instances of appeasement. With the Japanese invasion of Manchuria Britain was not in a position to act alone, and other powers did not help; besides, the League of Nations had been created to deal with such matters. Similarly with the Italian invasion of Abyssinia: no British interests were directly threatened, and being aggressive to Mussolini might drive him into alliance with Hitler. Mention the Hoare–Laval plan as an example of appeasement.

Britain felt some justification in allowing Germany to reverse some parts of the Treaty of Versailles.

Sum up by showing that, given the circumstances, the policy of appeasement was justifiable. Britain was not in a position to take action against the aggressors, and its interests were not being directly threatened.

1b This obviously links to the previous question. While appeasement was initially justifiable, circumstances changed. From the mid-1930s Britain rearmed and by 1939 was in a position to take action. Appeasement had proved not to work. Until March 1939, Hitler's actions were excusable, but not after Czechoslovakia.

One of the reasons for appeasement was the hope that Germany would prevent Soviet expansion. After the Nazi–Soviet Pact this reason disappeared.

There was the moral aspect. Hitler had broken his promise; none of Europe was safe. If Britain was to remain a great power then it needed to take action. Having said that Poland would be protected, Britain had to act when Poland was invaded.

The reason why Britain went to war after years of appeasement is that circumstances had changed.

The Labour government 1945–1951

Checkpoints

1 The war was over and the voters wanted social reform and reconstruction. They believed that Labour would give them this and the Conservatives would not.

2 Certain industries desparately needed rebuilding with massive investment. Only government could provide this, and in return it wanted control over the industries as part of its reconstruction plans.

3 They ensured that everyone, regardless of income, had access to important state services.

4 Under international pressure Britain's policy was to grant independence to countries ready for it (e.g. India) and prepare other countries for independence.

Exam questions

1 This question is very straightforward. You need to deal with the achievements thematically and then sum up overall achievement at the end.

Economic reconstruction. Look at the economic situation in 1945, explain what Labour did to improve matters and then make a comparison with the situation in 1951.

The formation of the welfare state. Explain what Labour did to create what is possibly its greatest achievement. It could also be seen as bringing in socialism, as with the policy of nationalization.

Foreign and colonial affairs. Show how Labour managed to maintain Britain's position as a major world power. Also show how it achieved the independence of India.

Evaluate the success of what Labour did in order to see whether it qualifies as 'achievements'.

2 Start by showing that Labour won a landslide victory in 1945 but only just lost in 1951. The change in fortunes was due to a gradual change in attitude towards the Labour government.

Explain the reasons why it won in 1945. It was seen as the best party for post-war reconstruction.

Briefly outline its policies and explain how it aroused some opposition.

Look at the situation in 1951. The voters were tired of 'austerity'. They wanted a change. The vote was not so much in favour of the Conservatives as against Labour policies now that the real work was done.

European history 1815–1894

This was a time of extraordinary change in Europe. The social and economic changes associated with the Industrial Revolution became more important as the century went on. Increasingly, these brought about pressure for political change as well. The ideas of liberalism and nationalism, although originating in the 18th century, had a profound influence on events across Europe in this period. This section will trace these developments as well as giving an indication of the problems that Europe faced as it entered the 20th century.

Exam themes

→ Reasons for political change.

→ The impact of individuals on the politics of the time.

→ Comparisons between important individuals.

→ The relationship between events in different parts of Europe.

Topic checklist

○ AS ● A2	AQA	EDEXCEL	OCR	WJEC
The Vienna settlement 1815	○			○
Russia 1815–1894	○		●	○●
France 1815–1848	○	●	●	
The 1848 revolutions	○		●	
France under Louis Napoleon	○		●	●
Italian unification	○		●	○
German unification	○	●	●	○
The French Third Republic	○			
Bismarck's Germany	○	●		○
Bismarck's foreign policy	○			●

The Vienna settlement 1815

The Vienna settlement of 1815 was an attempt to redraw the map of Europe after years of French control. The statesmen were aiming to prevent anyone dominating the continent in the way that Napoleon had done.

The 'twin evils' ●●●

The aim was to create a treaty that would be satisfactory to the majority of Europe and so secure a lasting peace. The settlement was also an attempt to control the twin 'evils' of **nationalism** and **liberalism**, which were held to be responsible for the upheavals of the previous two decades. Does the fact that the wartime alliance had fallen apart by the early 1820s mean that Vienna was a bad treaty?

The peacemakers ●●●

Their aims were:

→ Castlereagh (Britain) – devoted to the principle of **balance of power**, which in particular would mean resisting the territorial ambitions of Russia. France was the other main threat to future peace, so containment of the French was also necessary. Peace would benefit Britain commercially.
→ Metternich (Austria) – wanted a balance of power as well as a strong Central Europe (under Austrian control) as a barrier to Russia.
→ Tsar Alexander I (emperor of Russia) – wanted to use the congress to pursue Russian expansion into Poland. Totally opposed to any measure that could be seen to be promoting nationalism or liberalism.
→ Hardenberg (Prussia) – Prussia was weak after the Napoleonic wars and was indebted to Russia for liberating most of the kingdom from the French. Accordingly, Hardenberg had to follow the Russian line.
→ Talleyrand (France) – aimed to convince the allies that France was no longer a threat. He was also the chief exponent of the principle of **legitimacy**.

Guiding principles ●●●

Aside from their own specific aims there was agreement that all the negotiations should be based around certain fundamental principles:

→ Balance of power.
→ The need for a lasting peace after nearly two decades of conflict.
→ Compensation – a nation that lost territory under the provisions of Vienna should be compensated with land from elsewhere.
→ Legitimacy – the restoration to power of monarchs who had been dethroned because of the wars.
→ Containment of France.

Action point

Use relevant maps to see how Vienna changed the borders of Europe.

Checkpoint 1

What were the peacemakers likely to disagree about?
How do these disputes help us to understand why the wartime alliance had collapsed by the 1820s?

The territorial and political settlement ●●●

Some of the major provisions: Poland, Finland, Bessarabia to Russia; Saxony and the Rhineland to Prussia; Austria given Lombardy and Venetia; Belgium to Holland; Nice and Genoa to Piedmont; British colonial gains; German Confederation reconstituted; various legitimate monarchs returned to power.

The Concert of Europe ●●●

The 'Concert of Europe' is the term used to describe the various ways the major powers attempted to cooperate after 1815. Through working together they had defeated France and then produced a peace that was broadly acceptable to all. But what was to be the basis of future cooperation? By the end of 1815 there were two contradictory proposals:

→ Tsar Alexander's **Holy Alliance** (signed by most European sovereigns but crucially not the Prince Regent of Britain). Dominated by Russia, Austria and Prussia, it was an agreement to maintain the settlement of 1815 but more importantly it became a tool to crack down on liberalism and nationalism wherever they arose.

→ The **Quadruple Alliance**, signed by all the wartime allies but very much reflecting Britain's view that maintaining the Vienna settlement *did not* necessarily mean interfering in the internal affairs of European states (to crush liberalism and nationalism).

The congresses ●●●

Under the Quadruple Alliance the powers agreed to meet periodically:

→ **Aix-la-Chapelle 1818** – France readmitted to the concert of powers (the Quintuple Alliance).

→ Troppau and Laibach 1820–1821 – called in the wake of **liberal nationalist revolutions in the Italian and Iberian peninsulas**. The Troppau Protocol was agreed to by the Holy Alliance powers. Castlereagh conceded Austria's right to intervene in Naples but not in the name of the alliance.

→ Verona 1823 – to which the new British foreign secretary, Canning, sent only an observer. France was authorized to intervene in Spain despite British protests. Post-war cooperation was over.

"The principle of one state interfering in the affairs of another . . . is always a question of the greatest moral delicacy"

Castlereagh's state paper

Russia 1815–1894

Russia, in 1815, was an enormous multi-ethnic empire of incredible backwardness. In many ways Russia had never left the Middle Ages. The bulk of the huge population were **serfs**, the property of the Russian nobility, and still using extraordinarily primitive methods to work the land.

19th-century Russia

Industrial development was still in its infancy. Russia was an **autocracy**, the Romanov tsars having an extraordinary amount of personal power based upon the principle of **divine right**. A vast army, a brutal secret police, a huge civil service and the spiritual influence of the Orthodox Church maintained this power. The tsars of the 19th century attempted, using widely differing methods, to modernize Russia. Without doubt, Russia changed, but not necessarily in the way the tsars intended.

Alexander I (1801–1825)

Alexander had ascended to the throne in 1801. He was a paradoxical character, torn between ideas of liberalism he had acquired in his youth and the traditions of Russian autocracy. In the early part of his reign he had enacted various reforms, such as the abolition of torture and censorship as well as the creation of the permanent council, whose job was to advise the Tsar on government business. After 1815 Alexander continued to consider the possibility of liberal reforms but in practice became more reactionary. Secret societies were forming, dissatisfied with Alexander's failure to live up to his liberal reputation. Rather than make concessions, Alexander:

→ Banned study abroad and purged Russia's university system.
→ Brought back strict censorship.
→ Suppressed secret societies.

Nicholas I (1825–1855)

Nicholas, the younger brother of Alexander, had to deal with the army-led **Decembrist revolt** as soon as he became tsar. It aimed to bring about political and social reform (such as the ending of serfdom). It was brutally suppressed by loyal troops. Nicholas ruled according to the principles of '**orthodoxy, autocracy and nationality**'. Various reactionary measures were introduced. Most importantly, the secret police (the Third Section), which had been abolished by Alexander I, was re-established. Nicholas did see the need to modernize Russia socially and economically. Various reforms were introduced that would have been quite effective, but were not rigidly enforced:

→ Serfs could not be sold except as family units.
→ Encouragement of factory development.
→ The codification of laws that reminded nobles of their obligations to the serfs.

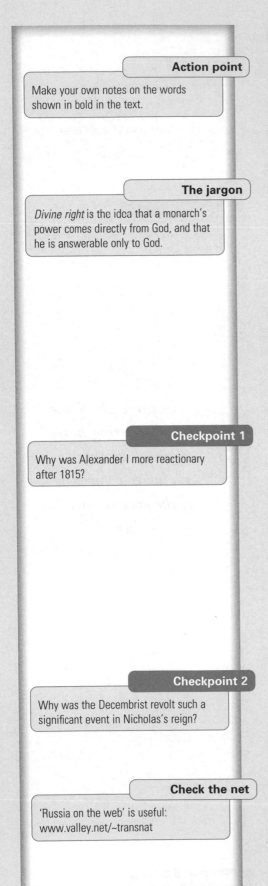

Action point

Make your own notes on the words shown in bold in the text.

The jargon

Divine right is the idea that a monarch's power comes directly from God, and that he is answerable only to God.

Checkpoint 1

Why was Alexander I more reactionary after 1815?

Checkpoint 2

Why was the Decembrist revolt such a significant event in Nicholas's reign?

Check the net

'Russia on the web' is useful:
www.valley.net/~transnat

The failure to abolish serfdom and the lack of political reform were causing great dissatisfaction by the end of Nicholas's reign.

Alexander II 'the Great Liberator' (1855–1881) ●●●

Alexander II came to the throne as Russia was being disastrously beaten in the Crimean War. The new tsar was forced to recognize the problems within the Russian system of government. The country was massively in debt. Crimea had shown the inefficiency of the army in both structure and operation. The civil service was inefficient and corrupt.

Industrial development was still severely limited, and there were 50 million disaffected peasants, bitter at the system of serfdom and mourning the loss of 600 000 people during the war.

The new tsar wished to save the autocratic system by reforming it:

→ Education – the universities were expanded and liberalized.
→ Legal system to include 'equality before the law' principle.
→ Modernisation of the army.
→ Local government – the creation of a new institution, the *zemstva* (local councils), elected by all local people.
→ The abolition of serfdom in 1861 – serfs became free peasants and received land from their former owners. The government compensated the nobility. Peasants had to repay the government for this land over 49 years (redemption payments). Village councils (the *mir*) were set up to administer the distribution of land and the organization of farming.

Alexander found these reforms only produced more agitation and so he returned to the repressive policies of his father and uncle. A new wave of opposition groups emerged such as the **Populists**, the **Nihilists**, **Liberals** and the **pan-Slavists**. On 1 March 1881 a member of one of these, the '**People's Will**', carried out the assassination of Alexander II.

Alexander III (1881–1894) ●●●

Unsurprisingly, the son of Alexander II continued with repressive policies. In particular the Jewish and Roman Catholic minorities suffered as loyalty to the state was identified with loyalty to the Orthodox Church. Deliberate persecution of non-Russian peoples within the empire (e.g. Finns and Poles) began in the 1890s. The growth of opposition political groups continued apace. The appointment of Sergei Witte as finance minister was significant as he embarked on a successful programme of industrial expansion.

"I am handing you command of the country in a very poor state"

Nicholas I to his son

Checkpoint 3

What were the limitations of these reforms? Why did they not end political opposition?

Test yourself

Summarize the reasons for and consequences of the policy decisions of the four tsars.

Exam questions   answers: page 99

1   To what extent did Alexander II solve Russia's problems? (45 min)

2   'There were more similarities than differences'. How far do you agree with this assessment of the policies of Alexander II and Alexander III? (45 min)

Examiner's secrets

In these questions, consider the motivation behind the policy of the tsars.

France 1815–1848

Following the defeat of Napoleon in 1814 the Bourbon monarchy was restored in 1815, and again following the defeat of Napoleon at Waterloo. From the beginning the regime was beset by problems. The unpopularity of Bourbon rule increased once Charles X succeeded Louis XVIII in 1824, culminating in the July Revolution of 1830. Louis Philippe, the Duc d'Orleans, then became king. The initial enthusiasm for his reign waned and he too was overthrown in the first of the 1848 Europe-wide revolutions.

The Bourbon restoration

The decision to restore the Bourbon monarchy was taken by the coalition of European powers responsible for the final defeat of Napoleon. It was insisted that Louis rule within the confines of a liberal constitution, the **charter of 1814**. Crucially, however, Louis still expressed a belief in **divine right**, and the king retained sole executive power (only he could initiate legislation, and he had a veto on any amendments proposed by parliament).

Increasing unpopularity 1815–1830

With a moderate constitution in place and France's undoubted economic potential, the Bourbon monarchy seemingly had a good chance of long-term survival. Why was it increasingly unpopular? Key factors:

→ The '**White terror**' of 1816 ordered by the **Ultra**-controlled government against former Bonapartists (supporters of Napoleon).
→ The assassination of the Duc de Berri. This allowed the Ultras to persuade Louis XVIII to backtrack from the liberal policies he had been pursuing between 1816 and 1820 (electoral system changed, censorship restored – carried out by Chief Minister Villele).

1824 saw the accession of Charles X. Charles was far more 'Ultra' in his political views. Key decisions:

→ **Compensation Law** (1825).
→ **Sacrilege Law** (1826).
→ Continuing press censorship.
→ Charles's refusal to select liberal ministers following their election victory in 1827 and his hostile attitude to parliament.
→ The appointment of the extreme Ultra Polignac as chief minister in 1829. His proposed Ordinances of St Cloud (or Four Ordinances) would have effectively destroyed the 1814 charter.

Also adding to the government's unpopularity was the severe economic depression France was suffering. Rioting began in Paris in July 1830 and Charles, lacking loyal troops, was persuaded to abdicate (the **July Revolution**).

Checkpoint 1

How did the circumstances of the restoration undermine the monarchy from the start?

Checkpoint 2

Did the charter satisfy any of the main political groupings in 1815?

"More royalist than the king himself"

Keith Randall on the Ultras

Checkpoint 3

What were the effects of Ultra-inspired policy?

The accession of Louis Philippe ●●●

The middle-class leaders of the July Revolution were clear in their desire to retain monarchical government in France. Louis Philippe, the Duc d'Orleans, was from an ancient French aristocratic family and related to the Bourbons. However, he held liberal views in politics, generally supporting the ideals of the French Revolution of 1789. This background made him acceptable to a broad cross-section of French opinion. On becoming king he enacted a series of reforms:

→ Alterations to the charter of 1814. The franchise was doubled to about 200 000.
→ Press freedom confirmed again.
→ The end of the Catholic Church's role as France's state religion.
→ The tricolour replaced the white flag of the Bourbons.

Checkpoint 4

How did the circumstances of Louis Philippe's accession create problems for him?

Increasing unpopularity 1830–1848 ●●●

Initial enthusiasm for the new monarchy soon dissipated. Key factors:

→ The unrepresentative nature of government and parliament:
    → Ultras excluded because of their political views.
    → Lower classes excluded by limited franchise.
→ The refusal of the government to intervene during times of severe economic hardship (the early 1830s and late 1840s).
→ Uninspiring **foreign policy** – successful in keeping France on good terms with other European powers but did not satisfy the public's wish for a return to the 'glory days' of Napoleon.
→ Louis Philippe's uninspiring character – the 'ordinary man'. Years of poverty and exile in his early life meant that he did not behave, dress, etc. in the way people believed a king should.
→ Press freedom led to a stream of hostile propaganda, including caricatures comparing the king's head to the shape of a pear.

Checkpoint 5

What was the reaction of the major political groups to these reforms?

Checkpoint 6

What similarities were there between the revolutions of 1815 and 1848?

Laws restricting open political gatherings led opponents of the regime to form the **Banquet movement**. These moderate reformers (e.g. Thiers) were frustrated by the king's refusal to consider any change in policy.

The government's decision to ban a meeting planned for February 1848 led to full-scale rioting on the streets of Paris. Following the refusal of the National Guard to fire on the demonstrators, Louis Philippe abdicated on 24 February 1848.

Exam questions   answers: pages 99–100

1   Why was it that revolution continued to be a factor in French history between 1815 and 1848? (45 min)

2   'Louis XVIII resisted the Ultras, while Charles X embraced them'. Is this a satisfactory explanation for the initial success but ultimate failure of the restored Bourbon monarchy? (45 min)

The 1848 revolutions

The revolutions of 1848 spread across most of the European continent. They were caused by the economic crisis of 1846–1847, which exacerbated existing social and political tensions. The revolutionaries were united by their belief in liberalism and nationalism but divided by their varying interpretation of these ideas. Despite the failure of revolutionaries to replace the existing regimes (except in France), Europe was never the same again.

Action point

Make your own notes on the words shown in bold in the text.

The jargon

Feudalism is a system of duties and responsibilities based on the ownership of land. Monarchs distribute land to the nobility in return for loyalty and soldiers in time of war. Peasants receive land from the nobility for their livelihood, but are then effectively owned by the nobles.

Checkpoint 1

What kinds of problem did these social and economic changes create?

Checkpoint 2

Why did the Frankfurt Parliament achieve so little?

Long and short term causes

Apart from the constitutional monarchies of Britain and France, Europe was a collection of states ruled by **absolute monarchs**, mainly along 'feudal' lines. This had been the case since the Middle Ages. By the middle of the 19th century, however, these societies were undergoing fundamental change:

→ Rapid population growth (dating from the late 18th century).
→ Rapid **urbanization** – towns were swollen from within but also by excess peasants from the countryside.
→ Rapid **industrialization** – industrial change led to the emergence of an urban (and class-conscious) working class, working for middle-class capitalists (the bourgeoisie).

In addition to these social and economic changes two major political ideas were increasingly espoused by an articulate, educated but excluded (in the political sense) middle class:

→ **Liberalism** – essentially human rights and freedoms, first put into practice during the French and American revolutions of the 18th century.
→ **Nationalism** – people of the same race and speaking the same language should have the right to form an independent state.

It is crucial also to consider the particular circumstance of 1846–1848:

→ Harvest failures of 1845–1846, leading to chronic food shortages across much of Europe.
→ Financial crisis – expensive food affected manufacturing. Consequent unemployment made it even more difficult for the masses to feed themselves.

France and the German states

The decision of King Louis Philippe to ban a hostile political meeting (the Banquet movement) led to rioting on the streets of Paris. An already unpopular monarch, Louis Philippe lacked loyal troops to defend his regime. By 24 February he had abdicated.

Events in France certainly acted as a catalyst in the German states. On 18 March Frederick William IV had granted a constitution, following widespread unrest. On 18 May, an elected assembly of nationalists and liberals from across the German states met for the first time at Frankfurt. Achieving little over the next year, the **Frankfurt parliament** was forcibly dissolved in June 1849. Germany was not united, and the rulers of the German states remained in power.

The Italian states

Rebellion in Sicily against the king of Naples actually preceded the February revolution in Paris. By the end of March there had been successful uprisings against Austrian rule in Lombardy and Venetia. In addition, the rulers of the independent (but Austrian-influenced) states of northern and central Italy had been forced to grant liberal constitutions. Most of these rebellions had been crushed by May, following the recovery of Austria from its own internal problems. In 1849 Mazzini declared a liberal republic in Rome, but this too was crushed by French troops in July, thereby restoring Pius IX to power.

Austria

Unsurprisingly, the revolutions in Austria's multi-ethnic empire were of a nationalist character. The uprising in Vienna itself was of a liberal nature and led to the resignation of Metternich in March 1848. An alliance of students and workers forced the emperor to flee and led to the creation of a constituent assembly, which passed various liberal reforms.

In October, loyal imperial troops surrounded Vienna and forcibly crushed the revolution. The Hungarians, under Louis Kossuth, were striving for independence from Austria, and were still fighting by April 1849. Austrian troops, having now dealt with events in Vienna, and aided by Russian troops, defeated the Hungarians in August. A similar nationalist revolt was crushed in Bohemia.

The significance of 1848

Despite the failures, 1848 was a turning point:

→ Constitutions in Prussia and Piedmont (crucial to future Italian unification) and the establishment of **universal male suffrage** in France and the encouragement of liberalism elsewhere, e.g. the Netherlands. Other regimes now saw the danger of authoritarian government. There was more awareness of the political consciousness of the masses.
→ In Austria, feudalism had been ended, and authoritarian government was never successfully re-established. The empire was now in decline.
→ The division between liberalism and nationalism. After 1848 nationalism became a tool of conservative leaders, e.g. Bismarck.

Checkpoint 3

What were the main reasons for the failure of the revolutions?

"divisions of interest between the respectable middle class . . . and the workers"

Peter Jones

Exam questions   answers: pages 100–101

1 Why were there so many revolutions in 1848? (45 min)

2 Why did a revolution succeed in France but fail in Italy in 1848–1849? (45 min)

Examiner's secrets

Both questions require you to show the link between socio-economic causes and political causes.

France under Louis Napoleon

Louis Napoleon, nephew of the great emperor Napoleon I, became president of the Second Republic, following the collapse of the July Monarchy in 1848. Having first got his term of office extended in 1851, he won popular support for his proclamation of the Second Empire in 1852. He then embarked on an ambitious programme of domestic and foreign policy until France's catastrophic defeat by Prussia, which led to his abdication as emperor in 1870.

From president to emperor

Napoleon won the presidential election of December 1848. This was in the main due to the fame of his family name among a largely illiterate and politically unaware population. Most French people were hostile to republicanism anyway, and Napoleon was perceived as the most anti-republican of all the candidates. It quickly became clear that Napoleon was not going to defend republican principles.

In December 1851 he carried out a *coup d'état*, which extended his term of office to 10 years. Crucial in his success:

→ Support of the army.
→ General support from all sections of society (shown by a plebiscite held just afterwards).

In November 1852 a second plebiscite approved the proclamation of the Second Empire.

From authoritarian to liberal empire

The constitution of 1852 gave Napoleon a huge amount of personal power. This system lasted until 1859 and is known as the **authoritarian empire**. The lower house of parliament met for only three months a year, and only the council of state, dominated by Napoleon, could initiate legislation. No newspaper could be published without government authority. In 1852 he promised that in the long term he would make political concessions. This began in 1859, leading to the creation of the **liberal empire**. Political prisoners were released in 1859, and this was followed over the next 10 years by a series of liberal measures. By 1869 there was limited parliamentary democracy in France, although Napoleon retained considerable powers. How can we explain this transformation?

→ Liberal dislike of authoritarian government.
→ Growing unpopularity of (increasingly unsuccessful) foreign policy.
→ Napoleon always intended liberalization (some historians argue).

Social and economic policy

1852–1870 was a time of great prosperity, due partly to world economic conditions but also to the success of Napoleon's policies.

Action point

Make your own notes on the words shown in bold in the text

The jargon

Coup d'état is an armed seizure of power. *Plebiscite* is a vote.

Checkpoint 1

Why was it so easy for Napoleon to bring republicanism to an end?

Checkpoint 2

How secure was Napoleon's position following the creation of the liberal empire?

Key measures:

→ Encouragement of free trade.
→ Encouragement of private enterprise, including setting up financial institutions that funded major commercial projects.
→ Improved communication – rail, road and canal building.
→ Urban renewal – especially of Paris.
→ Agricultural reform – scientific farming encouraged.
→ Workers' dwellings improved, friendly societies formed.

Foreign policy ●●●

Napoleon's foreign policy aimed to recreate the glory of his uncle's era. Inevitably, this meant seeking to undermine the main provisions of the (anti-French) Treaty of Vienna of 1815.

Partial success up to 1861:

→ **The Crimean War 1854–1856**. Reflecting Napoleon's desire to win Catholic support, France, in alliance with Britain and Turkey, entered into an ultimately successful war against Russia. France now appeared to be a driving force in European affairs. Austria's and Russia's anti-French Holy Alliance, which had existed since 1815, was now broken.
→ **Italy 1858–1860s**. Seeking to undermine Austria's role in Central Europe, France aided Piedmont in driving the Austrians from Lombardy in 1859. Napoleon was then overtaken by the events that led to the creation of a unitary Italian state. The resulting decline in the temporal power of the Pope caused much anger among French Catholics.

Failure after 1861:

→ **Mexico 1863**. An attempt to revive France's fortunes in the New World. Massive cost in money and manpower, leading to a humiliating French withdrawal in 1866.
→ **Wars of German unification 1866–1870**. Napoleon sought to ensure that France was compensated if there was any unification of the German states. This he failed to do following Prussia's defeat of Austria in 1866. Napoleon was then manipulated into war against Prussia, through the superior skills of Bismarck, over the **Hohenzollern candidature**. France's catastrophic defeat at Sedan led to Napoleon's abdication and the end of the Second Empire.

Checkpoint 3

What criticisms have been made of Napoleon's social and economic policy?

Checkpoint 4

Why was France so isolated by 1870?

Test yourself

Divide a blank sheet of paper in two. List Napoleon's successes and failures. Try to show the links between them. Which of the failures were most important in his downfall?

Exam questions   answers: page 101

1 'The fate of the Second Empire was sealed before the Franco-Prussian War'. Do you agree? (45 min)

2 Why and with what consequences did Napoleon III liberalize the Second Empire after 1870? (45 min)

Examiner's secrets

Q1 requires you to consider the most important reason for Napoleon's downfall.

Italian unification

Action point

Make your own notes on the words highlighted in bold in the text.

"It was only when the Austrian cat was distracted that the Italian mice could play"

Beales

Check the net

Look at 'windows on Italy' at www.mi.cnr/WOI/woindex.html

Checkpoint 1

Why was the rest of Europe no longer prepared to support Austria's role in Italy?

The term **'Risorgimento'** was first used in the 18th century. Literally it means 'rebirth', but historians use it to describe the growing national consciousness after 1815 – the desire to see Italy unified as one country. The Vienna settlement of 1815 placed the Italian peninsula under the control of the Habsburg Empire.

Up to 1848, various groups and individuals tried to unify the different states of Italy into one nation. However, these efforts all ended in failure. Italy was finally unified between 1860 and 1870 under Victor Emmanuel II, king of Piedmont.

Why did unification fail between 1815 and 1848?

There are three key reasons to explain this:

→ The role of Austria. Northern Italy was part of its empire, and a strong Austria was regarded as important by most of Europe as a barrier against France. Austria used its troops in 1820, 1831 and 1848 to crush nationalist uprisings.

→ Lack of cooperation between revolutionaries. Uprisings were directed against the rulers of individual states rather than coordinated across the peninsula as a whole. There was little agreement on the form that a united Italy would take – monarchy, republic or a federation under the Pope. To what extent would a united Italy be democratic?

→ The lack of popular support. To the peasantry of rural Italy the concept of a united Italy was completely meaningless.

Cavour and Piedmont

Cavour became prime minister of Piedmont in 1852 and had a crucial role in the eventual unification of Italy. Cavour had not set out to unify Italy but was clearly interested in extending the rule of Piedmont in northern and central Italy. In 1858 Cavour negotiated the **Plombières agreement** with **Napoleon III** of France.

The Piedmontese territories of Nice and Savoy would be ceded to France, and in return France would aid Piedmont in pushing the Austrians out of Lombardy and Venetia.

After provoking Austria into war the combined armies of France and Piedmont quickly pushed the Habsburg armies out of most of Lombardy (July 1859). Simultaneously, revolts broke out in the central states of Tuscany, Parma, Modena and the Romagna, the rebels aiming for union with Piedmont. Napoleon III, now worried about a Piedmont far stronger than he had envisaged at Plombières, signed the **Treaty of Villafranca** with Franz Josef, the Austrian emperor. Cavour resigned in disgust but returned to power in January 1860. Plebiscites were held in the central states, which voted in favour of union with Piedmont. In an attempt to appease the French, Piedmont ceded Nice and Savoy.

Garibaldi and the 'thousand' ●●●

Giuseppe Garibaldi was a passionate supporter of Italian unification. Heavily influenced by **Mazzini**, Garibaldi had been involved in several of the earlier revolutions in the Italian states.

Garibaldi now hoped to take advantage of what Cavour had achieved in the north in order to complete the unification process. In April 1860, with his volunteer army, the 'thousand', he left Genoa and first conquered Sicily and then the kingdom of Naples. This was a very worrying development for Cavour, deeply suspicious as he was of Garibaldi's republican and democratic views. He now took the view that if Italy was going to be united it would be on Piedmont's terms.

By September 1860, Piedmontese troops were occupying the Papal States. Garibaldi surrendered his conquests to Victor Emmanuel, and the kingdom of Italy (excluding Rome and Venetia) was proclaimed in March 1861.

Checkpoint 2

What were Garibaldi's qualities as a military leader? Why did he suppress the peasant uprising on Sicily, which he had earlier supported?

Unification completed ●●●

Taking advantage of the Austro-Prussian War, Italy was able to add Venetia to the kingdom in 1866. Similarly, when Napoleon was forced to withdraw his troops from Rome in 1870 (because of the war with Prussia) Italy was able to acquire its modern-day capital.

Summary ●●●

There are several crucial factors that help us to understand the unification of Italy:

Checkpoint 3

How important was national feeling in the unification of Italy?

→ Cavour – no unification was possible without the removal of Austria from the peninsula. Cavour's negotiation of the Plombières agreement was crucial in achieving this. His intervention in the south in the autumn of 1860 ensured that Italy was unified under the king of Piedmont.
→ Garibaldi – his intervention in the south forced Cavour to complete the unification process.
→ The role of other European powers. The direct intervention of France was crucial. With the obvious exception of Austria, the rest of Europe was either in favour or at the very least adopted a neutral attitude towards Italian unification

Exam questions   answers: page 102

1   Was Italian unification primarily the result of foreign intervention? (45 min)

2   'His only concern was the glory of his state.' Is this a fair assessment of Cavour? (45 min)

3   Why did Austria lose its primacy in Europe? (45 min)

Examiner's secrets

In Q1, don't forget the importance of foreign non-intervention.

German unification

Metternich, chief minister of Austria, a multi-racial empire, had a deep distrust of liberalism and nationalism. He used the German Confederation (set up in 1815) to clamp down on any attempt to create a united Germany. Prussia, the second-largest German state, was content to adhere to Austrian policy. The emergence of Prussia after 1848 as the dominant German state eventually led to the unification of all the German states (with the exception of Austria) under the Prussian King Wilhelm I in 1871.

Prussia and Austria

The emergence of Prussia as a leading economic and later military power is closely connected to the creation of the **Zollverein** (Prussian customs union). By 1836, 25 of the 39 German states were members of this free trade area. This was of great benefit to Prussia economically. By the middle of the 19th century Prussia was a major industrial power. Other reasons for this included:

→ Rapidly increasing population.
→ Good railway network.
→ Efficient civil service.

The growth in Prussian strength came at the same time as a weakening of Austria. Crucially, Austria was never a member of the Zollverein, which undoubtedly held back economic growth. In addition, there remained many unresolved problems in Austria's large multi-ethnic empire. The Austrians were increasingly isolated diplomatically in Europe, especially after failing to support Russia in the Crimean War.

The creation of the Zollverein encouraged supporters of German nationalism, who now hoped to see economic union lead on to full political unification. Significantly however, the nationalists were divided along political lines as well as on whether a united Germany would include Austria or not (**Kleindeutschland** or **Grossdeutschland**). This was clearly demonstrated in the failure of the 1848–1849 revolutions in Germany.

Bismarck

Key points:

→ Came from an aristocratic (Junkers) background.
→ Very hostile to liberalism.
→ Very hostile to Austria in the wake of the collapse of the **Erfurt union** (the Prussian union plan).
→ Appointed chancellor of Prussia in 1862 by Wilhelm I in order to push through disputed army reforms.

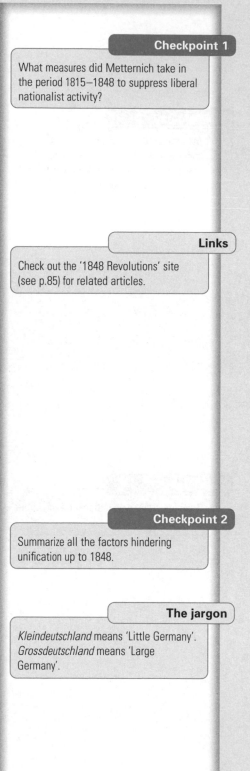

Checkpoint 1

What measures did Metternich take in the period 1815–1848 to suppress liberal nationalist activity?

Links

Check out the '1848 Revolutions' site (see p.85) for related articles.

Checkpoint 2

Summarize all the factors hindering unification up to 1848.

The jargon

Kleindeutschland means 'Little Germany'. *Grossdeutschland* means 'Large Germany'.

The wars of unification

Bismarck was determined to make Prussia the dominant German state. He was able to take advantage of increasing Prussian strength, as well as using his diplomatic skills, in order to unify the German states under Prussia. There are three major incidents to consider:

→ **War with Denmark 1864**. Bismarck induced Austria to sign an alliance with Prussia as the king of Denmark (Christian IX) had infringed an earlier agreement over the duchies of **Schleswig** and **Holstein** (part of the Danish kingdom but also members of the German Confederation). The Danes were quickly defeated. The duchies passed to Austria and Prussia, but there was no permanent agreement on their future.

→ **War with Austria 1866**. Bismarck saw that a war with Austria was inevitable. In addition, he had negotiated a secret treaty with Italy. He then provoked war with his proposals to place the future of Germany in the hands of an elected parliament, thereby taking advantage of liberal nationalist sentiment. Austria perceived this as an attempt to exclude the Habsburg Empire from German affairs. In the '**Seven Weeks War**' the results of Prussia's economic and military reforms were clearly seen in Austria's catastrophic defeat. Partial unification was achieved with the creation of the **North German Confederation**.

→ **War with France 1870–1871**. Bismarck had promised Napoleon III that France would not face a united Germany, which included the southern states. However, Bismarck did provoke war with France over the **Hohenzollern candidature**. The secret military alliances that Prussia had signed with the southern states were invoked following the French declaration of war. The French were quickly defeated and the German Empire, incorporating the southern states, was proclaimed in January 1871.

Summary

Germany was united in 1871 because of the interconnection of the following factors:

→ Prussian economic and military strength.
→ The desire of Prussia to assert its strength.
→ The decline of Austrian power.
→ German national feeling.
→ A favourable international situation.
→ The policy of Bismarck.

Exam questions answers: page 103

1 Why did Austria lose its primacy in Germany between 1848 and 1866? (45 min)

2 How important was nationalism in German unification? (45 min)

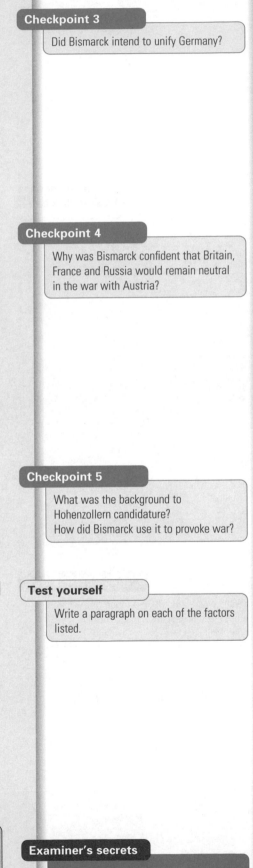

Checkpoint 3

Did Bismarck intend to unify Germany?

Checkpoint 4

Why was Bismarck confident that Britain, France and Russia would remain neutral in the war with Austria?

Checkpoint 5

What was the background to Hohenzollern candidature?
How did Bismarck use it to provoke war?

Test yourself

Write a paragraph on each of the factors listed.

Examiner's secrets

In Q1, discuss the role of Bismarck, including the importance of the Prussian army reforms.

The French Third Republic

The defeat and abdication of Napoleon III at Sedan led to the proclamation of a republic, the third in French history, in Paris on 4 September 1870. At times the chances of republican government surviving in France looked very remote indeed. The Third Republic did, however, survive major crises. Monarchy was not to make a return to France.

The shock of 1870–1871

France was finally defeated, by the Prussians, at the end of January 1871. The new German Empire insisted that France be represented at the forthcoming peace talks by a representative government. The subsequent elections for the National Assembly produced a chamber that was clearly monarchist in composition.

Adolphe Thiers negotiated the **Treaty of Frankfurt** (May 1871) for France. The treaty was harsh but not crippling for France, although the loss of Alsace and Lorraine was bitterly resented.

Anger against this royalist government grew in republican Paris:

→ Parisians feared a royalist restoration.
→ Parisians disliked the **social policies** of the government, which were very hard on the working classes.

This anger led to the declaration of the **Paris Commune** in March 1871 by a diverse collection of extreme left-wing revolutionaries. After a brutal siege French government forces broke the resistance of the rebels on 28 May 1871. Government troops killed at least 20 000 communards while the occupying German army looked on.

Monarchy or republic?

Thiers, now 'president of the French republic', had promised that the republic would be temporary. The supporters of monarchy were, however, bitterly divided between the **Bourbon** and **Orleanist** houses. A compromise whereby the Orleanist claimant would succeed the Bourbon Comte de Chambord failed when the latter insisted that France abandon the tricolour for the royalist white flag.

The republic consolidated 1871–1885

Support for the republic grew for the following reasons:

→ With the destruction of the Commune, radical, left-wing republicanism was eradicated as a force for a decade. Many monarchists were therefore won over to republicanism.
→ Thiers' conservative policies, which most people had thought could only come under a monarchy: tax policies that favoured the rich; no income tax; protectionism; quick repayment of reparations, which led to the withdrawal of German troops.
→ Divisions among the monarchists.
→ From 1879 republican supporters had a majority in the Senate – a range of legislation was passed designed to strengthen support for the republic.

Checkpoint 1

Why did the National Assembly elections produce a monarchist majority?

Checkpoint 2

Why was the Bourbon attitude to the flag of France important in the failure of monarchism?

"The Republic will be conservative or it will be nothing"

Adolphe Thiers

Checkpoint 3

How did this legislation strengthen the republic?

Internal threats to the republic ●●●

There were occasions after 1885 when the future of republican government in France once more seemed in doubt. Threats came from:

→ The radical right, wishing to avenge France's defeat by Germany (1870) and restore privileges to Church and nobility.
→ The radical left, who wished to see a republic far more socialist in nature. Many republican politicians seemed mostly concerned with serving middle-class interests. There were many strikes between 1906 and 1911, often met by government force. Gradually social reform was implemented.

The Boulanger affair

By 1885 France was suffering from a severe agricultural depression and there was also much discontent at failure in colonial policy. General Georges Boulanger gained huge popularity as minister of war between 1885 and 1887 by restoring pride in the army and threatening war with Germany to recover Alsace and Lorraine. The moderate republican government sacked him, fearing that he was about to become a new 'Napoleonic' figure. Huge demonstrations were staged in his support, and his supporters won a string of by-elections. At the crucial moment, however, he lost his nerve and fled abroad in 1889.

The Dreyfus case

In 1894 Captain Alfred Dreyfus, a Jewish army officer, was found guilty of selling military secrets to the Germans and sentenced to life imprisonment. It was discovered that a Major Esterhazy had forged one of the documents used to implicate him. However, he was acquitted in 1898. The 'anti-Dreyfusards' tried to use the Dreyfus case to discredit the republic. The involvement of the novelist Emile Zola led eventually to the pardoning of Dreyfus in 1899. The affair had divided France between supporters and opponents of the republic.

Survival of the republic ●●●

Key factors:

→ Resolute leadership in taking action and passing legislation.
→ Moderate political views of the majority of the people.
→ Success in foreign and colonial affairs.
→ Successful social and economic policy.

Exam questions   answers: pages 103–4

1 How do you account for the survival of the French Third Republic in the period 1870–1914? (45 min)

2 How successfully did the governments of the Third Republic deal with internal opposition? (45 min)

3 How far had France recovered in 1900 from the defeat in 1870? (45 min)

The jargon

Napoleonic means someone who would rule in the same way as Napoleon Bonaparte – as a military dictator.

Checkpoint 4

What was the significance of both the Boulanger and Dreyfus incidents?

Examiner's secrets

The examiner will be impressed if you can show that the republic survived through good fortune as well as the skill of republican politicians.

Bismarck's Germany

The German Empire was created in 1871 following the defeat of France at the hands of the Prussians. The architect of this unification process had been the Prussian chancellor Otto von Bismarck. Bismarck remained in power, as chancellor of Germany, for the next 19 years. Despite the creation of a unitary state, there were underlying divisions within the new country.

What kind of empire after 1871?

Key features of Germany's political system:

→ A **federal system** (the individual states retained much authority over their own affairs).

→ A parliamentary system – the Reichstag was elected by direct, secret and almost universal male suffrage; it could not initiate legislation but could reject the budget.

→ Bundesrat (state council), nominated by state assemblies; theoretically, it could change constitution; consent required to pass new laws.

→ A chancellor – the main initiator of legislation; had the power to appoint and dismiss ministers; responsible only to the emperor; could ignore the Reichstag.

→ A monarchy – the emperor could appoint and dismiss the chancellor; could dissolve the Reichstag; could declare war; possessed the right to interpret the constitution.

This system was also Prussian-dominated: the chancellor was also minister-president of Prussia. The Bundesrat was Prussian-dominated. This was not enough to satisfy Prussian ministers. In 1878 Bismarck therefore proposed the creation of new government ministries run jointly by the Reich (central) government and Prussia. Opposition from the other states in the Bundesrat led to this being dropped. Bismarck was never able to find a permanent solution to this force of disunity within Germany.

Economic policy

By the early 1870s German agriculture was being severely affected by cheap foreign imports. The **Junkers**, as well as industrialists, clamoured for protectionism. This was a chance for Bismarck to raise extra revenue for the Reich government, and, more importantly, to do it independently of the Reichstag (until this point Bismarck had been mainly reliant on Reichstag-approved taxation). This would also allow Bismarck to split with his long-term allies in the Reichstag, the **National Liberals**, who were long-standing advocates of free trade. In 1879 a Tariff bill became law.

Checkpoint 1

What do you think Liebknecht meant by this statement?

The jargon

Protectionism means protecting domestic industry by making foreign goods expensive, usually by tariffs on imports.

Checkpoint 2

Why did Bismarck want to end his partnership with the National Liberals?

The Kulturkampf

The term 'Kulturkampf' refers to the series of anti-Catholic laws passed by Bismarck in the 1870s. Bismarck disliked Catholicism because:

→ The Catholics of the west and south resented Protestant Prussia's domination of Germany.

→ Bismarck disliked the fact that Catholics' first loyalty might be to the Pope rather than to Germany.

→ Anti-Catholicism could strengthen ties with anti-Roman Catholic Russia.

The National Liberals, whom Bismarck relied upon for support at this time, were predominantly Protestant and favoured anti-Catholic measures such as bringing the Catholic education system under state control and enforcing a civil marriage ceremony.

Unfortunately for Bismarck, support for the **Catholic Centre Party** increased at the 1874 general election. Persecution of the Catholic Church actually increased its popularity. Bismarck's decision to end the Kulturkampf was also influenced by the following factors:

→ By the late 1870s, the possibility of a useful alliance with Catholic Austria was increasing.

→ Because of his switch to protectionism Bismarck had lost the support of the National Liberals. The Centre Party could be useful allies both in this and in his anti-socialist legislation.

Anti-socialism and the fall of Bismarck

The moderate socialist **Social Democratic Party** was a major political force by the 1870s. Bismarck succeeded in securing the passage of an anti-socialist bill, which banned the SPD, in 1879. Once again this did not have the desired effect. The SPD continued to operate illegally but effectively. Following the repeal of the law, the SPD gained over a million votes in 1890. Bismarck also tried to remove the appeal of socialism to the working classes through his '**state socialism**' measures. These included sickness insurance, accident insurance and an Old Age and Disability Act 1889. These measures were reasonably popular, but Bismarck still failed to win the political support of the urban working classes.

Wilhelm II became emperor in 1888, signalling the beginning of the end for Bismarck. Keen to stamp his own authority on government, Wilhelm was anxious to rid himself of the man who had dominated German politics for so long. Wilhelm's refusal to agree to a new anti-socialist law in 1890 led to Bismarck's resignation.

Checkpoint 3

Explain Bismarck's hostility to socialism.

Test yourself

Divide a page in two. List Bismarck's successes and failures.

Exam questions   answers: page 104

1   How successful was Bismarck in solving Germany's domestic problems between 1871 and 1890? (45 min)

2   How far were Bismarck's problems in Germany of his own making? (45 min)

Examiner's secrets

Both these questions require you to consider the idea that Bismarck caused more problems than he solved.

Bismarck's foreign policy

Action point

Make your own notes on the words shown in bold in the text.

Successful foreign policy was essential to guarantee the future of the German Second Reich, created in 1871. France was clearly looking for revenge after its humiliation in the Franco-Prussian War of 1870. Bismarck, chancellor of Germany, was under pressure from sections of his own people to pursue an expansionist foreign policy, while Europe generally was suspicious of this powerful new nation. Bismarck developed his own unique solution to these problems.

Bismarck's aims

Bismarck had clear aims in his foreign policy:

→ Peace through **conciliation** – Bismarck was aware that the rest of Europe was deeply suspicious of the new Germany. He aimed, therefore, to show that Germany was not a threat. At the same time, within Germany, Bismarck had to convince the army and German nationalists that such a low-key policy was in Germany's best interests.

→ France needed allies in a future war with Germany, therefore Bismarck aimed to keep France isolated.

→ To improve relations between Russia and Austria in their growing dispute over the Balkans, so keeping the support of both states.

→ To ensure that in any grouping of the major European powers Germany had the support of the majority of powers.

→ If a war broke out to try to ensure that Germany was not fighting on two fronts.

Checkpoint 1

Why did Bismarck not pursue a vigorous colonial policy?

Checkpoint 2

Why did Bismarck wish to improve relations between Austria and Russia?

Checkpoint 3

Why did Bismarck create the Dual Alliance? What were its strengths and weaknesses?

Bismarck's alliance system 1871–1882

Bismarck reasoned that the best way to achieve his aims was to construct a European alliance system with Germany at its hub:

→ The **Three Emperors League 1873** (First Dreikaiserbund) – Germany, Austria and Russia. This showed the diplomatic isolation of France, but it gave Germany no guarantees of support in a future war. Germany's weak position at this point was shown by the '**war in sight**' crisis of 1875. France's rapid recovery after 1870 led to intimidation by the Germans, an attempt to frighten the French government with the prospect of renewed war. Britain and Russia condemned Bismarck's actions.

→ The **Dual Alliance of 1879** – Germany and Austria. This was signed in the wake of the **Near Eastern crisis of 1877–1878** and the **Treaty of Berlin 1879** (which replaced the **Treaty of San Stefano**).

→ The **Three Emperors Alliance 1881** (Second Dreikaiserbund) – Germany, Austria and Russia.

→ The **Triple Alliance 1882** – Germany, Austria and Italy.

The system under threat 1882–1887

The Second Dreikaiserbund indicated a lessening of the tensions between Austria and Russia over the Balkans. These re-emerged in 1885, following the revolt in eastern Rumelia against Turkish rule. Unless Bismarck could keep on good terms with Russia, Germany would once again be facing the prospect of a Franco-Russian alliance. He therefore engineered the **Reinsurance Treaty** in 1887:

→ If Germany or Russia was at war with a third country the other power would remain neutral.
→ Germany recognized Russia's right to predominant influence in Bulgaria (part of the Balkans).
→ This did not apply if Russia attacked Austria or if Germany attacked France.

Bismarck had no intention of going to war with France. He hoped that this new treaty would prevent Russia attacking Austria. Bismarck was well aware of the flaws in the Reinsurance Treaty. In an attempt to strengthen Germany's position he encouraged the creation of the **Second Mediterranean agreement** in 1887:

→ The signatories were Britain, Austria and Italy (*not* Germany).
→ It was an attempt to prevent Russia precipitating a renewed crisis in the Balkans, mainly through increasing British naval presence in the area.

Checkpoint 4

What were the weaknesses of the Reinsurance Treaty?

Assessments of Bismarck's foreign policy

There are two main interpretations of Bismarck's foreign policy. In order to secure the future of the fledgling German Empire he sought to maintain European peace by keeping France isolated and to prove to the rest of Europe that Germany was not a threat to the *status quo*. This was undoubtedly achieved during his time in office.

During the period 1881–1886, Bismarck was clearly the most influential statesman in European affairs. On the other hand, it could be argued that Bismarck's foreign policy amounted to little more than 'crisis management'. In other words, his diplomacy secured Germany's interests in the short term but failed to solve some of the underlying problems:

→ The threat to Germany from France.
→ The Balkan issue, which still left open the possibility of a Franco-Russian alliance.

> *"Berlin was truly the diplomatic centre of Europe"*
>
> John Lowe

Test yourself

List Bismarck's international agreements, which resulted out of short-term necessity.

Exam questions — answers: page 105

1 'After 1871 Bismarck was unconvincing as an architect of peace.' Do you agree? (45 min)

2 Was Bismarck's foreign policy failing by the time he fell from power? (45 min)

3 'The signing of the Dual Alliance represented a diplomatic defeat from which Bismarck's foreign policy never recovered'. Do you agree? (45 min)

Examiner's secrets

Examiners are looking to see that you understand both interpretations of Bismarck's foreign policy.

Answers
European history 1815–1894

The Vienna settlement 1815

Checkpoints

1 There was a certain amount of common ground between Castlereagh and the leaders of the other victorious nations, particularly on the questions of balance of power and the need for peace. However, Castlereagh, reflecting the British political system, was nothing like so hostile to the ideas of liberalism and nationalism. As he made clear in his state paper, he did not favour intervention in the affairs of another country (if they had had a liberal revolution for instance) unless peace or the balance of power was threatened.

   When liberal revolts did break out in various parts of Europe, Britain was generally against intervention. This, coupled with George Canning's (Castlereagh's successor) general hostility to congress diplomacy in principle, led to Britain's withdrawal from European affairs in the early 1820s.

2 The principle of legitimacy was not always applied. This was because it was not always in the best interests of the powers to do so. For instance, many of the smaller German states were amalgamated because it was felt that this would provide a more effective barrier against the French. Norway was taken from Denmark and given to Sweden because the former had supported Napoleon. Belgium was united with Holland, rather than returned to Austria, again because this strengthened the *cordon sanitaire* (the barrier against future French expansion). For the same reason, Austria gained most of northern Italy.

Exam questions

1 The suggestion is that the great powers looked after themselves at Vienna. Show the examiner that you understand that this is what the essay is about. Make clear that this is a common criticism of the treaty, but on the other hand point out that many historians have argued the opposite, that the peacemakers did consider the wider issues.

   Demonstrate that there are clear examples within the terms of the treaty of powers acting in their own interests. Russia gaining Poland and Britain gaining various naval bases are clear examples, but point out that these two did more than anyone else to defeat Napoleon. A lasting peace would be one that satisfied Britain and Russia.

   Consider the principle of containment of France. Show how it could be seen as self-interest but also demonstrate that it would have been in the interests of the whole of Europe as well.

   Legitimacy – demonstrate that this was not always applied but this was usually to strengthen the barrier against France.

   Compensation – demonstrate that this was often applied in the interests of the great powers but point out again that it was necessary to create a peace that was as satisfactory to everyone as possible.

Balance of power – this certainly preserved the *status quo* in the interests of the great powers. The fact that no one power was dominant was in the interests of peace.

   Conclusion – the powers did act in their own interests but there is a lot of evidence to suggest that they were trying to create a lasting peace as well.

Examiner's secrets

Avoid long descriptions but include enough factual detail to show your knowledge.

2 This question requires you to analyse the role of the Vienna settlement in the failure of nationalist movements. Point out in the introduction that there are other factors.

   Give factual examples from the settlement itself to show that foreigners ruled many Europeans in 1815.

   Analyse the role of the congress system (a direct result of Vienna) in the failure of nationalism between 1815 and 1822, particularly in Italy.

   Demonstrate how Metternich used the German Confederation created by Vienna to crush nationalism in the German states in 1819.

   Point out that there were other reasons for the failure of nationalism, particularly the lack of national feeling across much of Europe at this time. In addition, be aware of the weakness of nationalist movements themselves.

   Point out that there were nationalist successes in Greece and Belgium in this period. Be aware that the great powers would not uphold the principles of Vienna if they felt it was not in their interests.

   Conclusion – sum up the argument that Vienna did play a significant role but there are other factors to consider.

3 You need to make clear that this essay requires you to examine the origins of the congress system. Were there indications of future disagreements? On the other hand, it could be argued that the system failed because of the particular circumstances facing the powers in the post-war world.

   Analyse the differences between the powers in 1815, particularly the political differences that existed between Britain and the European autocracies. Britain, as a constitutional monarchy, was likely to be more sympathetic to liberal nationalist revolts. Britain's primary concern would always be commerce. You could argue that opposition to France was the only point the powers could agree upon in 1815.

   Link to the previous paragraph by analysing the different blueprints for post-war cooperation, the Holy Alliance and the Quadruple Alliance. Explain how these differed.

   Look closely at the events of 1815–1822. Point out that, once France had been readmitted to the concert of powers in 1815, the alliance began to crumble. The alliance fell apart over the issue of intervention in the affairs of minor European nations (make sure you mention which). It can be convincingly argued that these differences did exist in 1815.

Assess the role of Canning in the collapse of the concert system. This was certainly a factor that could not have been predicted in 1815.

Conclusion – point out that some historians would argue that there was never a system at all. On balance, the evidence suggests that the differences between the powers made post-war cooperation very difficult.

Russia 1815–1894

Checkpoints

1 Alexander was increasingly under the influence of Metternich after the Congress of Vienna. Metternich, an avowed enemy of liberalism, did his best to frighten the Tsar out of any liberal notions. Disturbances at home and abroad (in Italy, Spain and Portugal) convinced Alexander that he had gone too far.

2 The memory of the Decembrist revolt lived with Nicholas for ever. The involvement of the nobility led him to distrust them. The reactionary nature of his reign is to an extent explained by this event.

3 To most Russian liberals the reforms did not go far enough. The legal system still treated peasants differently. Emancipation seemed to satisfy no one – the peasants remained impoverished and it angered much of the nobility. Agriculture remained backward. Alexander found that once reform had been granted the people wanted more – the liberals wanted a parliament and revolutionaries demanded the end of the autocracy altogether.

Exam questions

1 Make clear that the reign of Alexander was split into the reforming and the reactionary periods. Make clear that it is a bit too simplistic to see the former as a success and the latter as failure.

Discuss the importance of Alexander learning the lessons of the Crimean War. Clearly, he made an attempt to reform the autocracy.

Analyse the success of the reforms, especially the emancipation of the serfs.

Make clear the problems that still remained despite the backward economy: limited political reforms (only at a local level), etc.

Conclusion – he appeared quite successful at solving the perceived problems, but the discontent and terrorism at the end of his reign suggest that he had failed to solve the underlying problems of Russia. It could be argued that the autocracy was preserved for longer because of the actions that Alexander II took.

2 Make clear the general perception that Alexander II is seen as a liberal tsar, while his son, Alexander III, is seen as reactionary. Point out that this view is too simplistic.

Compare the circumstances of the accessions. Alexander came to the throne in the wake of the disaster of the Crimean War – reform was necessary. Alexander III became Tsar in 1881 because his father had been brutally

murdered – reform had created a threat to the autocracy. Both were fundamentally committed to the principle of autocratic government.

Alexander II's reign was certainly a reforming one to begin with (give details of the various reforms). You need to contrast this with the repressive policies of Alexander III.

Point out that in the last ten years of his reign, following the failure of reform, Alexander II carried out repressive policies that were similar to those of his son (give details).

Conclusion – at heart these tsars were both conservative. It was the circumstances they found themselves in that explain the differences in their policies.

> ### Examiner's secrets
>
> Demonstrate clearly the way in which events influenced the policies of the tsars.

France 1815–1848

Checkpoints

1 The fact that Louis XVIII was imposed on the French by the other powers of Europe to an extent undermined his position. There was certainly no wave of popular support for the Bourbon restoration.

2 The charter satisfied those moderates who wished to see a political system similar to Britain's. Clearly, it angered both the Ultras and those who wanted a more representative political system.

3 Ultra policy rapidly increased the unpopularity of Charles X among many of his people. They feared a return to autocratic monarchy.

4 Louis Philippe was a compromise king. He did not have the legitimacy of the Bourbons or mass support.

5 Like the charter of 1814, they were too radical for many and not nearly radical enough for others. They were in fact a very limited revision of the earlier charter.

6 Both revolutions occurred at a time of economic recession: the press played a role in both; both monarchs were unprepared; Paris as a hotbed of radicalism and a place of severe hardship for many was significant in both; both monarchs failed to satisfy the desire for political reform.

Exam questions

1 Make clear that this question requires the similarities between the revolutions of 1830 and 1848, but also the differences, to be analysed.

Middle-class frustration – limitations of the charters. Discuss Charles X's attempt to limit the 1814 charter and Louis Philippe's refusal to alter the charter of 1830.

Working-class discontent made worse by the economic crises of these times (show your knowledge of these), as well as the growing population. Analyse the particular socio-economic circumstances of Paris, especially by 1848.

Consider the role of the press and the government's attempts to control it.

Discuss the lack of preparation that both monarchs showed in the lead-up to the revolutions.

Point out the particular problems that Louis Philippe faced on foreign policy as well as his reputation as an 'ordinary man'.

Conclusion – were these revolutions inevitable or were they caused by the failures of the two kings? Attempt to provide an answer to this by summing up the evidence that you have discussed in earlier paragraphs.

Examiner's secrets

Do not describe what happened in these years. Stick to the causes of the revolutions.

2 Suggest that the statement in the question is too simplistic as an explanation of the revolution of 1830.

Explain how Louis XVII did get the Bourbon monarchy off to a good start by resisting the Ultras (give details), but there were other successes too in economic policy and foreign affairs.

Point out that after the assassination of the Duc de Berry, Louis began to embrace Ultra policy himself.

Argue that Charles X was much more closely linked to the Ultras and show this by giving details of the policies that he pursued, especially after Polignac was appointed chief minister.

Argue against the statement by pointing out that there were other reasons (than embracing the Ultras) behind the revolution of 1830 – particularly the economic crisis and Charles X's poor preparation for a potential revolution.

Summarize the argument. Clearly, Louis appreciated the dangers of pursuing Ultra policies in a way that Charles certainly did not. On its own this does not explain the collapse of the Bourbon monarchy.

The 1848 revolutions

Checkpoints

1 Rising population caused problems among Europe's peasantry. Primitive agriculture could not support everyone. The consequent move to the cities created its own problems, such as appalling living conditions. The exploitation of unskilled labour by unscrupulous employers meant that this new urban working class could be poorly paid, working in dangerous conditions, but out of work if there was an economic downturn. At the same time, living in this urban environment created a working-class consciousness.

2 The Frankfurt parliament achieved so little mainly because of its internal divisions. The delegates wanted to create a united Germany, but they could not agree on whether this should include Austria or not. Additionally, they argued about whether the constitution of a united Germany should allow elections through universal franchise or whether the right to vote should be limited to the propertied classes.

3 Disunity between the revolutionaries was crucial in Italy and Germany. In Germany and Austria the established autocratic rulers were never deposed. Once they had recovered their nerve, they were able to use force to put down the revolutions. The lessening of the economic crisis revealed the differences in aims between the middle-class leaders and the masses who supported the revolutions. Britain never gave any aid to the revolutions, while Russia actively helped the Austrians to put them down.

Exam questions

1 In your introduction point out that a series of events as complex as 1848 is caused by many interlinked factors. These can be categorized as political, social and economic.

Explain the social changes that Europe had gone through since the late 18th century. Discuss the consequences of these.

Discuss the consequences of industrialization.

Analyse the importance of the economic crisis of 1846–1848 to show that it exacerbated existing social and economic tensions.

Discuss the spread of the ideas of liberalism and nationalism. Link to the previous two paragraphs by explaining that the bulk of European society was extremely discontented with the status quo. Emphasize that the established rulers of Europe were not prepared to solve this discontent.

Explain the importance of the July Revolution in France as a catalyst for revolution elsewhere.

Conclusion – the changes of the previous half-century, coupled with the particular circumstances of 1846–1848, provide the key to 1848.

2 Explain in your introduction that the circumstances of the revolutions in France and Italy were very different. Give an indication of what these differences were.

Explain that in France discontent focused on one leader – Louis Philippe, whereas in Italy there were a series of revolutions directed against the individual rulers of particular states. In Italy, the revolutionaries did not work together.

The French revolution of 1848 was focused on Paris. The problems of industrialization were particularly acute here, and consequently working-class consciousness was well developed. This guaranteed the involvement of the Parisian masses. In Italy, the middle-class revolutionaries clearly had different aims from the peasant masses, whose support tailed away once the economic crisis eased.

Italy was a sphere of international interest. Austria believed that it had a right to rule there. Once Austria's own revolution had ended, Austrian troops played a key role in repressing the uprisings in Italy. France too intervened to end the Rome republic in 1849. No European power had the right to intervene in France.

Discuss Louis Philippe's poor preparation for a potential revolution.

Conclusion – re-emphasize the argument and make a judgement on what you consider to be the most crucial difference.

France under Louis Napoleon

Checkpoints

1 There had never been mass support for republicanism in France. The 1848 revolution had been centred on Paris, where republicanism *was* strong. The power vacuum of 1848 allowed a republic to be established. The left-wing republicanism of the early months was frightening to France's property owners (which included the peasant masses). Louis Napoleon's conservative (and at times anti-republican) policies were popular. The fact that he was a directly elected president allowed him to claim that he had a personal mandate from the people to end the constitution.

2 There is no doubt that Napoleon was not as popular in the late 1860s as in earlier years, due to foreign and domestic policy failures. The creation of the liberal empire was an attempt to win support. However, there is little to indicate that his rule was seriously under threat. It was the Franco-Prussian War that brought him crashing down.

3 Napoleon's social and economic policies did not really do a great deal to help ordinary people. This was particularly true of the urban renewal programme in Paris. France's industrial development was not as impressive as in other European countries.

4 France's foreign policy had left it isolated. Aiding Piedmont over Italian unification had angered Austria, while defending the Pope's secular power in Rome created hostility from the new Italian kingdom. Relations with Russia had not been good since the Crimean War and were made worse by Napoleon's support of the Polish revolt of 1863. Bismarck clearly saw France as a barrier to his plans for Prussia. Britain too was suspicious of Napoleon, believing that he was trying to upset the European balance of power in France's favour.

Exam questions

1 Make it clear in the introduction that you understand the question, which is suggesting that the Second Empire would have collapsed even if France had not gone to war with Prussia.

Examine social and economic policy. The overall failure to improve the lives of ordinary people indicates that the Second Empire was becoming more unpopular.

The liberalization of the political system indicates that this was a regime that was becoming desperate. By passing these reforms Napoleon was also creating more open opposition. On the other hand, point out that some historians argue that such liberalization was part of Napoleon's long-term plans.

Analyse foreign policy. The overall failure of this created opposition at home and left France without friends in Europe (give factual examples).

Conclusion – despite the growing opposition was Napoleon about to be overthrown in 1870? The evidence suggests not (crucially, the army was still loyal). What actually caused Napoleon to abdicate in 1870? Surely this was defeat by the Prussians?

2 This question requires you to consider the motivation behind the liberalization of the French political system.

Examine the authoritarian empire of the 1850s. This was acceptable at the time, coming after the chaos of the 1848 revolution and the unpopularity of the Second Republic. There was a great deal of support for the 'strong man' leadership style at this time, particularly so following France's success in the Crimean War.

From the late 1850s Napoleon began to liberalize the political system (show your factual knowledge of these changes). Examine the view that these changes were always intended by Napoleon. It could be argued that he needed evidence of opposition at home before he could win over opponents of reform within his own cabinet. The unfortunate death of the Duc de Morny (a liberal) also delayed reform.

Consider the opposite view that the decision to liberalize the regime was brought about *because* of the opposition. Make clear the rising tide of discontent because of failures in social, economic and foreign policy. Perhaps Napoleon was naturally more comfortable with authoritarianism.

Discuss the consequences. Liberalization certainly led to much greater criticism of the regime, especially from radical republicans. It could be argued that this made Napoleon even more desperate for foreign policy success in order to increase his popularity. This led him into the disaster of the Franco-Prussian War.

The evidence is inconclusive on the reasons for change. Make a judgement on which interpretation you find the more convincing.

Italian unification

Checkpoints

1 Austria got no support from Russia because of its failure to support the Russians during the Crimean War. Disputes over the future of the German states were souring relations with Prussia. France under Napoleon III was looking to undermine Austria's position in Italy. Britain was sympathetic to the cause of Italian nationalism.

2 Garibaldi had an extraordinary ability to inspire the men under his command, and he was skilled in the tactics of guerrilla warfare. Garibaldi sided with the landlords in Sicily

in order to restore order quickly. He was motivated above all else by his desire to achieve Italian unity. Order on Sicily was crucial before he could launch a successful invasion of the kingdom of Naples.

3 Nationalism was important in the way that it inspired the crucial figure of Garibaldi. However, Italy was not united as a result of popular national feeling. The concept of Italy did not exist for the peasant masses of Italy.

Exam questions

1 This question implies that the main reason for unification was the active involvement of foreign powers. In your introduction, make it clear that there are other factors to consider.

Analyse the importance of France in Italy in 1859. You could also mention the role of the British navy in aiding Garibaldi's invasion of Sicily.

Show that foreign *non-intervention* was also important. Explain the reasons behind Russia and Prussia failing to support the Austrians. Demonstrate that events abroad in 1866 and 1870 allowed Italy to complete unification through the acquisition of Venetia and Rome.

Explain the importance of Cavour in bringing about Italian unification. In particular, focus on his diplomacy.

Discuss the role of Garibaldi in creating the unitary Italian state.

Conclusion – summarize the argument that there are many other factors to consider.

2 The quote reflects the view that Cavour was only concerned with Piedmontese expansion. Suggest that this is too simplistic.

Argue that Cavour was a Piedmontese nationalist first and foremost. He encouraged economic developments in the 1850s. He wished to create a northern Italian kingdom under Victor Emmanuel II. This was clearly the motivation behind the French alliance and subsequent war with Austria.

Analyse his attitude to Italian unity. He was prepared to cede the territories of Nice and Savoy (to France) in order to gain French acceptance of Piedmont's annexation of central Italy. This demonstrates his lack of commitment to the idea of Italian unification. Point out his negative opinions of the economically backward south.

Examine Cavour's attitude to Garibaldi's invasion of the south. You could argue that Cavour intervened in southern Italy in order to make sure that Italy was unified on Piedmont's terms.

Discuss Cavour's commitment to stable constitutional government. In the 1850s he acted decisively to prevent a return to autocracy. He certainly wanted to extend his moderate liberalism to other parts of the Italian peninsula. Autocratic rule of the northern and central states was something he wanted to bring to an end for ideological reasons.

Conclusion – Cavour was certainly motivated primarily by his desire to aggrandize Piedmont. To say that this was his only motivation is going too far.

3 This is a straightforward causation question. In your introduction, indicate the general areas of your analysis.

Analyse the economic decline of Austria after 1848. Focus on the significance of Austria's non-membership of the Zollverein. Consider the difficulties that Austria was having in holding on to its multi-ethnic empire.

Consider the reason for Austria's diplomatic isolation.

Discuss the role of Cavour in ending Austria's rule in Lombardy as well as the work of Bismarck in ending Austrian control of Venetia in 1866.

Point out that, having lost control of northern Italy, Austria was in no position to prevent Garibaldi's invasion of the south.

Conclusion – which was the most important factor? Consider the idea that Austrian domination of the Italian peninsula was not seen as crucial by the rest of Europe, as had been the case earlier.

German unification

Checkpoints

1 Metternich used the German Confederation, set up in 1815, to pass legislation such as the Carlsbad Decrees (1819) and the Six Acts (1832) to crack down on liberal nationalist activity. These led to the control of teaching in German universities as well as censorship of liberal publications.

2 The opposition of the two most powerful German states, Austria and Prussia, to unification is crucial. In the period up to 1848, the arch-reactionary, Metternich, dominated German affairs. In addition, liberal nationalists were divided in their aims and on the methods to achieve them.

3 This is a very difficult question to answer! Like Cavour in Piedmont, Bismarck was looking to aggrandize his state. In this sense he was a Prussian nationalist. He skilfully manipulated European events in order to achieve Prussian expansion, and used nationalistic feeling in order to achieve this. Finally, he did take the chance to complete unification in 1871, but he never had a plan to do so.

4 Bismarck could be confident that Britain would not support a backward, autocratic state like Austria. In any case, Britain did not have the land army to do this. Bismarck had made French neutrality a near certainty by making vague promises of territorial compensation to Napoleon III. Russian neutrality had been virtually guaranteed since the Crimean War (when Austria had failed to lend Russia support). In addition, he had won Russian favour by supporting its repression of the Polish revolt in 1863.

5 The Hohenzollern candidature concerned the choice of the next monarch of Spain. Bismarck proposed a German, Leopold of Hohenzollern. This caused outrage in France. Napoleon III adopted a very aggressive tone towards Prussia in order to appease his own people. This was used by Bismarck to whip up anti-French nationalistic fervour in

the German states. After Bismarck's alteration of the Ems telegram, Napoleon was manipulated into declaring war on Prussia, for which Bismarck now had popular support.

Exam questions

1 In your introduction, make it clear that Austria had been the dominant German state up to 1848. Briefly outline the main reasons for Austria's decline.

Discuss the way in which the relationship with Austria changed after 1848. Before 1848, Prussia had been content with Austria's domination of policy in the German states. Austria was responsible for the collapse of Prussia's Erfurt union in the 1850s. This was the beginning of Prussia's desire to dominate the German states.

Explain the increasing strength of Prussia – mention the Zollverein and the extent of Prussia's industrialization.

Link to the previous paragraph by analysing the decline of Austria. Mention its economic problems, the difficulties in maintaining its multi-ethnic empire and its growing diplomatic isolation in Europe.

Discuss the role of Bismarck. You should stress the importance of the Prussian army reforms; his manipulation of Austria into war in 1866; the way in which he guaranteed the neutrality of other powers.

Conclusion – summarize the argument and try to come to a judgement on the most important factor.

2 In your introduction, state that nationalism was important but that on its own it does not provide a satisfactory explanation of German unification.

A useful comparison could be made with Italy. Make clear, in contrast to Italy, that there was genuine nationalistic feeling among a large proportion of the population. The German language (again in contrast to Italy) already united most of the states of the confederation. The increasingly urbanized nature of German society was aiding the spread of nationalist ideas, especially among the middle classes.

Link to the previous paragraph by demonstrating how Bismarck took advantage of this latent nationalist feeling to whip up enthusiasm for his wars against Denmark and France. These Prussian victories were crucial in achieving German unification.

Now go on to state that there are other factors to consider. Begin by pointing out that it was Bismarck's clever diplomacy that created the situations through which Prussia achieved German unification.

Discuss growing Prussian strength and the decline of Austria.

Demonstrate how the international situation was favourable, especially in the way major European powers stayed neutral at crucial times.

Conclusion – summarize the argument and make a judgement on the significance of nationalism.

The French Third Republic

Checkpoints

1 The monarchists' desire to end the war with Prussia, in contrast to the republicans, is the crucial factor. This made the monarchists much more in tune with the moods of the people.

2 After a century of revolution the Bourbons showed how out of touch with reality they still were. The desire to have the traditional royalist flag sent out the wrong message to the people of France. It evoked memories of autocratic monarchy and the repression that went with it. This made a Bourbon restoration unacceptable, and the monarchists were unable to agree on any alternative leader.

3 Popular decisions such as the return of exiled veterans of the Commune and the legalisation of trade unions were made. Much was done to reduce the power of the Church in French society, especially in the area of education. Thus the power of a powerful anti-republican force was reduced.

4 Both these long-running sagas divided the nation ever more into supporters and opponents of the republic. Yet on both occasions the republic triumphed. The anti-republican elements of Church and army were reduced in their influence. There was a gradual acceptance of the principle of republican government.

Exam questions

1 In your introduction, make it clear that the republic survived through a combination of good fortune and sensible policy decisions.

Demonstrate that a return to monarchy seemed likely after 1871 and then explain the reasons for France's rejection of a monarchical form of government.

Explain the significance of the destruction of the Paris Commune in that it led to the removal of radical republicanism for a decade.

Analyse the successful policy decisions of a succession of republican governments. Focus on social and foreign policy and demonstrate how the influence of anti-republican elements was reduced.

Discuss the significance of internal crises such as the Boulanger and Dreyfus affairs in the long-term survival of the republic.

Conclusion – make it clear which aspects of the republic's survival were due to good fortune and which can be credited to republican politicians.

2 In your introduction, make it clear who were the main opponents of the Third Republic. Give an indication of the methods used to deal with opposition but point out that success was not total.

Demonstrate that the Paris Commune was a threat itself to republican government. Its destruction gave moderate republicanism a chance to flourish.

Discuss how the opposition of the Church and army was dealt with through successful legislation. Highlight the success in dealing with the Boulanger and Dreyfus incidents, which allowed a further curb on the influence of anti-republican institutions.

Analyse the success of the republic in dealing with threats to the republic from socialism and communism through social legislation. Point out that this success was not total, strikes and riots still being common.

Conclusion – given how unlikely the long-term survival of the republic seemed in 1871, it must be argued that the Third Republic dealt very successfully with internal opposition. You must point out, however, that problems still remained.

3 In your introduction, give an indication of the problems facing France in 1871 following the Prussian defeat. Indicate that on the whole France had recovered.

Show that the destruction of the Paris Commune was important in the creation of stable government. Point out the success of the early republican governments in paying off reparations to the Germans.

Analyse the success of the Third Republic in building up support for republican government through popular legislation (social, economic and foreign policy).

Explain the significance of the Boulanger and Dreyfus affairs in securing the future of the republic.

Point out that problems still remained by 1900, such as the poor relations that existed with Germany and the threat to the republic from the radical left wing.

Conclusion – point out that 30 years of relatively stable government are testament to the recovery of France, even if there were still weaknesses in the republican system.

Bismarck's Germany

Checkpoints

1 He meant that Bismarck had created a political system that was a façade. It appeared to be democratic but in reality left huge power with the chancellor and the emperor.
2 Bismarck's alliance with the National Liberals was always an uncomfortable one. Their aim of creating a true democracy in Germany was not one that he shared. By the late 1870s he was looking to create a new alliance with the Centre Party in order to fight the socialist threat.
3 Like Catholicism, socialism was an international movement. In theory at least, socialists' first loyalty was not to Germany but to the international socialist movement. Obviously, their ideas on the redistribution of wealth were not ones that a conservative such as Bismarck could possibly share.

Exam questions

1 In your introduction, make it clear that Germany's problems stemmed mainly from it being a recently created country – to a certain extent by force. There was potential for disunity.

Focus on the 1871 constitution. Argue that this gave Bismarck the power to hold the country together. On the other hand, point out that he never successfully dealt with Prussian desires to remain the dominant German state.

Bismarck perceived the Catholic south as a problem. Demonstrate how his attempt to limit Catholic influence failed.

The urban working classes felt alienated from the regime. Did either Bismarck's anti-socialist legislation or his 'state socialism' succeed in overcoming this problem?

Analyse the success of his protectionist economic policies. As Germany was already industrialized and had a large internal market, these policies were beneficial.

Conclusion – Bismarck's control of Germany was supreme. However, it could be argued that he failed to reconcile important groups to the new German Empire.

2 Indicate in your introduction that there is evidence to support this assertion, but on its own it is too simplistic.

The clash with Prussia was a result of the 1871 constitution. This was probably unavoidable. The constitution was a compromise. By not allowing Prussian domination the unity of the rest of the empire was made more secure.

The dispute with the National Liberals was clearly engineered by Bismarck for his own political reasons.

The Catholic south was certainly not as loyal a part of the empire as Bismarck would have liked. However, anti-Catholic legislation increased disunity.

Anti-socialist legislation increased support for the SPD.

Conclusion – Bismarck certainly made underlying problems worse. However, to say that they were of his 'own making' implies that these problems were created by the chancellor, which is going too far.

Bismarck's foreign policy

Checkpoints

1 Bismarck wished to prove to the rest of Europe that Germany was not a threat. An active colonial policy would have alarmed Britain in particular.
2 Bismarck wished to reduce tension between Russia and Austria over the Balkans because this would avoid Germany having to take sides over the issue. Turning his back on Russia, for instance, could have led to the creation of an anti-German Franco-Russian alliance.

3 German–Russian relations had been soured by the Near Eastern crisis. Bismarck therefore turned to Austria in order to create a reliable military alliance. However, Austria was in decline as a major European power and there was also a danger that Russia might sign an alliance with the French.

4 The problem with this treaty was that, in the event of Franco-German war, Russian neutrality was not guaranteed.

Exam questions

1 The statement implies that Bismarck was unsuccessful in his attempt to guarantee European peace.

Demonstrate that Bismarck was aiming to preserve peace in Europe as this would safeguard the future of the German Empire.

Argue that his policies did help to preserve peace in Europe. Use clear factual examples (e.g. the Dual Alliance; the Second Dreikaiserbund) to prove this, either through improving relations between nations or threatening them through German strength.

Look at the same events from a different angle – that Bismarck's foreign policy was no more than 'crisis management'. Particularly focus on the Reinsurance Treaty.

Analyse the prospects for peace in 1890. What problems still remained?

Conclusion – 19 years of peace were impressive, but had Bismarck created a strong system that would guarantee peace in the future?

2 The question implies that Bismarck's foreign policy was successful early on but less so by 1890.

Argue that he was successful throughout his time in power, since he achieved his aim of preserving European peace. Demonstrate how he solved crises as they arose by alterations in his alliance system (give factual examples).

Argue that the policy can be seen as failing by 1890 because of the threats to European peace that still existed.

Argue that it was, in fact, failing right from the beginning because Bismarck never sought to find long-term solutions to the problems that were clearly there in 1871. The Near Eastern crisis and the Dual Alliance demonstrated the fragile foundations on which Bismarck's foreign policy rested, and this was 11 years before his resignation.

Conclusion – depending upon the criteria used, Bismarck's foreign policy could be seen as a total success or a continual failure.

3 1879–1885 is often seen as the high point of Bismarck's diplomacy. By 1890 his alliance system was falling apart. It is possible to perceive this eventual failure at the time the policy was supposedly working most successfully.

Examine the strengths of the Dual Alliance – a reliable ally and knowledge of it eventually forced Russia back into Bismarck's alliance system in 1882.

On the other hand, the Dual Alliance tied Germany to a weakening partner. It indicated to the Russians that in the long term Germany would side with Austria on the Balkan issue.

Point out that it is wrong to blame the Dual Alliance as the most important reason for the weakening of Bismarck's foreign policy. His anti-Russian stance at the Congress of Berlin is important. Argue that his policy of friendship with both Austria and Russia was doomed to failure from the beginning because of the inevitable clash in the Balkans.

Argue that since Bismarck maintained European peace his foreign policy could be viewed as a success.

Conclusion – to see the Dual Alliance as the fundamental reason for the weakening of the alliance system ignores the longer-term factors that were at work.

European history 1895–1945

This period of European history is dominated by political upheaval. The two world wars were the pivotal events in the first half of the 20th century. They are indelibly linked to the imperialist struggles of the great powers and to the rise of extremist mass political movements, most notably fascism and communism. The conflicts that these forces precipitated were to shape not only the major European events to 1945 but also those of the 50 years to follow. Much of the period was apparently dominated by powerful leaders, and this has led historians to debate how far the course of events, both inside states and internationally, was dictated by their objectives and planning.

Exam themes

→ The causes of the world wars of 1914–1918 and 1939–1945.

→ Reasons for the rise of mass political movements (communism and fascism).

→ The nature of communist and fascist states – the totalitarian model.

→ The role of key individuals in shaping political events, e.g. Hitler, Stalin, Mussolini.

→ Different 'schools' of historical interpretation – the intentionalist vs. structuralist debate.

Topic checklist

○ AS ● A2

	AQA	EDEXCEL	OCR	WJEC
Causes of the First World War	○●	●	○	○●
Results of the Great War	○●	●	○	○●
Nicholas II: Tsar of Russia	○●	○	○	●
Russia: 1917–1924	○●	○	○●	●
Fascism in Mussolini's Italy	○●	○●	○	●
The Weimar Republic	○	○	○	●
Hitler's Germany 1933–1945	○●	○●	○	●
The USSR under Stalin	○●	○●	●	●
International relations: 1930s 1	●	○●	○●	○●
International relations: 1930s 2	●	○●	○●	○●

Causes of the First World War

The debate about the causes of the First World War essentially revolves around the question of Germany's relative responsibility. While there is a broad consensus about the importance of Balkan nationalism, the alliances forged by the European powers and the arms race, the same cannot be said for Germany's role. For some, the war was a product of the general breakdown in international relations in 1914. For others, like Professor Fritz Fischer, Germany went to war with a specific expansion programme in mind.

Great power alliances

Under Bismarck, Germany's policy in Europe was built around the isolation of France. While not fully successful by 1890, Bismarck nevertheless pursued a cautious foreign policy that avoided outright provocation of the great powers:

→ He was against German overseas conquests that might annoy Britain.
→ He wanted Austria-Hungary firmly under German control to restrain it in the Balkans and played down German interests in Turkey, which risked uniting Russia and Britain. With his departure, these cautious policies were abandoned.

Action point

Make your own notes on the words shown in bold in the text.

Weaknesses of Wilhelmine diplomacy included:

→ An alliance was signed between France and Russia in 1893, making a two-front war with Germany possible.
→ Britain was driven towards France by the Kaiser's naval policy, ending the era of 'splendid isolation' by signing the **Entente Cordiale** (1904). By 1907, the **Triple Entente** with Russia had been concluded.
→ Germany's chief alliance partner under the Dual Alliance was Austria-Hungary, whose objectives in the Balkans risked conflict with Russia. Germany's policy also had the goal of potential influence over Polish provinces of Russia's empire.

The potential for war

Secret diplomacy was the hallmark of the alliances. As a result, Germany and Austria-Hungary began to fear **encirclement**.

Checkpoint 1

How else did Germany contribute to tension over arms?

Anglo-German naval rivalry

By 1898 the Kaiser had set Germany on a course of naval expansion, epitomized by the German Navy Law of 1900. This policy seemed to threaten the overseas interests of Britain as well as its own security. Production of the *Dreadnought* encouraged a direct German response as well as growing militarism in Britain, as seen in the Navy League demand 'We want eight and we won't wait'.

Balkan nationalism ●●●

The most obvious clash of interests in the Balkans was between Austria-Hungary and Serbia:

→ Austria's fears were of pan-Slav or pan-Serb nationalism, which could split the Dual Monarchy and destroy the empire.

→ The focus for these fears was Serbia's designs on Bosnia and Herzegovina, annexed from the Ottoman Empire in 1908 (though administered by it since 1878).

→ These provinces were an integral part of Serbia's dream of a Yugo Slav or south Slav state.

→ After territorial gains by Serbia in the second Balkan crisis of 1912–1913, Austrian fears of Serbia's growing political and military stature intensified the desire to quell pan-Serb nationalism.

Assassination in the Balkans ●●●

On 28 June 1914, the murder of the Habsburg heir, Archduke Franz Ferdinand, by Serb nationalists triggered a conflict that was to draw in the rival alliances:

→ Germany backed the Dual Monarchy's ultimatum to Serbia, which was designed to snuff out Serbian independence.

→ Russia backed Serbia, not only on the grounds of common Slav heritage but also in order to preclude the Austro-German domination of the Balkans, the Black Sea and the Straits.

Germany's declaration of war on Russia led to France's entry under the Triple Entente and that of Britain on 4 August 1914.

The jargon

Nationalism is the desire of a race to rule itself, which arises out of a sense of racial or national identity.
Pan-Slav means 'embracing all Slavs'.

Check the net

You will find further information about the causes of the First World War at www.sky.co.uk/history

Checkpoint 2

What part did Belgium play in Britain's decision to go to war with Germany?

Exam questions   answers: page 128

1 'The causes of the First World War lay in the Balkans.' To what extent is this view accurate? (45 min)

2 'Germany had a clear programme of territorial expansion before 1914, which made war inevitable.' How far can this view account for why war broke out in August 1914? (45 min)

Examiner's secrets

In Q2, make sure you address *both* main issues, not just the first one.

Results of the Great War

> *"The Germans are going to pay every penny: they are going to be squeezed . . . until the pips squeak"*
>
> Lloyd George

The 1914–1918 war was to have lasting consequences not only for the defeated powers but also the victors. Four empires were to fall as a direct result of the conflict, and the seeds of the Second World War were to be sown.

Consequences for Germany

Of all the defeated powers, Germany's perception of its own humiliation was perhaps the greatest. It was this that was to shape its domestic affairs and foreign policy over the following two decades.

A republican Germany

The immediate consequence of Germany's huge battlefield losses in 1918 was a revolution that ended the Wilhelmine monarchy and created a republican system (the Weimar Republic).

Public reaction to Versailles

The war guilt clause ran counter to the common German view that they had fought a defensive war to prevent encirclement. German nationalism, epitomized by figures like Ludendorff, began to propagate the 'stab in the back' myth that was to destabilize the Weimar Republic from the right.

The severe economic provisions imposed upon Germany, justified by its 'guilt', further aggravated resentment of the terms. The weight of **reparations** precipitated the Ruhr crisis of 1923 and began German reliance upon US loans – **Stresemann**'s 'dancing on a volcano'. Some historians also believe that the poor economic performance of the European powers after the war can in part be blamed on Germany's inability to act as a buoyant market, much as Keynes suggested at the time.

Self-determination and the new states

US President Wilson's belief that the frontiers of Europe should be redrawn to allow all races to rule themselves was pursued to a limited degree in practice. Nine states were created from the old empires:

→ Czechoslovakia, Yugoslavia, Austria and Hungary were carved from the Habsburg lands.
→ Poland, Finland, Lithuania, Latvia and Estonia emerged from Russia (where the tsar had been deposed as a result of the war's effects upon his nation and a Bolshevik regime had come to power in 1917) and Germany.

Problems

The inclusion of so many German speakers inside the borders of both Poland and Czechoslovakia was to lead the Weimar governments to seek a policy of gradual adjustment in the Versailles terms.

Checkpoint 1

Why did Ludendorff argue that the German army could have won the war?

The jargon

Self-determination is the right of a people to decide for themselves which country they belong to or what sort of government they have.

Under Hitler, such gradualism was abandoned in 1938–1939 with the justification of reuniting all German speakers in one Reich. These states were too weak economically and strategically to withstand aggression.

The creation of these new states after the war also had wider implications:

→ They reinvigorated the Asian and African nationalist movements.
→ The Indian independence movement gained momentum.

Consequences for Turkey ●●●

Turkey was laid open to attack from Greece, which saw the chance to reclaim Asia Minor, lost in 1453. After the Treaty of Sèvres virtually divided Turkey between Greece, Italy and France, Turks rallied to **Kemal**, with these effects:

→ In Greece, Constantine was forced to abdicate as a result of Greek defeat at Sakarya.
→ Turkey became a republic under Kemal and embarked on a programme of modernization and reorientation towards the West, while abandoning imperialist ambitions.

Consequences for the victors ●●●

Britain found itself suffering severe economic problems by 1920–1921, with unemployment of two million. The heavy burden of war debt repayment to the USA was in part responsible and contributed to rapid economic growth in the USA. This fuelled competition for British overseas markets.

Italy had joined the Allies in 1915 principally in the hope of territorial gains. These were to be largely disappointed at the Paris conferences. Resentment, coupled with a large war debt and a backward southern economy, combined with industrial unrest to produce political instability. These were the circumstances that led to the rise of Mussolini and fascism.

The USA was dominated by **isolationist** sentiment. The defeat of the Treaty of Versailles on the floor of the Senate was followed by the 1935–1937 Neutrality Acts, further distancing the USA from world affairs. Despite being tied to the European powers through war debt and the necessity this brought about to stabilize Germany (Dawes/Young plans), the USA's reluctance to support peacekeeping through the **League of Nations** crippled that body from the start.

Watch out!

It is a common error to state that Germans were to be found in the north of Czechoslovakia. They were German-speakers, formerly of the Austro-Hungarian Empire.

Checkpoint 2

What had been the main effects of Sèvres on Turkey?

Test yourself

Make a list of each key nation. Write out a series of bullet points that show the effects of the war on each.

"Are we making a good peace? Are we? Are we?"

diary of Harold Nicolson, British delegate to Versailles

Exam questions   answers: page 129

1 'The post-war settlement laid the foundations for war in 1939.' How accurate is this view? (45 min)

2 'An unwarranted punishment imposed for revenge.' Is this an accurate view of the Treaty of Versailles? (45 min)

Nicholas II: Tsar of Russia

> *"The world should be surprised that we have any government in Russia, not that we have imperfect government"*
>
> Sergei Witte

Action point

Make your own notes on the words shown in bold in the text.

The jargon

The *proletariat* is a term most often used by Marxists to describe the industrial working class, who are seen as the instrument by which socialism will be established.

The jargon

Liberals wished to establish constitutional government under which political and civil liberties would be protected.

Nicholas II was the last of the Romanov dynasty, which had ruled Russia since 1613. His regime was in many ways a medieval institution that was placed under pressure by the forces unleashed by modernization. However, this does not mean that its overthrow was inevitable. More than any other factor, it was to be the First World War that brought the Tsar's government down.

The nature of the tsarist autocracy

The theoretically absolute rule of the Tsar allowed for no compromise or consultation over the governance of the vast Russian Empire. He exercised total power over all the functions of the state: executive, legislative and judicial. This model of power was derived from a conception of divine right. The Tsar was the 'father' of his people, chosen and guided by God. However, until the development of a more centralized bureaucracy in the 1860s, the practical administration of policy was often conducted by local gentry and the clergy. Nicholas II was firmly convinced that only autocracy could hold Russia together. The alternative was anarchy and the disintegration of the empire.

A nation in transition

In certain respects Russia was changing very rapidly as a nation by the time Nicholas took the throne in 1894. The state-interventionist policies of Sergei Witte had led to huge increases in the production of iron, coal, petrol and textiles. By 1900, Russia had the fastest rate of economic growth in the world. A massive railway boom, symbolized by the 4 000-mile Trans-Siberian Railway, acted as a motor to growth. However, both the new urban **proletariat** and the peasantry were becoming increasingly discontented:

→ The proletariat had to endure terrible living and working conditions in the few areas and large factories in which they were concentrated. This led to a growing politicization of industrial workers and their support for either the Social Democrats or the Social Revolutionaries (SRs).
→ The peasantry too were becoming more restless by the 1890s. Rising population and taxes placed burdens on peasant landholdings. By 1901–1902, serious crop failures had translated into many uprisings.

The 'revolution' of 1904–1907

The humiliation of the **Russo-Japanese War** lit the touch paper for constitutional reform in Russia. A wave of strikes that paralysed the autocracy brought together liberals and workers and forced the Tsar to concede a new constitution under the October manifesto of 1905. This was designed to give to the Duma a genuine say in governing the state.

However, from the start Nicholas set out to undermine it:

→ Nicholas gave the State Council a veto over the Duma.
→ The Tsar himself could veto any legislation, dissolve the Duma before the end of its term and govern by decree.

This clearly failed to meet aspirations for constitutional government.

The impact of the First World War ●●●

At first the war united large sectors of Russian society. However, military defeat and the Tsar's association with it as commander-in-chief did much to undermine public support for the regime.

→ In 1915, he managed to disillusion most of the educated classes by rejecting a national government drawn from the 'Progressive Bloc'.
→ In 1916, the proletariat joined them, largely because of inflation and shortages of food and fuel. The political vacuum caused by the 'ministerial leapfrog' in Petrograd led to strikes and the mutiny of the garrison. The Tsar was forced to abdicate on 2 March 1917.

Why did Nicholas survive in 1905 but not 1917? ●●●

There are some striking similarities between the situations in 1905 and 1917. In both cases, popular unrest arose partly out of military failure, and liberal and proletarian objectives coincided. Nicholas survived in 1905 because the army remained basically loyal, allowing him the option of repression. He also made concessions that were sufficient to head off more radical demands. His survival also owed much to the work of two able ministers, **Witte** and **Stolypin**.

But in 1917 he had lost the loyalty of the army. The 2.8 million wounded and 1.8 million dead placed the reliability of the army in serious doubt. The garrison at Petrograd was the key to his loss of control in the city, though some historians point out that it could have been dealt with by other troops who were still obedient to the Tsar. However, as noted above, the army command could no longer predict with any accuracy the response of the rank and file, so this course of action was highly dubious.

For many, it was Nicholas' abandonment by his generals that guaranteed his fall. For some of them he was now an obstacle to victory, and his abdication would serve to prevent revolution rather than bring it about. This willingness of the elite to sacrifice the Tsar was a crucial difference from the position in 1905.

Check the net

You'll find plenty of information about the causes of the February Revolution at www.historytoday.com

Checkpoint 1

To whom does the term 'Progressive Bloc' refer?

Test yourself

After you have read these pages, take a sheet of paper and list the key differences between 1905 and February 1917.

Checkpoint 2

How could Nicholas' abandonment by his generals be seen as an attempt to limit a social revolution in Russia?

"A war in Europe would be a very useful thing for the revolution but it is hardly possible Franz Josef and Nicky would give us this pleasure"

Lenin, 1913

Exam questions   answers: pages 129–30

1   How did the Tsar survive the 1905 revolution? (45 min)

2   Why was the Tsar forced to abdicate in February 1917? (45 min)

Russia: 1917–1924

The jargon

The *Kadets,* or Constitutional Democratic Party, were supporters of Western-style constitutionalism. Most of their support came from the emerging middle class. *Soviets* were councils, which became increasingly influential in 1917 as oppositional forces to the Provisional Government.

Checkpoint 1

What was the significance of the Kornilov affair?

The February Revolution of 1917, which deposed Nicholas II, ushered in the Provisional Government. This was to be short-lived, falling in the October Revolution instigated by the Bolsheviks. We will deal first with why the provisional administration was overthrown, then with why the Bolsheviks could consolidate their power in an apparently hostile environment.

The fall of the Provisional Government

To understand the failure of the Provisional Government and its leader Alexander Kerensby, we must first understand that it had been brought to power in order to avert a more radical social revolution. However, it was undermined by its own weaknesses, its inability to deal with the demands of the masses and by the machinations of the Bolshevik party.

The nature of the Provisional Government

The government increasingly resisted the demands of the peasantry for land, of the workers for improved conditions in the factories and of the rank and file for an end to the war. This was due to the dominance of the **Kadet Party** within the governing coalition, which sided with the interests of the landowners. They were philosophically opposed to state control of the economy and favoured a military coup to restore order. This served to shift power towards **the soviets** as the public came increasingly to ignore the Provisional Government.

The demands of the people

One of the central problems for the new government was an almost complete collapse in obedience. Seizures of land in the countryside were gathering pace by October 1917, workers' demands became more radical in response to a disintegrating economy (calls for workers' control became more commonplace), and the army became alienated over the **Kornilov affair**.

The Bolshevik party

At the start of 1917 the Bolsheviks appeared perhaps the least likely to take power in Russia by the end of the year:

→ Their membership was a paltry 10 000, while their influence within the soviets was far eclipsed by both the Mensheviks and the Social Revolutionaries (SRs).

→ The Bolsheviks became almost a party of protest, reaping the benefits of popular discontent with the socialist parties that had collaborated with the Provisional Government.

→ Government failure to deliver the demands of the masses – peace, bread and land – allowed the Bolsheviks to claim they were acting on behalf of the soviets. This helps to explain why much of the army rank and file stood by and allowed the Bolshevik takeover to succeed in October 1917.

The consolidation of Bolshevik control ●●●

In the elections to the Constituent Assembly of November 1917, the Bolsheviks polled a mere 24% of the popular vote. They were far outstripped by the SRs, whose 48.1% easily established them as the majority party in Russia. Despite this apparently hostile environment, the Bolsheviks were able to entrench their hold on the Russian state for four principal reasons:

1. A divided opposition

Russia from 1917 was effectively a system in a state of terminal collapse. The economy was in turmoil; the chief preoccupation of many became survival. In a system where town was pitted against countryside for control of food supplies and where the army's discipline had fallen apart there was simply no united front against Bolshevik control. Leftist opponents were likewise divided among themselves, and support for the Whites seemed to be tantamount to supporting counter-revolution – in itself a prospect sufficient to deter many.

2. The civil war

As noted above, the White oppositional forces were viewed by many as endangering the gains made by workers and peasants. This drove them into the arms of the Bolsheviks during the civil war period as the best guarantors of those achievements. **The Whites** themselves were never a very potent threat, because:

→ Their armies were weak compared with the Red Army.
→ They were ideologically divided, encompassing monarchists and supporters of liberal democracy.
→ They commanded little support among many minorities due to their strong Russian nationalism.

3. The New Economic Policy

The regime was stabilized politically by the reversion to capitalism under the **New Economic Policy** (**NEP**). This ran in tandem with intensified political repression, which effectively neutralised opposition.

4. A channel for social mobility and advancement

The development of the party apparatus enabled many to attain occupations and a standard of living that were not available to those who were not party members.

Check the net

You'll find more information about the Bolshevik takeover at www.historytoday.com

Checkpoint 2

What were the objectives of the Whites?

"[The Bolsheviks] were motivated by utopianism . . . by a vision of world socialism. If people did not agree they would have to be educated"

Darby, 1998

Exam questions   answers: page 130

1   'The Provisional Government was doomed to failure from the start.' How accurate is this statement? (45 min)

2   Why were the Bolsheviks able to consolidate their hold on power between 1917 and 1924? (45 min)

Examiner's secrets

In Q1, begin by outlining the weaknesses of the provisional government.

Fascism in Mussolini's Italy

Checkpoint 1

What were Italy's African ambitions in the late 19th century?

Checkpoint 2

How did the PR system destabilize Italian democracy after 1919?

Check the net

You'll find more information on Mussolini's rise to power at www.bbc.co.uk/education/modern

While the rise of Fascism in Italy cannot be divorced from the person of Mussolini himself, it is also true that its success required an environment conducive to its growth. This was provided by the crisis of Italian liberalism, socio-economic problems and the failure to achieve great power status following the 1914–1918 war.

The crisis of Italian democracy

Between 1859 and 1870 a united Italian kingdom was created, characterized by a limited monarchy and a liberal parliamentary constitution. Attempts to create an Italian empire in North and East Africa from the 1880s were frustrated, intensifying resentment towards the imperial powers of Britain and France. Italy's economic backwardness further contributed to the rise of Italian nationalism before the First World War. This ascribed the country's ills to the corruption of the political class that dominated **liberalism**. Though the nationalist movements failed to gain significant popular support prior to 1914, they did forge close links with the business community, Catholics and conservatives, and these were to help spawn fascism after the war.

1918–1922: The post-war crisis

Despite fighting alongside the victorious powers from 1915, Italy in 1918 was in some respects on a par with the defeated nations:

→ The economy was afflicted by rapid inflation and rising unemployment.
→ A divided party system was encouraged by proportional representation (PR). The two largest parties in 1919, the PSI and the Partito Popolare Italiano (a Catholic party) were unable to cooperate and guide Italy into a new democratic age.
→ Industrial unrest fuelled fears of communism, as did soaring trade union membership between 1918 and 1920.
→ Many felt an acute sense of national humiliation after Italy failed to gain African and Middle Eastern colonies from the post-war settlement.

When the Fascist Party or PNF was officially established in 1921, it appeared to offer to many Italians a vehicle for the destruction of a discredited liberal elite.

The rise to power 1922

Mussolini became prime minister in October 1922. Conservative forces within Italy facilitated his rise to power.

→ Leading liberals like Prime Minister Giolitti believed a coalition that included the Fascists would bring the movement under control and eventually neutralize it as a threat to the liberal system.
→ Business and large landowners saw in the party the promise of stiffer regulation of labour.

- → The Vatican hoped for an end to the long-running conflict between Church and state.
- → The King was unwilling to challenge a proposed march on Rome by the Fascists for fear of inciting civil war and possibly because of fascist sympathies in the army.
- → Many Italians were fearful of left-wing violence and the possibility of communist revolution.

Despite presiding over a coalition for two years, Mussolini began to lay the foundation for dictatorship with the **Acerbo Law** of 1923 and during 1925–1926 it was fully established. Opponents like **Matteotti** were ruthlessly eliminated.

The corporate state ●●●

One of the key features of Italian fascism – claimed to be unique – was the creation of the **corporate state** between 1925 and 1939. This was to bring workers, managers and employers together. However, there is strong evidence to suggest that the corporations came to take decisions primarily in employers' interests. For example, from 1928 workers' representatives on corporations were actually fascist officials, often favouring industrial interests. Because of this, many historians have taken issue with the regime's self-described totalitarianism. The need to tailor many economic policies to the concerns of business removed from the party the control required for a totalitarian state.

Foreign policy ●●●

Noted earlier were the attempts in the 1880s and 1890s to seize colonies in Africa. A broad consensus has now formed that Mussolini's foreign policy was always expansionist in character, and in this respect a degree of continuity with the late 19th century can be seen. Despite ruthless measures in Libya between 1922 and 1932, Mussolini's hand was stayed in Abyssinia by the effects of the Depression. However, with the conflict of 1935 his policy took on a new, more aggressively ideological aspect. Aggression was the means of replacing the decadent, failing empires of Britain and France and demonstrating that fascism was the dominant new force in geopolitics. His involvement in the Spanish Civil War, his neutrality over the status of Austria and the 'Pact of Steel' wedded Mussolini to German foreign policy. Despite hesitating over participation in the war, in spring 1940 Italy was dragged into a war it was not equipped to fight.

> **The jargon**
>
> The *Acerbo Law* was an electoral reform of July 1923 that gave the leading party or alliance in an Italian general election two-thirds of the seats in parliament.

> *"My objective is simple. I want to make Italy great, respected and feared"*
>
> Mussolini

Exam questions   answers: pages 130–1

1   'Italian fascism was simply one variation of totalitarianism.' How far is this view supported by the experience of the Mussolini dictatorship after 1925? (45 min)

2   'The appeal of fascism lay in protecting agrarian and industrial interests from the threat of socialism.' Do you agree? (45 min)

Examiner's secrets

The Weimar Republic

The Weimar Republic of 1919–1933 is often seen as a failure because of its inability to entrench democratic values among a big enough proportion of the German people. The absence of such support can in part be seen to have provided fertile ground for Germany's turn to extremist politics from the late 1920s.

The founding of the republic

The German revolution brought to power a '**Weimar coalition**', which from the start relied upon an active compromise between bourgeois and socialist forces, which had been in conflict during the empire. The parties that formed the governing coalitions comprised:

→ **SPD**: which under Ebert had rejected the wide-ranging change in German society favoured by the KPD (and to a lesser degree the USPD) in favour of a moderate democratization of the German state.
→ **Centre** (**Zentrum**), **Democrats** (**DDP**) and **German People's Party** (**DVP**): these were all non-socialist parties committed to the defence of private property rights and the interests of German private enterprise.

These four parties formed nine governments between February 1919 and the end of 1923, but the SPD was to withdraw from active government for much of the period thereafter. These basic ideological differences were to divide the parties most committed to developing democratic norms.

The constitution

The tensions in the Weimar party system were in large part a product of the constitution, which established a **proportional system** for parliamentary elections. The horse-trading required for the formation of new governing coalitions did much to alienate many German voters from parliamentary democracy.

The role of the **presidency** was also crucial. The extensive use of emergency decrees under Article 48 led many Germans to see the president as an 'emperor substitute', further undermining already fragile support for the parliamentary system.

Successes of the Weimar Republic

Successes included:

→ Maintenance of democratic structures in the face of extremist challenges 1919–1924.
→ The defeat of the **Spartacist** threat in 1919.
→ The crushing of the Bavarian Soviet the same year, followed by the failure of the **Kapp putsch** in 1920, may be said to have bought the new system time in which to begin to win over more of the German people to democratic values.

Action point

Make your own notes on the words shown in bold in the text.

The jargon

Proportional representation or *PR* describes a range of electoral systems that, to varying degrees, allocate seats approximately in proportion to the percentage of the vote won by a party.

Checkpoint 1

What kind of government did the Spartacists wish to establish in Germany?

→ Enhancement of German security to the east: the Rapallo Treaty might be said to have safeguarded Germany from a Polish attack in the east at the time of the Ruhr invasion of 1923.

→ Normalization of relations with Germany's western neighbours: Locarno 1925 improved relations with France.

Failures of the Weimar Republic ●●●

Included:

→ Continued power and traditions of the old army: the Freikorps were allowed to form the basis of the new Reichswehr, under the command of the old officers. Anti-republican forces were therefore in control of the armed forces.

→ Maintenance of the imperial bureaucracy: another focus of opposition to democratic norms.

→ Failure to prepare the German people for the Versailles terms meant that the nationalist 'stab in the back' myth more easily gained a foothold.

The 1929–1933 crisis ●●●

Division among the Weimar coalition parties

By the time **Brüning** took office, the willingness to compromise between the bourgeois parties and Social Democrats had all but ended. Class conflicts now divided the democratic forces irreparably.

Brüning's deflationary policy

Brüning's tight monetary and fiscal policies stoked the public discontent upon which extremism grew, while alienating Hindenburg and the Reichswehr as a result.

Manoeuvring on the right

The conservative establishment's readiness to hand power to Hitler can be seen as:

→ An act of naivety, especially by **Hindenburg** and **Schleicher**, who both believed he could be controlled through a nationalist coalition.

→ A desperate effort to head off the Bolshevik threat by the conservative forces most threatened by republicanism.

Check the net

You'll find information about the strengths and weaknesses of the Weimar Republic at www.history today.com

Checkpoint 2

Why would the preservation of the old civil service be a practical obstacle to the success of the new republic?

"By 1932 the collapse of the Weimar Republic had become inevitable; Hitler's triumph had not"

Stern, 1972

Exam questions answers: pages 131–2

1 Why was the Weimar Republic able to resist anti-democratic forces in the 1920s but not in the 1930s? (45 min)

2 'The Weimar Republic was predestined to failure because the German people retained a belief in authoritarianism.' Discuss. (45 min)

Hitler's Germany:
1933–1945

Action point

Make your own notes on the words shown in bold in the text.

Checkpoint 1

What threat to Hitler's position did the death of Hindenburg remove?

The jargon

Intentionalists see the pursuit of political goals by strong leaders as central to what happened. *Structuralists* question the ability and power of the leaders to direct events and prefer to emphasize more general factors like economic, political and social causes.

The nature of the Nazi dictatorship continues to cause debate. Marxists interpret the Nazi state as one devised to protect the interests of capital. The view of the 'totalitarian school', that it was similar to the Stalinist model of communism in important respects, has been challenged by the 'new orthodoxy', which stressed the rapid industrialization and urbanization of German society, leading to the rise of the *volkisch* ideology.

Power and consolidation

The decisive step towards dictatorship came with the passage of the **Enabling Act** in 1933. The legal transfer of legislative and executive powers to the chancellor for four years was to usher in what was initially a chaotic new model of state authority in which the party sought to impose its authority upon the organs of government. The key to extending Hitler's control was a process of **Gleichschaltung** or 'coordination'. This involved:

→ Subordination of the state governments by January 1934.
→ Creation of the German Labour Front to replace independent unions.
→ Integration of right-wing organizations like the Stahlhelm into the party.

With the effective neutralization of the SA in June 1934 (the **Night of the Long Knives**) went the possibility of an army coup. Hitler's power was consolidated. His decision to weld together the offices of president and chancellor following Hindenburg's death was simply a formal recognition of his control.

The nature of the dictatorship

Some historians have challenged the once common view of Nazi Germany as a totalitarian state. Instead, a chaotic web of competing power centres has been advanced as the key feature of the regime. Consequently, the Nazis were unable to control the state as in Soviet Russia, and bodies like the bureaucracy continued to retain considerable autonomy. Some historians have argued that Hitler had no clear blueprint for the creation of a Nazi state and without the underpinning of the regime by Himmler, through the **Gestapo** and the **SS**, it might well have collapsed.

The intentionalist/structuralist debate

Historians have disagreed about why the Nazi state was characterized by such chaos and disorder:

→ Intentionalists see it as a deliberate means of consolidating Hitler's position.
→ Structuralists (or 'functionalists') stress the absence of a clear strategy for creating a Nazi state. This was inevitably going to cause administrative chaos.

Economic policy ●●●

Lacking a coherent economic strategy, Hitler at first maintained many of the policies of the Papen and Schliecher governments:

→ Under Schacht's full dictatorial powers, deficit financing was expanded to facilitate German rearmament.
→ By 1936, however, Schacht was being by-passed in favour of Göring, whose Four-Year Plan introduced **autarky** for the first time.

Historians like Overy have seen this as the decisive step towards German war mobilization.

Racial policy ●●●

Race was of central importance to Hitler's vision of the new German community:

→ The initial period of harassment, encompassing legislative acts against the Jews like the Nuremberg Laws of 1935, lasted from 1933 to 1938.
→ This gave way to an escalation of violence, with *Kristallnacht* and Hitler's notorious threat in 1939 to annihilate the Jews of Europe. With the Wannsee Conference of 1942, the 'Final Solution' of **genocide** was introduced.

The intentionalist/structuralist debate

Once again opinions are sharply divided on the origins of Hitler's anti-Semitic policy.

→ Intentionalists view the formulation of policy as deliberate, part of a long-term aim to murder the Jews.
→ Structuralists stress the chaos of the Nazi state and ascribe the escalation of 1938 onwards to bureaucratic infighting and to the pressures of war, which led to ever more radical proposals.

Check the net

You'll find information on the economic and racial policies of the Nazi regime at www.bbc.co.uk/education/modern

The jargon

Autarky is a policy of economic self-sufficiency by a nation, freeing it of reliance upon imported goods.

Checkpoint 2

What were the main steps taken against the Jews by the Nuremberg Laws?

The jargon

Genocide is the systematic elimination of a race.

Exam questions   answers: pages 132–3

1   How far can Germany under Hitler be said to conform to the model of totalitarianism? (45 min)

2   'Hitler's long-term goal was the genocide of the Jews in Europe.' What evidence is there to support or challenge this view? (45 min)

"In the Soviet Union ... [Hitler] envisaged the eventual settlement of 100 million Germans"

Williamson, 1994

The USSR under Stalin

As with Nazi Germany, there has been an extensive debate among historians about the nature of the Soviet state under Stalin. The principal area of controversy has been whether the USSR during its Stalinist period can accurately be described as totalitarian.

A totalitarian state?

Intentionalist historians have tended to see the USSR under Stalin as a totalitarian state. They have stressed the power of the party apparatus and its ability to terrorize society. Control of education, the mass media and propaganda allowed for mass indoctrination.

Structuralist historians have rejected the totalitarian model. They have focused on those groups in Soviet society who benefited from the regime and therefore actively supported it – such as the military, party bureaucrats and Komsomol ('young communist') members. The autonomy of the bureaucracy is emphasized, downplaying the role of Stalin in initiating and coordinating the purges and mass terror.

Intentionalists have criticized this approach for marginalizing the 'guilt' of Stalin and the Politburo for the regime's crimes.

Economic policy

In agriculture the key policy of the Stalinist regime was **collectivization**. This entailed:

→ The 'liquidation' of the more prosperous peasants or *kulaks* as a class.
→ Confiscation of land from poorer peasants who had seized it in 1917.
→ The creation of huge state farms alongside the collectives. In the latter, families retained small plots of land for growing their own food or raising a cash crop.

Although there were still about nine million peasants outside the collective farm sector in 1934, by 1937 virtually all of them had been collectivized.

The effect of the collectivization programme was famine. Terror had been used to coerce the peasantry into collectives. Their reaction, particularly in the case of the *kulaks*, was to slaughter their livestock and burn their crops. The famine this created was made worse by the requisitioning of grain from the countryside to feed the Red Army. The number of deaths brought about by the famine is thought to be between 7.2 million and 8.1 million.

In industry, the New Economic Policy (NEP) introduced by Lenin was also abandoned. Under the First Five-Year Plan, between 1928 and 1932, the USSR embarked on a concerted drive towards rapid industrialization. Though targets for production were often missed, the country appeared to make prodigious gains in heavy industry, though at the cost of neglecting consumer goods. Other features of the industrialization strategy included:

The jargon

The *kolkhozes* (collectives) and *sovkhozes* (state farms) meant the end of private farming. Several villages were generally lumped together and declared to be a collective.

Peasants were divided into poor, middle and rich by the Bolsheviks. The rich peasant or *kulak* had enough land to produce a surplus and so in Western European terms would be classed as modestly well-off.

Checkpoint 1

Why had the NEP been introduced?

→ The rejection of egalitarianism, as wage differentials grew from 1931.

→ Greater control over the labour force. Laws allowing for prison sentences for violations of 'labour discipline' were introduced in 1931, and the internal passport system was increasingly used from 1932 to control labour deployment.

→ Falling living standards for many workers from the Third Five-Year Plan of 1938–1941, as defence expenditures rose to 18% of GDP.

The nature of the five-year planning system

While the impression was created of one master plan there was in reality no such thing. In practice, a mass of lower-level plans were formulated, which the central authorities then attempted to coordinate. The system was very successful in focusing resources on key goals but was inefficient and wasteful in other respects. Labour could be coerced to work but not to work well.

The terror ●●●

The 'show trials' are one of the darkest pages of the Stalinist era. The foundations for the great purges of 1936–1938 had been laid in 1928–1934, when a number of show trials were held that provided scapegoats for the economy's failings.

Three major show trials were held between 1936 and 1938. All were designed to eliminate old Bolsheviks who might threaten Stalin's position. The first saw Kamenev and Zinoviev shot, while Bukharin and Rykov were eliminated in the third. However, the purges were far more extensive than just the party hierarchy. The military was also assaulted from 1937. The execution of Marshal Tukhachevsky was followed by a great blood-letting of the Red Army command.

Though the Ezhovschina or Ezhov times (named after the head of the NKVD to 1938) were particularly brutal, the terror state remained a fundamental feature of the Stalinist system for much longer. According to McCauley (1995), the total number of executions in 1937–1938 was 681 692, though smaller peaks of repression occurred in 1930–1933, 1942 and 1945–1946. It appears that a further purge was being planned by Stalin at the time of his death in 1953. The same imperatives to meet plan targets applied to the secret police as to any other sector.

Check the net

You'll find more information on Stalin's policies for collectivization and industrialization at www.bbc.co.uk/education/modern

Checkpoint 2

Why would intentionalist historians see the use of the purges as clear evidence of a totalitarian state?

"Stalin's course [was] . . . charted by Lenin"

Pipes, 1994

Exam questions answers: pages 133–4

1 'The Stalinist system was a totalitarian system.' To what extent does this statement account for the nature of the Soviet state under Stalin? (45 min)

2 'The Stalinist system of terror was an aberration from the Leninist model of 1917–1924.' Do you agree? (45 min)

International relations: 1930s 1

The causes of war in 1939 used to be commonly ascribed to one main factor: Hitler. However, historians like Overy argue that the international system of great power relations during the 1930s must be examined in order to fully appreciate its causes. In this section we deal with the roles of Britain and France in particular, while the following section (pp. 126–7) analyses the part played by Hitler.

Origins of appeasement

Appeasement can be seen as continuing a tradition of British diplomatic policy stretching back to the 19th century. Overy has described it as:

> '. . . a policy of adjustment and accommodation of conflicting interests broadly to conform with Britain's unique position in world affairs' (1998).

Essentially, both Britain and France were seeking in the 1930s to preserve the existing system of international relations and their interests within it, first and foremost their empires. Chamberlain operated on the basis of maintaining the '**balance of risks**', avoiding a simultaneous challenge to British interests in key parts of the globe.

A policy with limits

Such a policy of protecting British national interests clearly implied limits. For example:

→ Japanese expansionist aims in Asia would be accommodated only to the point that Britain's interests in China were not threatened.
→ Italian aggression against Abyssinia did not interfere with British mercantile or military aims, but moves against Malta and Egypt surely would.
→ Considerable sympathy existed in Britain for German complaints against the Versailles Treaty. These were accommodated through arrangements like the Anglo-German naval agreement of 1935. While the French were understandably less willing to do this, there were also limits to how far Britain was prepared to go.

Problems with appeasement

One of the main faults in the appeasement strategy was that both Britain and France were conducting it from a position of relative weakness:

→ Neither was militarily strong enough to use force if required.
→ Each was constrained by the strength of pacifist opinion at home.
→ Both were more fearful of the Soviet than the fascist threat.

Checkpoint 1

What areas of the world was Chamberlain principally concerned with protecting through the balance of risks strategy?

Checkpoint 2

Why would these weaknesses in the British and French positions lead the nationalistic powers towards greater aggression?

Appeasement abandoned: 1938–1939

The **Munich agreement of 1938** is often seen as the turning point in the policy of appeasement. In large part this is due to the markedly more aggressive stance of German foreign policy that it brought about. It was the confirmation that Hitler needed of Britain and France's essential weakness, seen by him as their tacit acceptance of German expansionism to the east. To those intentionalist historians who believe there existed a blueprint for aggression, this opened the door to the first stage of Hitler's imperialist ambitions – '*Mitteleuropa*'.

The blame for this dangerous miscalculation can partly be laid at the door of Britain and France. Their failure to spell out clearly the limits of appeasement can be seen to have encouraged German aggression to the point where their own interests became directly threatened. Poland provided the moment that was most preferable for a declaration of war, not least because of the state of military preparedness in Britain and France by September 1939 (see below).

British and French rearmament

The level of Franco-British armaments helped to determine the timing of the war. Rearmament had been a feature of states as large as Russia since 1929, preceding that of Germany, and of many weaker nations like Czechoslovakia and Poland. However, both Britain and France felt constrained until the late 1930s by:

→ Fears of precipitating another economic crisis by diverting resources into rearmament.
→ The possibility that this then might lead to labour unrest and civil disorder.
→ Commitments to social expenditures (e.g. British leaders like Baldwin and Chamberlain had committed themselves to extensive house building and welfare spending in 1935).

All these factors encouraged the use of appeasement into 1938, when rearmament was begun in earnest. However, both the British and the French felt that the pace of rearmament could only be supported economically to 1939.

Check the net

You'll find more information about appeasement at www.historytoday.com

Checkpoint 3

What part did the Munich agreement play in preparing the ground for the Nazi–Soviet Pact of 1939?

Examiner's secrets

In a question like 2, an examiner will expect you to examine both sides of the issue but, having done so, do not be afraid to come down on one side at the end of the essay. So long as your case is supported this will score you extra credit for independent thought.

Exam questions   answers: pages 134–5

1 'Britain and France went to war to defend Poland.' How far does this account for the motives of both powers? (45 min)

2 'War could have been avoided by challenging Hitler militarily over the Rhineland invasion in 1936.' What are the strengths and weaknesses of this view? (45 min)

International relations: 1930s 2

Hitler's objectives in foreign policy undoubtedly contributed to the outbreak of war in 1939. The preceding pages have noted how appeasement led Hitler to miscalculate over the timetable for expansionism. However, most would not challenge the view that there was a vision of conquest, which was likely to risk war at some point.

Hitler's foreign policy objectives ●●●

In 1961, A. J. P. Taylor set out the view that Hitler was essentially a pragmatist in foreign affairs, taking advantage of situations as they arose. He lacked any premeditated plan for war and was pursuing the goal of restoring German national pride, which so many of his predecessors had also sought.

However, others, like Richard Overy, have repudiated this view, seeing Hitler's foreign policy as a two-stage programme for territorial expansion.

Stage one – *Mitteleuropa*

This stage is seen as dependent upon German military strength and diplomatic opportunity for its execution but is nonetheless part of a coherent and specific plan. Essentially a pan-German vision, *Mitteleuropa* would be created from the reunification of German speakers in Czechoslovakia and Poland as well as the *Anschluss* with Austria. In 1938–1939 these steps were achieved. Exploitation of resources within each state would allow for the pursuit of stage two.

Stage two – *Lebensraum*

In a secret meeting at the Reich Chancellery in November 1937, Hitler set out his aim of achieving *Lebensraum* to the east, at the latest by 1943–1945. While some have pointed to his omission of Russia as evidence of his primary concern with Germany's frontiers, others have seen no more in this than an opportunistic playing to his audience of generals.

Historians like Overy are of the view that *Lebensraum* was a consistent part of Hitler's world view from the 1920s and that it would provide the key to making Germany a world imperial power. This approach, stressing an ultimate objective to dominate not only Europe but Asia too, is a clear departure from A. J. P. Taylor's view of Hitler as a 'pragmatist', lacking a premeditated plan.

Anti-communism

Hitler's anti-Bolshevist rhetoric is a consistent feature of the Nazi ideology. To many, his commitment to a 'crusade' in the east was in large part driven by a determination to eradicate what he saw as the forces of barbarism. Gaining *Lebensraum*, especially in the Soviet Union, would be part of his great historical mission to extend civilization and Western culture to the 'inferior' Slavic races.

Action point

Make your own notes on the words shown in bold in the text.

Checkpoint 1

In which parts of Czechoslovakia and Poland were German speakers to be found?

Anti-Semitism

In Hitler's mind the 'threat' of 'International Jewry' and that of Bolshevism were simply two sides of the same coin. Consequently, some historians have viewed the commitment to genocide as being primarily driven by the desire to eliminate Russian Jewry.

Economic motives for expansionism ●●●

The world economic crisis in the 1930s contributed to the breakdown of international peace. The three major powers most committed to **aggressive nationalism** were all driven, to an extent, by the belief that their populations would only be secured through conquest:

→ Germany had seen many of its economic resources, such as coal and iron deposits, depleted by the Versailles settlement.

→ Italy was economically underdeveloped to begin with, partly through a lack of basic raw materials.

→ Japan was likewise short of natural resources before its invasion of Manchuria in 1931.

To Hitler, the root cause of economic conflict was the unequal distribution of territory and political power. Economic concerns therefore became politicized in the Third Reich and provided a further justification for military expansionism.

The United States and the USSR ●●●

US isolationism also played its part in destabilizing international peace. Roosevelt, fearful that the isolationist lobby would undermine the New Deal, pursued a policy that undermined the League of Nations (just as it had been by US non-involvement since 1919.)

The USSR's decision to sign the **Molotov–Ribbentrop** (**Nazi–Soviet**) **Pact** in 1939 opened the way for Hitler's invasion of Poland. However, its significance lies not only in the assurance it gave Hitler of Soviet non-intervention against Germany. It also convinced him that a German–Polish conflict would remain localized, and Britain and France would stay neutral. As noted in the preceding two pages, he failed to see that Poland would provide a platform upon which French and British interests could be defended, at just that point when their military power was at its peak.

Exam questions   answers: page 135

1 'The outbreak of war in 1939 was accidental.' To what extent do you agree? (45 min)

2 'Hitler was a pragmatist in foreign policy – he took opportunities as they presented themselves.' To what extent does this explain Hitler's foreign policy successes to 1939? (45 min)

Check the net

You'll find more information about Hitler's anti-Semitic policies at www.sky.co.uk/history

The jargon

Aggressive nationalism is the glorification of one's country and a desire to strengthen it by conquest.

Checkpoint 2

What were the main terms of the Nazi–Soviet Pact?

Examiner's secrets

The examiner will be impressed if you can show an awareness of the different interpretations of Hitler's foreign policy proposed by figures like Taylor and Overy.

Answers
European History 1895–1945

Causes of the First World War

Checkpoints

1 Germany had further contributed to tension over armaments through its 'testing' of the Entente Cordiale in Morocco in 1905 and then in the Agadir crisis of 1911. The latter incident almost led to war between Britain, France and Germany, until the Kaiser was forced to back down and accept French supremacy in Morocco.

2 Belgium's neutrality in any war had been guaranteed by the Treaty of London (1839). Britain, as well as Prussia, had signed this document. A neutral Belgium had been Britain's idea because it had always wanted to keep an area near the English coast out of hostile hands. Twice before, in 1702 and 1793, it had gone to war to prevent an enemy conquering the area. When Germany invaded France through Belgium in 1914, Britain declared war on Germany in defence of Belgian neutrality.

Exam questions

1 This question is asking for an evaluation. The words 'To what extent' should immediately alert you to the importance of other factors besides that identified in the title. You need to state this clearly at the beginning of your answer.

Explain the predominant role of Austria-Hungary in the Balkans and put this into some context – refer to the 19th-century development of Habsburg power.

Explain Austro-Hungarian anxiety over the rise of pan-Slav nationalism and the part played by Serbia as a potentially destabilizing factor upon the Dual Monarchy.

Link the issue of Slav nationalism to Austria-Hungary's reaction over the Sarajevo assassination – show how the ultimatum to the Serbs was a device designed to restrain Balkan nationalism. Note the support of Russia for Serbia and the part this played through the alliance system in broadening a regional conflict.

Explain how there were other factors besides Balkan nationalism that created the potential for war, e.g. the alliances.

Explain the role of Germany in heightening tensions in Europe over its ambition for great power status

Conclusion – return to the evaluation demanded in the title. Make a judgement about the relative importance of the factors you have examined and whether problems in the Balkans – while not the sole cause – may have been the most significant cause.

2 This question is presenting the thesis about the causes of the First World War advanced by figures like Fritz Fischer. A good start would show an awareness of this and contrast it with the other main 'school', those historians who ascribe the war to a general breakdown in international relations rather than to Germany in particular.

Explain how the Fischer thesis can be substantiated. Focus particularly on the aims of the Kaiser for territorial expansion. You could talk about Germany's frustrated ambitions in much of Africa (the Moroccan crises of 1905–1911 would provide good examples. Show how the Kaiser's designs on the Polish provinces of the Russian Empire might risk war through the alliance system.

Explain how historians like Fischer believe that Germany deliberately provoked a conflict in 1914 as a 'now or never' opportunity to weaken the influence of Britain and France as continental powers. Contrast this case with the contrary position, which sees Germany as simply one contributory factor among several to the outbreak of war – and not necessarily the most important. Explain how the alliance system, militarism in Britain and fears of Slav nationalism by the Habsburg monarchy also helped to tip Europe into war.

Conclusion – you must confront the two main issues in the title – did Germany have a programme of territorial expansion to 1914 and if so, did it make war 'inevitable'? You might agree with the first proposition but not the second! If you challenge the second statement you must give some thought to how the Balkan conflict had already drawn Russia into a regional war through the alliances before Germany's direct involvement.

Results of the Great War

Checkpoints

1 Ludendorff's claim that the German army had been 'stabbed in the back' or betrayed was at first sight inconsistent. It was the failure of Ludendorff's offensive of 1918, costing one million German casualties, that had finally cracked the Central Powers. It was also Ludendorff himself who had admitted in October 1918 that peace had to be sought. To understand how this can square with his later claims, one must remember that Ludendorff was a German nationalist who harboured a deep-seated hatred of democracy. To blame the loss of the war on the Weimar Republic was to associate the new democracy itself with defeat, a tactic designed to foment political disorder.

2 Sèvres was very harsh on Turkey. It took away nearly all its land in Europe and put the Turkish straits under League of Nations control. Its Arab lands in the Middle East were turned into mandates controlled by Britain and France, and armies from Britain, France, Italy and Greece occupied what remained of Turkey – an area known as Asia Minor.

Exam questions

1 You will notice that while the question refers to 'the foundations for war in 1939', it does not mention Germany by name. This question is intended to get you thinking about the effects of the post-war settlement in destabilizing peace on a broader canvas than Germany alone, though Germany will feature in a major way in your answer.

Explain how the motives of the victorious powers were coloured by the desire both to preserve peace and to punish those they held responsible for the war. Apply these criteria to Germany's treatment at Versailles. You must show a consequence for the destabilization of peace by 1939 in each reference to a treaty provision, e.g. the loss of German-speakers in West Prussia and Posen contributed to Hitler's objective of reunification, which ultimately led to the invasion of Poland in September 1939.

Explain how the impact of the settlement on other powers contributed to the potential for war: Turkey's ability to overturn Sèvres set a precedent for challenging the settlement, and the institutions like the League of Nations that had been established by it; US isolationism contributed to unchecked aggressive nationalism by Germany, Italy and Japan in the 1930s.

Explain how the foundation for later war might have been laid, but this by no means made war inevitable. Other causes were to contribute to the collapse of peace by 1939. Material from the sections titled 'Hitler's Germany' and 'International relations: 1930s' would be relevant here. For example, show how Hitler's expansionist policies were not solely a function of the post-war settlement (you could mention his commitment to racial war in the east) or how the policy of appeasement might have been modified or replaced, with effect upon the development of events.

Conclusion – you must explicitly address the issue 'How accurate', basing your judgement upon the argument you have constructed in the essay.

2 The question is asking whether the statement is an 'accurate' view, and there are two distinct issues that you must address – whether the Treaty of Versailles was 'unwarranted', and whether it was imposed for 'revenge'.

Explain first the motives behind the imposition of the treaty. Particularly stress that even among the French, who were motivated more than the other victors by considerations of revenge, it was not the only influence. The determination to maintain peace should be explained.

Make specific links from these motives to the provisions of the treaty.

Explain and analyse the issue of 'unwarranted'. Unwarranted from whose perspective? Look at the above from the point of view of the French and then the Germans. Explain how the differing interpretations by each of the treaty's 'fairness' depended very much upon their own wartime experiences, fears of future aggression and concepts of national pride.

Conclusion – the treaty may have appeared to be justified at the time to powers like France that imposed it. Its danger for maintaining peace in the long term lay in the different perception of it by those upon whom it was imposed.

Nicholas II: Tsar of Russia

Checkpoints

1 The term 'Progressive Bloc' refers to a body of opinion in Russia in 1915 that was composed of two-thirds of the Duma, a sizeable proportion of the State Council, some government ministers and much of the press. Its objective was to create a national government as the first step towards a constitutional democracy.

2 Generals like Krymov were quite clear that the army had withdrawn its support for Nicholas because retaining him risked a social revolution that would be virtually impossible to control. The Tsar's abdication can therefore be seen as part of a strategy by the army and bourgeoisie to avoid a broader revolution.

Exam questions

1 You could start off by mapping out the surface similarities between the 1905 and February 1917 scenarios. Both seemed to arise out of military failure. Both seemed to be based on the coincidence of proletarian and liberal interests. Yet the Tsar survived the first situation but not the second.

Explain how the two situations were different in important respects. The first key difference was in the lack of coordination of the Tsar's political opponents in 1905 compared with 1917. This might offer an opportunity to question whether the 1905 situation really qualifies as 'revolutionary' in the true sense. The liberals were trying to press for constitutional government, whereas the workers were more concerned with working conditions. Neither at that point had the aim of deposing the Tsar as the means of achieving these goals. In 1917, both saw the Tsar as an insurmountable barrier to their goals.

Explain how the Tsar made timely concessions in 1905 but not 1917. Talk about the October manifesto, and the creation of the Duma, which created an outlet for constitutional aspirations, despite their limits. Discuss Nicholas' refusal to entertain a national government in 1916.

Explain how the Tsar was able to use force to keep control of the state in 1905 because he retained the support of the military. In 1917, he had lost the confidence of his generals.

Conclusion – the Tsar was able to survive, but the grievances that emerged in 1905 were not solved and were to re-emerge in 1917.

2 This question is quite similar to Question 1. Again, a contrast with 1905 can help to illustrate the importance of key factors in bringing about the Tsar's abdication – the position of the political opposition, the Tsar's own reaction and management of the political challenge, and his ability to control opposition through repression. An evaluation of the relative importance of these factors is crucial. Was Nicholas' loss of his generals' support the most significant factor, or the position of the army rank and file?

Russia: 1917–1924

Checkpoints

1 Kerensky formed a second coalition government on 24 July 1917. It had a socialist majority, but the Kadets were still in a very influential position. Kerensky then appears to have plotted with General Kornilov, the new commander-in-chief, for the use of army troops against the Bolsheviks and to restore order in the capital. Fearing that Kornilov intended to overthrow him, Kerensky then carried out a double-cross. He armed the Bolsheviks, Kornilov's troops deserted and the general was arrested. The significance of this event was that it discredited Kerensky on both left and right while providing the Bolsheviks with the means to conduct a *coup d'état*.

2 The Whites were a disparate coalition, united by their opposition to the Bolsheviks but by little else. They included ardent monarchists and supporters of liberal democracy. The Whites became more authoritarian and reactionary as the civil war went on – and less attractive as a political alternative to the Reds.

Exam questions

1 Begin by identifying the main weaknesses of the Provisional Government.

Explain why the government itself was really an attempt to stave off a more radical social revolution. Talk about the role of the Kadets within the administration and their aims.

Explain how this led the Provisional Government away from the demands of the workers, soldiers and peasants.

Explain how their unwillingness to support these demands contributed to a collapse in obedience. Talk about the lack of control over Russian society, which afflicted the Provisional Government from the outset.

Explain how the Kornilov affair weakened Kerensky's position with both left and right and contributed to army disillusion. Connect to the army rank and file's unwillingness to defend the Provisional Government in October 1917.

Explain how the Bolsheviks were able to exploit the unpopularity of the socialist parties that participated in the Provisional Government. Explain their alignment with the Soviets.

Conclusion – these factors made it highly likely that the Provisional Government would fail. The disintegration of state authority over the masses would alone have posed a major obstacle. Coupled with the government's reluctance to end the war and address rural and urban concerns, it was built on sand.

2 Begin by setting out the scenario that faced the Bolsheviks in November 1917, at the time of the elections to the Constituent Assembly. Note their minority status.

Explain how divided opposition assisted the Bolsheviks in retaining and consolidating power. Talk about the context of the revolutionary environment. Stress the lack of unity in the army as well as among rival political groups.

Explain how the civil war might be considered to be the most important reason for the Bolsheviks' survival. The role of the Whites as counter-revolutionaries and mobilizers for the Red Army should be examined.

Explain how the opposition forces – particularly the Whites – were far less effective and less numerous than the Reds.

Explain how the adaptability of the Bolsheviks assisted their survival. The NEP and its restoration of a degree of economic stability should be examined.

Explain how the bureaucratization of the party began to create a wider base of support for the regime among those who benefited directly from it. Talk about the development of the *nomenklatura*.

Conclusion – the Bolsheviks were in a precarious position initially but were helped by the inability of the opposition to mobilize support. Their hostility to the gains made by peasants and workers allowed the Bolsheviks to present themselves as guardians of the revolution.

Fascism in Mussolini's Italy

Checkpoints

1 At the end of the 19th century, Italy had sought territory in Africa. After failing to make inroads in North Africa it turned to the east, annexing Eritrea in 1885 and part of Somaliland in 1889. Leaders like Francesco Crispi (prime minister 1887–1891 and 1893–1896) wished to establish a protectorate in Abyssinia, an ambition dashed in 1896 after Italy's defeat at Adowa. This did much to discredit the liberal system but not the imperialist dream, which Mussolini sought to advance, partly to expunge the shame of 40 years before.

2 A PR system guaranteed coalition government. Given the inability of the two biggest parties to cooperate, government instability was the consequence.

Exam questions

1 As with question 1 in the 'Hitler's Germany' section (p.121), begin by establishing the main features of the totalitarian model.

Explain the Mussolini regime's own self-described totalitarianism.

Explain the steps that were taken to establish single-party rule in Italy. Talk about the initial coalition phase of 1922–1924, giving way to a Fascist monopoly on power – the role of the Acerbo Law, the cementing of party control 1925–1926.

Explain the part played by the use of terror – the murder of Matteotti in 1924, the use of the OVRA.

Explain how the totalitarian model has been challenged since the 1960s. The Mussolini regime has been viewed by many historians (as opposed to political scientists from the 1940s–1960s) as falling far short of the totalitarian ideal.

Explain how the regime had to compromise with and accommodate particular forces in Italian society that prevented the formation of a true totalitarian state. The corporate state could be used to illustrate the need to enlist the support of Italian business. Another example might be the continued hold of the Vatican and Catholic Church over education and the private consciences of believers. The Lateran Accords of 1929 with the Papacy could be seen as an acceptance of the limits to state control over the Italian populace.

Explain how use of the mass media and propaganda was of limited effectiveness in the countryside as opposed to the urban centres.

Conclusion – the Fascist state under Mussolini was one characterized by conformity but not the total commitment of sizeable sectors of the population needed for the mobilization of society in a totalitarian state.

2 Begin this question by setting out the background to the rise of fascism in Italy. You need to highlight the weaknesses of the liberal system prior to 1914, in particular stressing the rise in Italian nationalism.

Explain how the post-1918 period was dominated by economic problems. Talk about the prevalence of inflation and unemployment and the growing industrial unrest occasioned by the growth in unionism. Point out the fears of socialism among the business class.

Explain how large landowners also wished to see a firmer line over labour unrest, which the establishment liberal parties appeared unable to provide.

Explain how the Fascist Party did act to contain these perceived threats once in power through the creation of the corporate state.

Explain how the appeal of the PNF was not exclusively its hostility to socialism and worker radicalization. Talk about the crisis of national identity occasioned by the post-war settlement of 1919 and its contribution to the declining faith of business and agrarian interests in the liberal parties. In this sense, these interests were drawn to fascism by the same influence that drew those of other classes to the movement.

Conclusion – the rise of fascism in Italy was a product of a series of factors. While fear of socialism certainly attracted large landowners and industrialists to the party, their support alone cannot account for its rise to power. It also gained support because of the crisis of the old system of liberalism and the atmosphere of national humiliation that had been festering since the end of the 19th century.

The Weimar Republic

Checkpoints

1 The bureaucracy was the mechanism through which the administration of the new state would be conducted.

The hostility of the old imperial civil service towards democracy would create a barrier to the effective implementation of government policy. In addition, the willingness of the SPD to accept the bureaucracy's conservatism persuaded some potential supporters to veer towards the extreme left – the KPD – or the USPD as vehicles for achieving more radical societal change.

2 The German communists, or Spartacists, sought to establish a government like the Russian model after 1917. Overthrow of the government in a revolution was to be followed by the formation of councils of workers (or 'soviets'), which would then introduce socialist reforms.

Exam questions

1 Establish a clear introduction, pointing out that the republic that emerged out of Germany's defeat ushered in a period of democracy lasting 14 years, only to be replaced by a dictatorship.

First tackle the issue of the republic's survival against anti-democratic forces in the 1920s.

Explain the ability of the 'Weimar coalition' to conserve parliamentary government to 1930, allowing for the development of democratic values in Germany.

Explain how revisionist historians like Holtfrerich have argued that even hyper-inflation in 1923 helped the republic by wiping out significant amounts of debt and leading to the introduction of the Rentenmark, a motor to economic growth (though you might point out that this is a minority view!).

Explain the successes in foreign policy (Rapallo, Locarno, League membership, Kellogg–Briand) that contributed to German security and minimized (between 1924 and 1929) the appeal of nationalism.

Explain the division on the extreme right and the inability of the extremists to enlist widespread popular support.

Now move on to an analysis of the weaknesses of the republic that paved the way for the failures of the 1930s.

Show the other side of some of your earlier arguments. For example, hyper-inflation helped debtors but it harmed investors, who lost their savings, destroying the faith of many Germans in democracy. The humiliation of Versailles continued to rankle – many Weimar politicians were identified with national humiliation. The PR system alienated many voters. The constitutional provision for emergency decrees via the president helped to entrench authoritarian attitudes.

Explain the importance of the Depression as a turning point for Weimar. The role that unemployment played in increasing support for the Nazis should be shown within the context of Brüning's deflationary policy.

Explain the disunity of the Weimar coalition parties and how it contributed to Brüning's increased use of emergency decrees, which served to undermine parliamentary government.

Explain the fear of communism among conservatives in the Reichswehr, the bureaucracy and around

Hindenburg. Examine its part in the plan to 'control' Hitler in government. Stress the lack of faith in democracy among all these elements.

Conclusion – the contrast between the 1920s and 1930s is that in the 1930s the economy was in a much worse state than in 1919–1924. Democracy from 1930 was in the hands of elements that did not strongly support it. The extremist forces on the right were far more unified in the 1930s than earlier and seemed to offer competent solutions to Germany's problems.

2 First establish a view about the inevitability argument. The assumption that failure was not inevitable presupposes that the republic could have survived had some factors been different.

Explain why the republic might be said to have been likely to fail. Of these factors, the authoritarianism mentioned in the title should be dealt with first.

Examine the argument that the German people were not accustomed to democracy, given the Wilhelmine past.

Broaden out the argument above to examine anti-democratic values within the Reichswehr, the bureaucracy and the bourgeoisie. Connect to the fear of Bolshevism following the Russian Revolution of 1917.

Explain the features of the Weimar constitution that might be said to have strengthened authoritarian attitudes, e.g. the role of the presidency as an 'emperor substitute'; PR and its effects on views of parliamentary democracy.

Explain how failure was not inevitable, only likely, because of these weaknesses. You need to focus on the short-term factors of 1929–1933 to illustrate how failure might have been avoided, e.g. greater unity between the Weimar coalition parties in the face of growing extremism; clearer understanding by the conservative establishment of the dangers posed by the Nazis to German democracy.

Explain why these short-term factors happened as they did, e.g. the conservative establishment was hostile to democracy anyway, so had no clear view of the need to defend it; their principal concern was Bolshevism, not fascism.

Conclusion – the failure of the Weimar Republic was made certain in 1932–1933 by the loss of support for the Weimar coalition parties and the bypassing of parliamentary government. But this did not mean that Hitler was the only alternative. This was made reality only by the complicity of the conservative elements within the German government itself.

Hitler's Germany 1933–1945

Checkpoints

1 Upon Hindenburg's death, Hitler amalgamated the offices of chancellor and president into 'Führer and Reich Chancellor'. This cemented his hold over the Reichswehr (army), which he had gained with the elimination of the SA on the Night of the Long Knives.

He was now officially supreme commander of the German armed forces, secure against the threat of an army coup. He was secure too against the removal from power that Hindenburg could have engineered. The president had held the power both to appoint and dismiss the chancellor. Now this independent voice was gone.

2 The main provisions of the Law for the Protection of German Blood and German Honour were to forbid marriage and sexual relations outside of marriage between Jews and 'Aryan' Germans. The Reich Citizenship Law removed from Jews their status as German citizens and therefore all of their political and civil rights.

Exam questions

1 A good start to this essay would be to set out the essential features of a totalitarian state. The surface parallels to Soviet Russia should be noted.

Explain in detail how some of the features described above were used to portray Nazi Germany as totalitarian until the late 1960s–1970s, e.g. the process of *Gleichschaltung*; the role of the Enabling Act in eliminating opposition to the party through abolition of rival parties, unions, independence of local government structures, right-wing extremists like the Stahlhelm.

Explain how full control over the state apparatus might be said to have been achieved with the loyalty of the Reichswehr, the installation of Nazi officials in the bureaucracy and the subjugation of the judicial system.

Explain how Nazi ideology was promoted through the education system, the Hitler Youth movement, control of mass media and propaganda.

Explain how this model of totalitarianism was promoted by political scientists in the post-war period (Hannah Arendt). As historians began to investigate the nature of the Nazi state, a division of opinion arose.

Explain how the anti-totalitarian school views the Nazi state. Set out the difference between them and the totalitarians.

Explain how Hitler's own decision-making process was supportive of internal party and bureaucratic rivalries (duplication of tasks and functions; playing off the vested interests in one department against another).

Explain how Nazi economic policy could conform to this model, e.g. initial incoherence; reliance on the policies of prior governments; the independence of Schact to 1936.

Explain how historians in the anti-totalitarian school disagree over why the Nazi State was chaotic. Set out the intentionalist vs. structuralist debate.

Conclusion – the question asks 'How far'. You must reach an evaluation based upon the evidence you have proposed in your answer.

2 Start by setting out the key role played by Hitler's policy towards the Jews in the history of the Third Reich. The six million dead as a result of the Holocaust is an event so awful that it demands a rationalization.

Explain how there is a division between intentionalist and structuralist historians over the causes of the Holocaust.

Explain the intentionalist case. Begin with Hitler's anti-Semitism in *Mein Kampf* and his persecution of the Jews once in power from 1933 to 1941. The boycott of Jewish businesses in 1933, the removal of Jews from the pro-fessions, the Nuremberg Laws of 1935 and the violence of *Kristallnacht* could all be said to form a clear and premeditated pattern.

Explain how Hitler's statement in 1939 about the destruction of Europe's Jews could be viewed as a prophecy of his future intentions. These intentions were put into practice once the Russian campaign was underway, as Hitler's anti-Semitism was also driven by his detestation of communism. As he equated the two, elimination of the Jews served to remove the menace of communism to the east while also removing the '*Untermenschen*' or 'sub-human' races.

Explain how structuralists would challenge this view of Nazi policy as a deliberate plan for the murder of the Jews. Show how they would see genocide as a symptom of a chaotic state structure. Bureaucratic 'one-upmanship' led to the escalation of anti-Semitism far beyond what was originally planned.

Explain how earlier instances of anti-Semitism could be seen not to have been part of a strategy for eventual elimination, e.g. the Nuremberg Laws can be viewed as a sop to more extreme elements in the party, who wished to go even further. As such, they should be seen as a consequence of party management rather than a pre-meditated racial policy. For example, exile to the island of Madagascar seems to have been considered prior to 1942.

Conclusion – having set out evidence for both sides you should try to evaluate at least one of the positions, e.g. the structuralist argument about Madagascar can be countered by pointing out that it was abandoned once the USSR had been invaded and the chance to eliminate Bolshevism became a reality. Likewise, one might challenge how serious a proposition it really was.

The USSR under Stalin

Checkpoints

1 The NEP was introduced in 1921 because of the failure of 'war communism' in the preceding three years. Grain requisitioning had led to falling production; nationalization had not halted the decline in industry. To head off popular discontent (especially peasant riots), an element of capitalism was needed to revive the economy.

2 Intentionalist historians generally subscribe to the view of Stalinist Russia as a totalitarian state. Therefore, the use of terror as a mean of enforcing the control of the Communist Party is of great importance. In the years 1923–1953, 39.1 million people were sentenced by the regular courts. McCauley has calculated that this is the

equivalent of every third citizen being sentenced for non-political crimes. Intentionalists would point to this as evidence of how far the party was able to reach into people's lives and manipulate the judicial system to its own ends.

Exam questions

1 As with the questions about Nazi Germany and Fascist Italy, begin by setting out the main components of the totalitarian model.

Explain how intentionalists support the totalitarian thesis. Talk about control of education, terror, pro-paganda, etc. as features of the Stalinist state.

Explain how structuralists differ. Talk about the marginal role of Stalin personally and of the central state in being able to control society.

Contrast these two cases through an examination of the system in key areas.

Explain how the drive towards industrialization and collectivization can be seen as part of a centralized, coordinated drive by the party and Stalin personally.

Talk about his role in formulating the five-year plans and in forcing through the collectivization of agriculture.

Explain how both of the above programmes can be presented as non-centralized. Talk about the myth of the single plan and the existence of local plans, which would prove extremely difficult to coordinate from the centre.

Explain the limits to coercion in the workplace. Talk about the inability of the regime to induce true commitment from the workforce to achieving plan targets after 1938.

Explain how the use of terror and purges can be presented as symptomatic of a totalitarian state. Talk about the extent of terror and its use against the general population as well as the party hierarchy, the bureaucracy and the military.

Explain how the terror can be presented as an uncoordinated by-product of a bureaucratic state (the structuralist case).

Conclusion – having presented the differing interpretations of the Stalinist state, make a judgement about its status based upon the argument you have constructed.

2 Again you could build your argument around the contrast between the intentionalist and structuralist cases.

Explain how intentionalists see continuities within the Soviet system under both Lenin and Stalin. The creation of the Cheka by Lenin and the use of imprisonment without trial would, they argue, lay the foundation for the apparatus of repression under Stalin. The slogan of the Cheka under Lenin was after all 'Every Russian has been, is or will be, in prison'.

Explain how the organs of repression were further developed by Lenin during the civil war period.

Explain how structuralists would reject both the idea of continuity between the policies of Lenin and Stalin and the idea that Stalin's policies were formulated in a systematic and coordinated way (see question 1). Talk about the difference in the extent and use of terror under Stalin compared with under Lenin.

Explain how one of the prime targets of terror under Stalin was the party itself, rather than external opposition, as it was under Lenin.

Conclusion – reach an evaluation. Was the use of terror 'in the nature of the beast', or did the Stalinist regime mark a departure in its use of terror from what had gone before?

International relations: 1930s 1

Checkpoints

1 Chamberlain's strategy of maintaining a 'balance of risks' was based on avoiding a simultaneous challenge to those areas around the globe that were of key importance to Britain. This essentially meant containing threats in Europe, the Mediterranean and India.

2 One of the principal weaknesses of appeasement was the fact that the nationalist powers failed to perceive that there were limits to the policy. In this respect, Britain and France can be held to blame for not articulating this reality forcefully or unambiguously, though one could argue that even had they done so the nationalist powers would not have believed them. They saw appeasement as a sign of weakness, and it confirmed their belief that the old empires were in a state of perpetual decline, ready to be replaced by new ones of their own making.

3 The absence of the USSR from the four-power Munich conference and the decision of that body to hand the Sudetenland to Hitler helped to push Stalin towards the 'marriage of convenience' – the Nazi–Soviet Pact. The apparent willingness of Britain and France to 'direct' Germany towards Russia (coupled with France's blatant abandonment of the France–USSR Pact, which had pledged to support the Czechs) left Stalin seeking short-term insurance against German attack.

Exam questions

1 Start off by noting that Britain and France declared war on Germany in September 1939, not the other way around. Their publicly declared reason for this action was Germany's infringement of Polish sovereignty. Was this their chief motive? What were the others?

Explain how the policy of appeasement was adopted by Britain and France to try to preserve their status as world powers and (especially in the case of Britain) the security of their empires.

Explain Overy's view that appeasement was part of a trend in British diplomacy stretching back to the 19th century.

Explain the idea of a 'balance of risks' and how Britain and France always assumed that appeasement had parameters.

Explain the perception of appeasement by the nationalist powers in the 1930s and how it did not square with that of Britain and France.

Explain how some intentionalist historians see Munich as Britain's and France's great miscalculation. Talk about the idea that Hitler had a two-stage plan for territorial expansion that would make Germany a world imperial power able to challenge Britain and France (*Mitteleuropa* and *Lebensraum*). Examine the idea that Munich gave Hitler the confidence to pursue these aims.

Explain how Hitler's attack on Poland can be said to have offered Britain and France the best opportunity they were going to get to check Germany's expansionism.

Conclusion – great powers usually act because their interests are in some way threatened. Britain's and France's' interests were under potential threat by Germany, and Poland offered the best moment to try to restrain German expansionism.

2 Start off by connecting the statement to critics of appeasement. The Rhineland is often spoken of as one of the early 'tests' of the Western powers – a test that they failed. Evidence in support of this view lies in the fact that Hitler himself instructed his forces to withdraw immediately from the demilitarized zone should Britain and France contest his action. His forces were not strong enough for a confrontation at that point. His gamble was rewarded with appeasement, which simply led to escalating demands in Austria, Czechoslovakia and finally Poland.

Explain how this view would seem to be convincing. Hitler's own words seem to suggest that he would have been checked by a military response in 1936.

Explain how Hitler might have viewed Britain and France as being serious about limits on appeasement had he been challenged earlier. This might have avoided the danger of his seeing them as declining and vulnerable empires.

Explain how this view can be challenged. It assumes that action in 1936 would have prevented war rather than delay it.

Explain how Hitler's foreign policy is seen by intentionalists as an ideologically driven set of imperatives. The desire to achieve a pan-German state in Central Europe, followed by expansion to the east, was underpinned by anti-communism and anti-Semitism. His belief in these goals was so central to his world view that eventually he would have challenged the interests of Britain and France in pursuit of them.

Explain how Britain and France were ill-equipped to confront Hitler in 1936. Their own forces were stronger, but their governments were constrained by the strength of pacifist feeling among their own electorates. The threat of communism was also a barrier to action, as Nazi Germany seemed to offer a safeguard against Bolshevism.

Conclusion – military confrontation over the Rhineland in 1936 may have deferred war but was unlikely to prevent it.

International relations: 1930s 2

Checkpoints

1 The Sudetenland region of Czechoslovakia had formerly belonged to the Habsburg Empire. The 3.5 million German speakers to be found there provided Hitler with his pretext for further territorial demands. These were promoted through deliberate provocations staged by the Nazi Sudeten leader Henlein, in concert with Berlin. Germans were to be found in Poland because of the transfer of West Prussia and Posen in 1919. In the preceding 124 years, Poland had had its territories shared out between Russia, Austria, Hungary and Prussia. Some of Germany's land was therefore being 'recovered' by the Poles.

2 The Nazi–Soviet Pact was publicly a 10-year non-aggression pact between Germany and Russia. However, a secret section (unknown till 1946) stated that eastern Poland, Latvia, Estonia and Finland would be left in the USSR's sphere of interest (i.e. would be taken over).

Exam questions

1 Start by examining the concept of 'accidental' outbreak. This view arises because of the evidence that Hitler was surprised when Britain and France declared war on Germany over Poland. In that sense, Germany's involvement in a much broader war than anticipated might be deemed accidental.

Explain how a distinction must be made between Hitler's willingness to wage war to the east and his avowed intent to avoid war with Britain and France if possible.

Explain how intentionalists like Overy do not see the war as accidental, in the sense that Hitler was planning war against states in Central and Eastern Europe. Talk about the ideas of *Mitteleuropa* and *Lebensraum*.

Explain how an economic rationale could also be said to underpin Hitler's expansionist plans. Contrast the intentionalist case with Taylor's thesis that Hitler's foreign policy was not based on any plan for war but was opportunistic and part of a trend in German foreign policy.

Explain how the Taylor thesis can be challenged, e.g. Overy's contention that Hitler's foreign policy was distinctly different in its view of Germany as a world imperialist power.

Conclusion – examine the idea that even lacking a clear plan for war (Taylor), the nature of Hitler's foreign policy aims was always likely to bring about conflict. Also examine the idea that Hitler's aims were eventually going to endanger the interests of Britain and France, so his hopes for avoiding war with them were at best misguided and at worst hopelessly ignorant of their desire to maintain their global positions.

2 This question is similar in substance to question 1. The idea of Hitler as a pragmatist is essentially the Taylor thesis. An opportunistic foreign policy is a rejection of the intentionalist view of historians like Overy. As in question 1, both schools need to be examined within the context of the evidence.

Explain the differences between the Taylor and Overy positions.

Explain the strengths and weaknesses of each, e.g. there is some evidence to support the idea that Hitler 'gambled' in challenging Britain and France's resolve (the Rhineland; the *Anschluss* 1938).

Having explained the pros and cons of each case, the issue of 'to what extent' must be addressed. How far does Hitler's pragmatism explain his success to 1939? Talk about the other factors that also contributed to his success, e.g. the willingness of Britain and France to use appeasement to 1939; their inability to challenge him militarily until pacifist opinion had been reduced in the face of German expansionism; the rate of rearmament of the Western powers.

Explain how other counterweights to German influence were ineffective, e.g. the League of Nations; US isolationism; the USSR's complicity in the Polish invasion.

Explain how other nationalist powers assisted Hitler, e.g. Italy's complicity over Austria.

Conclusion – it is true to say that Hitler pursued his objectives pragmatically. This does not entirely account for his success in achieving them.

20th-century world history

Many people believe that the events of the 20th century were the most dramatic since recorded history began – a view which is exaggerated by their relatively recent nature. What differed about the events of the 20th century was the technological advances leading to a globalization of politics and international affairs. This section follows the main events of the century and traces the development of new political ideas such as communism. The presence of superpowers and weapons of mass destruction are an underlying theme for the 20th century.

Exam themes

→ The changing role of the USA in world affairs.

→ The development and influence of communism.

→ The Cold War.

→ The declining influence of European empires.

→ The end of the Cold War.

Topic checklist

○ AS ● A2

	AQA	EDEXCEL	OCR	WJEC
The results of the Second World War	○	○●	○	●
The origins of the Cold War	○●	●	○●	○●
US foreign policy 1917–1953	○●		○	○●
US domestic policy 1930–1990	○●	○●	○●	○●
China under communism	○●	●	○	○●
Chinese foreign policy	○●	●	○	○●
Soviet foreign policy	○●	●	○	○
US foreign policy from 1953	○●	●	○	○●
The end of European empires	○●			○
The recovery of Western Europe	○	●	○	○
The end of the Cold War	○	●	○	○●

The results of the Second World War

> *"The awful ruin of Europe with all its vanished glories"*
>
> Winston Churchill

The end of a military conflict is usually the scene of much rejoicing; this was certainly the case in Europe on 8 May 1945. However, with hindsight we can see that many problems were only just beginning.

The immediate problems of economic chaos and the relocation of hundreds of thousands of refugees and prisoners of war (POWs) had to be solved before Europe – and indeed the world – could rebuild.

Economic distress

It is well worth noting the scale of destruction in terms of both human life and infrastructure that was caused by the 1939–1945 war. The war had lasted for 2 000 days and on average cost the lives of 500 Europeans every hour.

→ Millions of people had lost their homes and possessions.
→ A quarter of all houses in Germany had been destroyed.
→ Warsaw, Belgrade and Leningrad had been devastated.
→ Harbours and the road system had been smashed.
→ Railway lines had been destroyed by Allied bombing.
→ Agricultural production had been similarly affected. In 1945 wheat production was only 30% of what it had been in 1938.

These problems could not be solved quickly and put the immediate post-war relations between the victors under enormous strain.

The problem of refugees

The refugee question was the most immediate concern as the victorious powers approached the post-war world.

There were over 8 million refugees (officially referred to as displaced Persons or DPs), who had been displaced for a variety of reasons:

→ Thousands had been released from Nazi concentration camps.
→ Many more had fled their homes during the war as their homelands were invaded, by either Nazis or Communists.
→ The Soviet occupation of Eastern Europe at the end of the war led to further voluntary emigration.

The refugee question was an enormous concern in all the areas of conflict; however, it was in Europe that the major powers were confronted with the issue. The UN Commissioner for Refugees was responsible for caring for DPs; however, the problem was not solved for many years.

Action point

Look at a map of the different areas of fighting in the Second World War. Consider how the refugee problem was added to by the changing political scene in the post-war world.

Peace treaties ●●●

The Potsdam conference had stated that the foreign ministers of the major powers would meet to discuss peace terms, and so in accordance with this decision the ministers met in Paris during 1946. Representatives of 21 countries were present at the conference, but the conference had no decision-making powers and could only advise the representatives of the three major powers, the USA, USSR and Britain.

→ **Italy** ceded land on its borders to France and Yugoslavia and the Dodecanese islands to Greece. Trieste was declared a free UN territory. Italy lost its former colonies Ethiopia and Libya.

→ **Finland** and **Romania** ceded land to the USSR and Bulgaria, while **Hungary** ceded territory to Romania.

→ **Italy**, **Romania**, **Finland**, **Hungary** and **Bulgaria** had to pay **reparations** in varying amounts to their neighbour countries.

→ No treaties were signed with either **Germany** or **Austria**, mainly because the USSR was already exploiting their resources. Eventually, in 1955, a treaty that promised permanent neutrality was signed with Austria.

Denazification ●●●

The most serious job of reconstruction had to be undertaken in Germany. Inevitably, this involved the physical reconstruction of the cities destroyed by Allied bombing but more significantly the eradication of all traces of Nazism.

The four zones of occupation attempted to deal with the problem in different ways. The Soviets used Nazis who they believed could help them (such as scientists) and sent the rest to Siberia, the French attempted to re-educate a race that they believed were all tainted with Nazi beliefs, while the British did little to deal with the problem at all. Only the Americans pursued denazification seriously, conducting a massive survey of ideas and beliefs and arresting 170 000 people.

The process of re-education was seen as equally important to punishment; after all, there were 7 million former Nazi Party members in Germany at the end of the war. Schools were rebuilt and reorganized, Nazi teachers were sacked, and textbooks were rewritten. In the Soviet zone, one form of propaganda was replaced by another.

Exam question   answer: page 160

How far did the involvement of the major powers in the Second World War reduce their impact on the post-war balance of power? (45 min)

Action point

Remind yourself of the various peace treaties at the end of the First World War and consider whether the Allies had learned any lessons from mistakes made at the Paris peace conference of 1919.

"It is a fundamental part of these proceedings to establish for all time that international law has the power to declare that a war is criminal"

Sir Hartley Shawcross

Checkpoint

How could the Nuremberg war trials be justified? What arguments could be used against such trials?

Examiner's secrets

It would be unusual to come across an exam question that focuses specifically on the conditions in Europe at the end of the war. However, it is an integral part of any question on the causes of the Cold War.
There are endless details you could research to quote figures of civilians and military personnel killed during the war. Some will be useful, but you should remember that the main object of your essay is to analyse the consequences of these statistics rather than recount them.

The origins of the Cold War

Action point

Make some notes on the development of communism in Russia. You should try to build a pattern of development from the theories of Marx to their reinterpretation by Lenin to fit Russian conditions in 1917. Marxist Leninism, as it was referred to, was then adapted again by the next Soviet leader, Stalin. By 1939, he had produced a very different approach to Soviet development.

"The Russians trust the United States more than they trust any power in the world"

Harry Hopkins (US Secretary of State), 1945

Action point

Make notes on the definitions of the following terms:
➜ Marxism
➜ Socialism
➜ Communism
➜ Bolshevism
➜ Marxist Leninism

Although first used to describe Anglo-German relations between 1898 and 1914 and then again to refer to the frosty relationship between France and Germany in the 1930s, the **Cold War** usually refers to the conflict between the USA and the USSR from 1945 to 1989.

A 'cold war' is a state of permanent hostility between two nations that never erupts into an armed conflict or a 'hot war'. This conflict dominated world politics from the end of the Second War to the late 1980s.

Ideological differences

The Cold War has often been described as a war of ideas and as such it revolves around the contrasting ideologies of the protagonists.

➜ Communism in the Soviet Union was derived from the writings of Karl Marx and adapted for use in Russia by Lenin. In short, it involves the ownership of all means of production by the state rather than individuals. Implicit within Marx's teachings was the idea that communism would spread over the entire industrialized world. This notion was what the United States sought to avoid.
➜ Capitalism allowed private enterprise to operate in all industrial spheres in the belief that more wealth would be generated by the profit motive.

Clearly, the two ideologies had entirely opposite aims.

Soviet/American relations 1917–1941

Although the USA welcomed the revolutions in Russia in 1917 in the belief that they would bring about democracy, it was soon alarmed by the spread of Bolshevik ideas.

The USA, with the assistance of its allies, made an unsuccessful attempt to defeat the new Bolshevik regime immediately after the end of the First World War.

The background of hostility between the two nations is shown by the fact that the USA did not open diplomatic relations with the USSR until 1933.

Soviet/American cooperation 1941–1944

The USA helped the Soviet government well before they joined the war themselves. Through the **Lend-Lease** scheme, the Americans lent more than 10 million tons of equipment to the Soviets.

The Alliance itself began when Germany declared war on the USA after the Japanese attack on Pearl Harbor in December 1941. The Grand Alliance, as it was called, was more accurately referred to by the Russians as the '**anti-Hitler coalition**'. This seems to sum up the practical nature of the agreement to enter into an alliance.

Major cracks appeared in the alliance during the war, concerning these two issues:

→ British and American reluctance to open a **second front** against Germany until D-Day, June 1944.
→ The Americans' refusal to involve the USSR in the **Manhattan project**, developing the atom bomb.

Soviet/American peace aims 1945 ●●●

The end of the war brought a hasty end to the uneasy alliance. Both nations had emerged from the conflict as the world's dominant powers, now referred to as **superpowers**. They shared a desire for peace and reconstruction, but their specific aims were different:

→ Roosevelt wanted no empires or spheres of influence in the world.
→ Stalin's primary concern of Russian security could only be achieved, he believed, by developing a buffer zone of **puppet states** on Russia's western border.

The specific problems were as follows:

→ **Poland** – Polish borders had been the cause of much discussion at the wartime conferences. Stalin believed that he had the right to extend the Soviet border westwards into what used to be Poland. This had been privately agreed at Tehran, though the compromise of Yalta meant that Stalin got his way but promised to hold free elections in Poland. The subsequent failure to hold these elections soured relations between the powers.
→ **Germany** – the division of Germany caused inevitable problems over the utilization of coal in the western sectors, the question of reparations and also the problem of Soviet exploitation of their sector.
→ **The economy** – the termination of the Lend-Lease scheme in May 1945 caused further ill feeling. Stalin had hoped that financial aid could continue, at least in the short term. The USSR refused to join the IMF and the World Bank because of this dispute.

Exam questions   answers: pages 160–1

1 How far was the United States responsible for the Cold War? (45 min)

2 Explain why the wartime allies were enemies by 1946. (45 min)

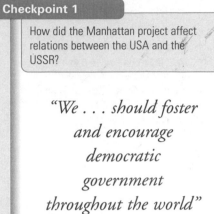

Checkpoint 1

How did the Manhattan project affect relations between the USA and the USSR?

"We . . . should foster and encourage democratic government throughout the world"

Harry Hopkins

Checkpoint 2

How did Stalin's idea of 'socialism in one country' affect his view of Western Europe?

"Whoever occupies a territory also imposes on it his own social system"

Stalin

Don't forget

You should focus on the underlying cases of the Cold War as outlined here but also link these factors to the early examples of Cold War hostility mentioned throughout this section, such as:
→ The Truman doctrine as a response to the crises in Greece and Turkey
→ The conversion of Czechoslovakia to communism
→ The Chinese Communist Revolution
→ The Soviet development of the atom bomb

Examiner's secrets

You must be familiar with the various terms used during the Cold War. Especially confusing are those relating to Russian political beliefs. You will find that these terms are very similar but often misused. Using them correctly gives an examiner a good impression of your background knowledge.

US foreign policy
1917–1953

Action point

You should make some brief notes on the presidents of the USA from Wilson to Roosevelt. Make sure you are aware of the pattern of Democrats, Republicans and back to Democrats. Does this appear to affect the involvement of the USA in world affairs?

Action point

Remind yourself of the pressure exerted on Germany by the Allied blockade and how this led to the sinking of the *Lusitania* and ships like it.

"I hate war"

F. D. Roosevelt

Check the net

You can find biographies of all US presidents at www.peoriaud.k12.az.us/resources/presidents

The United States of America was a reluctant participant in world affairs in the early part of this century. Yet by the middle of the century, the USA had emerged as the dominant superpower, pursuing an active foreign policy in distant and seemingly unrelated parts of the globe.

The USA in the Great War

The American nation, and **Woodrow Wilson** in particular, were in two minds during the Great War for the following reasons:

→ The accepted policy of American **isolationism**, which preserved commercial interests and avoided unnecessary costly wars.
→ Historic ties with Great Britain and the idea that a common language encouraged alliance.
→ A significant and influential American population of German origin.
→ Anti-tsarist sentiment among the many Polish and Russian communities living in the USA.
→ The belief that the British blockade of German ports was illegal and prevented **free trade**.
→ The blockade led to a reduction of trade with the central powers and an increase in commerce with the Allies. This suggested to many that the USA effectively supported the Allies.
→ Unrestricted U-boat warfare and the sinking of the *Lusitania*.

However, when America eventually joined the Allies in 1917 and contributed over a million and a half troops by August 1918, its contribution proved decisive financially and militarily. This was an important moment in the 20th century, as it marked the end of purely European conflicts and the beginning of world politics.

Boom years and isolationism

America had played a vital part in prompting German demands for an **armistice**; however, the USA quickly withdrew from international diplomacy. There were a number of reasons for this:

→ American losses in the Great War.
→ American fears that communism would spread through contact with Europe.
→ The immigrant population of the USA had fled from European misrule and did not want to become involved once again in European politics.

Consequently, even though the **League of Nations** had been the idea of Woodrow Wilson, the USA never joined. During the 1920s the USA concentrated on economic interests, which led it to lend money to Germany through the **Dawes plan** in 1924. The 1930s found America in the grip of the **Depression**, and Roosevelt saw no reason to abandon the policy of isolationism.

The USA in the Second World War ●●●

In keeping with the policy of isolationism, the USA did not join the Second World War until the unprovoked Japanese attack on Pearl Harbor in December 1941. However, from the outset America had clearly supported the Allies through the sale of weapons and supplies. This had meant the end of American observance of the **Neutrality Acts** and the adoption of the **Cash and Carry plan**. When Britain ran out of money a new scheme, **Lend-Lease**, was devised, lending Britain equipment that theoretically would be returned after the war. This scheme was extended to include the USSR in 1941. In August 1941, the **Atlantic Charter** took cooperation with Britain a stage further.

Once the USA had formally joined the war on **11 December 1941**, its involvement was complete and crucial to the eventual success of the Allies in Europe, but especially in the Pacific against Japan. US involvement in the peace preparations saw a major change in world politics, the US being determined to play an active role in world affairs.

The USA in the post-war world ●●●

In the early years of the Cold War, American foreign policy could be summed up by the notion of *containment*. The subject should be divided between events in Europe and Asia:

→ **Europe** – the threat of communism was first seen in **Greece** and **Turkey**. This worried Americans, as they believed that communism would spread to the Middle East. This led to the famous **Truman doctrine** in 1947, in which the USA promised to support 'free peoples' of the world against attempted 'subjugation' by outside pressures. The USA feared that communism would thrive on the poverty in Europe after the war and therefore devised the **Marshall Plan**, a huge programme of economic assistance to avoid this possibility. The formation of **West Germany** shortly after the crisis of the **Berlin airlift** further marked American attempts at containment, as did the formation of **NATO** in 1949.
→ **Asia** – the USA also feared the spread of communism in Asia and devoted much attention to containment in this area. It supported **Japan**'s recovery and democratization, attempted to prevent the communist victory in **China** and tried to preserve the independence of non-communist **South Korea** in the **Korean War**, which reached a stalemate in 1953.

Exam questions answers: page 161

1 How successful was the American policy of containment between 1945 and 1953? (45 min)

2 Discuss the view that the United States played a crucial but reluctant role in international affairs from 1914 to 1945. (45 min)

Action point

Make notes on the various forms of aid that the USA gave to Britain and the USSR before joining the war against Hitler. It is important to realize the background to these important events in the American Congress. Roosevelt's defeat of the isolationists in Congress paved the way for the entry of the USA on to the world stage.

"We must begin the great task that is before us by abandoning once and for all the illusion that we can ever again isolate ourselves from the rest of humanity"

F. D. Roosevelt

Checkpoint

How did the Marshall Plan aim to prevent the growth of communism?

Action point

You must make comprehensive notes on all of the Cold War conflicts that are mentioned here in bold type. Your notes should focus on the causes and consequences of each conflict rather than a narrative account of the conflict itself.

Examiner's secrets

The failure of the League of Nations and the causes of the Second World War are popular exam questions. You should consider this area in the light of American domestic politics as well as in your work on the breakdown of international diplomacy in the 1930s.

US domestic policy 1930–1990

The USA has been described as a **melting pot**, where different immigrant populations integrate to produce a culture greater than the sum of all the constituent parts. This view has been challenged by the difficulties of assimilation demonstrated by 20th-century American history. Since 1930, these problems have been **economic**, **social** and **political**.

The Depression and the New Deal ●●●

Roosevelt's response to the Depression became known as the '**New Deal**' and can be summarised as follows:

→ The **100 days** – the first actions of the New Deal were to restore confidence in the banks and restructure the American financial system. The Beer Act repealed prohibition.

→ The **alphabet agencies** – these measures, so called because of the acronyms they were known by, attempted to solve many of the specific problems of the 1930s. Agricultural problems, unemployment and working conditions were all dealt with by the many different agencies.

→ **Opposition to the New Deal** was vociferous and sustained. The Republicans argued, with some success, that many of the alphabet agencies extended federal control over areas that should be controlled by state law. The **Supreme Court's** opposition to the New Deal prompted Roosevelt to threaten to alter the composition of the Supreme Court itself. This proved unpopular even with Roosevelt's supporters in Congress. The second New Deal saw the Supreme Court take a more moderate line.

The New Deal certainly solved the immediate problems of the Depression. However, it was the onset of European war in 1939 and the boost to US industry that really brought America out of the Depression.

The post-war economy ●●●

Industrially, the USA emerged from the war as the dominant superpower, the recovery continuing due to the demand created by the **Cold War** and the **space race**. The American economy benefited from legislation to make strike action less likely (**Taft–Hartley Act**), and by the 1970s the USA produced 25% of the world's wealth.

Agricultural production continued to increase after the war, and overproduction continued to cause problems; the government subsidized and stockpiled produce, but it was not until the poor world harvests of the 1970s that the problem was relieved.

Regional poverty and unemployment continued, particularly in areas such as the Appalachians and among the Californian immigrant population. While much of the USA prospered, these regional differences caused much concern.

Action point

The New Deal is a complicated area and one that has many terms to learn. You should aim to make notes on all of the different alphabet agencies. Pay special attention to the TVA, as this is regarded as the main success of the New Deal.

"I pledge you, I pledge myself, to a new deal for the American people"

F. D. Roosevelt

Action point

The alphabet agencies were created during the 100 days. However, it is easier to learn the different features of the New Deal by separating the agencies from the immediate acts to restore the banking system.

"The chief business of America is business"

Calvin Coolidge

Action point

Remind yourself of the structure of government in the USA. You must be sure of the different roles and responsibilities of the president, Congress and the Supreme Court.

The Civil Rights movement

Segregation was practised throughout the USA, although it was beginning to be challenged by the 1950s. The Second World War went some way towards integrating white and black communities during the conflict, as did the migration to northern cities, yet after the war President Truman's attempts to improve the legal position of the black population were vetoed by Congress.

The conflict erupted over the issue of desegregated schools in 1954 and once again with the **Montgomery bus boycott** of the following year. Legislation was passed in 1964–1965 (**Civil Rights Act**, Voting Rights Act) that encouraged leaders like **Martin Luther King** to extend the campaign further. Many different movements pursued different methods, but the situation would not improve until the black population achieved economic equality as well as an end to segregation. This has yet to be achieved, and tensions still exist.

Imperial to imperilled presidency

Arthur Schlesinger coined the phrase '**imperial presidency**' to describe the increasing powers of the presidency during Roosevelt's period in office. The escalation of the **Vietnam War** in the 1960s and President Nixon's subsequent widening of the conflict into Cambodia and Laos in 1970 meant that the American public lost confidence in the presidency. This problem was exacerbated by the **Watergate scandal** in 1974.

Consequently, Congress has exerted far greater control over the presidency since the mid-1970s. President Ford commented on the '**imperilled presidency**'. This can be seen by the low legislative success rate experienced by both Ford and Carter in the 1970s (75–78% under Carter, compared with Johnson's 93% and Kennedy's 88%).

The 1980s saw the rise of the political right with **Reagan's monetarist control** of the economy and the return of power to the states and away from federal control.

The increase in **arms spending** throughout the 1980s led to the increase in the US **deficit**. The end of the Cold War in 1989 relieved this pressure, but the focus of American domestic politics remains a commitment to low taxation and minimal federal intervention.

Action point

You should be able to make comprehensive notes on the various personalities of the Civil Rights movement. The consequences of Martin Luther King's assassination in 1968 should also be considered.

"We hold these truths to be self-evident, that all men are created equal"

American Declaration of Independence, quoted by Martin Luther King in 'I have a dream . . .'

Action point

Make notes on the careers of Presidents Truman, Kennedy and Johnson.

Checkpoint 1

Consider the many consequences of the Vietnam War in the light of American foreign policy as well as domestic affairs.

Checkpoint 2

How did the Watergate scandal affect the views of many Americans about the presidency?

Exam questions   answers: page 162

1   Why did America elect Franklin Roosevelt four times? (45 min)

2   How far has the USA lived up to its reputation as a melting pot where many different immigrants can prosper? (45 min)

China under communism

China has nearly one-fifth of the world's population. European fears that Communism would spread after the Second World War were increased significantly with the formation of the People's Republic of China in 1949.

The background to communism

The **1911 revolution** brought the Kuomintang to power, led by Sun Yat-sen and subsequently Chiang Kai-shek. The problems they faced were as follows:

→ Continued control of the **warlords**.
→ Ineffective government increasing existing **poverty**.
→ **Natural disasters** such as poor harvests and floods.
→ Failure to deal with Japanese attacks.
→ The growth of **communism**, led by the influential Mao Tse-tung.

Inspirational achievements like the **Long March** and the guerrilla war against the Japanese convinced many that communism was the way forward for China.

This eventually culminated in the defeat of the Kuomintang in 1949 and China's conversion to communism.

Early years of communism

As had been the case in Russia in 1917, the main reason that the peasants supported communism in China was their demands for **land**, therefore land was redistributed to the peasants in the first year of communist control, thus increasing Mao's popularity. Other initiatives included:

→ **Cooperatives** were set up gradually throughout the 1950s; this slowly improved agricultural methods and productivity.
→ **Industrially**, there was much development: previously foreign-owned businesses were taken over by the Communist Party, and inflation was controlled by a system of central fixed pricing.
→ The **USSR** offered considerable help to Mao in the early years of communist control. This took the form of money, expertise and equipment. The Soviet theme was continued in 1952, when Mao launched his **First Five-Year Plan**.
→ **Education** and **health** were slowly improved, both with a slant towards communist **propaganda**. Women were given a new role within society and encouraged to work alongside men.
→ The '**hundred flowers**' campaign encouraged criticism of the government, until a wave of negative responses brought about its demise.

Action point

Study China's geographical position on a world and Asian map. Think about the trading influences of European empires and the significance to China of the growth in power of the USSR and Japan.

"Political power grows out of the barrel of a gun"

Mao Tse-tung

Checkpoint 1

Marx originally believed that communism would emerge in an industrial society. Consider how Industrialized both the USSR and China were before they became communist states. Why then did communism develop in these societies?

"I have witnessed the tremendous energy of the masses, on this foundation it is possible to accomplish any task whatsoever"

Mao Tse-tung

The Great Leap Forward

Mao's criticisms of the development of a new middle class in China, profiting from their expertise in agriculture and industry, led to the 1958 initiative, which rewrote the targets of the previous year's Second Five-Year Plan. The features of the Great Leap Forward were as follows:

→ **Communes** – a development from the earlier system of cooperatives. The vast scale of the communes meant that major projects were undertaken. Mao based his plans on the 'tremendous energy of the masses', thus ordinary people built schools, bridges and dams and operated backyard blast furnaces. By the end of 1958, there were 26 000 communes in China.

→ **Propaganda** – the drive to increase production was accompanied by a huge propaganda campaign to convince the people that they were working for the future of their country.

→ The Great Leap Forward had **limited success** – a lack of experience, the absence of Russian experts after their withdrawal in 1960 and a succession of bad harvests meant that progress was limited. These factors led to Mao's resignation.

The Cultural Revolution

The drive to return Chinese communism to its roots began in the summer of 1966. Mao once again felt that the experts were taking over China, so he encouraged the young to become activists.

Reorganization caused chaos, and the zealous **Red Guards** coerced into basic jobs the middle managers they felt responsible for inefficiency. Not only did this frequently involve intimidation and violence but it also meant that production of food and manufactured goods fell dramatically.

China since Mao

Mao's death led to a power struggle in China, which was eventually resolved in favour of Hua Guofeng and Deng Xiaoping. Jiang Qing, Mao's widow, and three associates, known as the **Gang of Four**, attempted to take control but were eventually tried and imprisoned. The harsher elements of Maoism were relaxed under Deng Xiaoping and China began to make genuine economic progress. However, there are still questions about individual freedoms, which erupted on an international scale during the student demonstrations of 1989.

Exam questions   answers: page 163

1   Compare the motivation behind the Great Leap Forward and the Cultural Revolution. (45 min)

2   How far has communism solved the problems faced by China in the 20th century? (45 min)

Checkpoint 2

Try to make a comparison between the development of Chinese and Russian communism. What parallels can be drawn between the experiences of Lenin, Stalin and Mao in attempting to advance their countries' industrial and agricultural production?

Check the net

There is lots of information on Maoist China at www.gettysburg.edu/~s345972/glf.html

Test yourself

Take a blank piece of paper and make a list in two columns: successes of Chinese communism and failures of Chinese communism.

> *"Let a hundred flowers bloom, let a hundred schools of thought contend"*
>
> Maoist slogan

Examiner's secrets

Questions on the Great Leap Forward and the Cultural Revolution will ask you to balance their industrial success or failure with the effect they had on morale and the consequent propaganda that surrounded these initiatives.

Chinese foreign policy

Checkpoint 1

How would comments like that quoted above concern Western powers?

Initial friendship between communist China and the USSR came to an end with the death of Stalin, which left China without the support of a major world power. This isolationism was not to end until the détente of the 1970s.

Taiwan and Tibet

Four themes run through Chinese foreign policy:

→ A long-standing fear of foreign intervention.
→ Alignment with similar poor Third World countries.
→ An uneasy relationship with other communist countries.
→ Distrust of the United States after the latter's support for Chiang Kai-shek.

The defeated Kuomintang retreated to the island of **Taiwan** in 1949. The USA supported the Taiwanese government as part of its policy of containment throughout the Cold War. China's place on the United Nations Security Council was taken by Taiwan because of American opposition to communism.

China's invasion of **Tibet** in 1950 led to disputes with the West but also with Tibetan neighbour India. This erupted into a small-scale war in 1962 over the construction of a road to allow the Chinese military greater access to the province. China made small gains, but the situation did not escalate.

Korea and Vietnam

Part of the American justification for their policy of **containment** and therefore involvement in the Korean War was the communist takeover of China the previous year.

The escalation of the Korean War led to Chinese troops invading North Korea in 1951 to force the combined American, South Korean and UN forces back to the **38th parallel**. Truman's dismissal of MacArthur avoided war between China and the USA. China had made an important statement about its intentions to oppose foreign intervention in Asia.

China also opposed American involvement in the **Vietnam War** by sending aid to the North Vietnamese forces. Although the Chinese never sent troops it was clear that this was once more a conflict between the USA and China. Once again, the American withdrawal in 1975 seemed to boost Chinese military confidence.

Relations with the USSR

Relations between the USSR and China have often been strained. There are several reasons for this tension:

→ Mao did not agree with Soviet coexistence with capitalism in Europe under Khrushchev from 1953.
→ Mao felt that the Soviet Union treated China as an inferior communist power.

→ Mao believed that Russian communism had become corrupt and divorced from its roots in the soviets.
→ The two countries share a 4 000-mile border, over which there had been many disagreements in the past.

The initial period of cooperation ended in 1960, when the Russians withdrew their advisors from China. The situation grew more serious in 1969 with the Ussuri River dispute.

Relations with the USA ●●●

American opposition to Mao's communist China was immediate. The philosophical objections to communism were exacerbated by the concept of the **domino theory**. The USA soon opposed China practically by supporting Chiang Kai-shek in Taiwan and ensuring that China played no part in the United Nations.

These tensions were increased by Korea and Vietnam, and at one point it seemed that an American nuclear strike on China was possible. Mao himself pragmatically called the atom bomb a 'paper tiger', believing that China would emerge from a nuclear war as the world's dominant power through sheer weight of numbers.

The **détente** of the 1970s improved relations between the two countries. President Nixon made a watershed visit to Peking in 1972. The reasons for this détente are as follows:

→ The American **withdrawal from Vietnam** pacified the Chinese government.
→ The Americans realized that a rigid policy of containment was not feasible in Asia.
→ Chinese relations with the USSR had deteriorated so that it was in their interests to be on better terms with the West.
→ Diplomatic pressure had mounted through the 1960s, and China had been allowed to join the **UN** in 1971.
→ The failure of the **Great Leap Forward** had made the Chinese turn to the West for more heavy industrial goods.

Action point

Remind yourself of the changes in power in the Soviet Union. How did Khrushchev differ politically from Stalin, and why would this affect relations with China?

"The USSR enforces fascist dictatorship at home and carries out aggression and expansion abroad"

Mao Tse-tung

Checkpoint 2

Explain carefully what is meant by the domino theory. How is this linked to containment and the American Cold War attitude to China and the other Asian communist powers like North Korea and Vietnam?

Test yourself

Revise the Cold War in geographical sections: Europe, Asia and Latin America.

Exam questions   answers: pages 163–4

1 Examine the relationship between the USSR and the People's Republic of China. (45 min)

2 'China's foreign policy since communism has been dictated by its experiences before communism.' Discuss. (45 min)

149

Soviet foreign policy

Action point

Remind yourself of the geography of the USSR. The combination of frozen seas to the north and only indirect access to the world's oceans in the south presented Russia with a logistical and defensive problem. Equally, the enormous land borders the USSR shared with its neighbours made defence more difficult.

"We do not want to be beaten. Russia was ceaselessly beaten for her backwardness . . . we must make good this lag in ten years. Either we do this or they crush us"

Stalin

Checkpoint 1

What was Stalin's primary goal when he became the leader of the USSR?

Checkpoint 2

Consider how the USSR's role in the build up to the Second World War may have influenced relations between the victors in the post-war world.

We do not want a single foot of foreign territory but we will not surrender a single inch of our territory either.

Stalin

We can see from these words that Soviet foreign policy under Stalin differed from the Marxist idealism of Lenin. Yet in the aftermath of the Second World War the USSR was increasingly keen to expand territory and influence throughout the world.

Socialism in one country

The immediate consequence of the **October Revolution** for the Russian people was an end to their participation in the Great War. However, British, American and French support for the White armies in the **civil war** that followed the Great War set the tone for relations with the new communist country.

Lenin believed in the Marxist principle of expanding socialism throughout the world and consequently set up the **Comintern** (1919) to spread Marxist ideas. Lenin also arranged the **Treaty of Rapallo** with Germany in 1922 to give the USSR at least one ally in Europe, while in the east, Soviet support for Sun Yat-sen's Chinese Nationalists led Lenin to believe that he could encourage communism through the back door.

After the death of Lenin in 1924, Stalin's belief that the world was not ready for communism led to a dramatically different foreign policy.

Stalin's foreign policy 1924–1945

Stalin improved the Soviet diplomatic position by opening relations with Britain, France and Italy in 1924. This became more important as Soviet influence waned in the east with the arrival of Chiang Kai-shek in China and Japanese militarism in the 1930s over Manchuria.

In Europe, Stalin pursued a policy of cooperation and signed the Kellogg–Briand Pact in 1928 and accepted an invitation to join the **League of Nations** in 1934. However, British and French **appeasement** of Hitler in the late 1930s led Stalin to believe that he could not trust the West, and in 1939 the **Molotov–Ribbentrop Pact** was a surprise treaty with anti-communist Germany.

Stalin remained neutral as war developed in 1939 but strengthened Soviet defences by the conquest of **Finland** in 1940. The inevitable Nazi invasion of the USSR in the summer of 1941 led to the uneasy alliance between the Soviets and the Western powers: Britain, France and subsequently the USA. The eventual Soviet victory was hard-fought and costly (it has been estimated that as many as 20 million citizens and soldiers died as a result of the war), but morale-boosting victories at **Stalingrad** and **Leningrad** did much to increase the standing of Stalin in the eyes of the Russian people.

Control of Eastern Europe

The many events in the Cold War in Europe can be divided into those that increased tension and those that improved relations between the superpowers. First, those that increased tension:

→ Soviet conquest and exploitation of Eastern Europe.
→ The Truman doctrine, Marshall Aid and atomic rivalry.
→ The creation of Cominform in 1947.
→ The Berlin airlift of 1948 and increased Soviet control of the Eastern bloc.
→ The development of the Iron Curtain separating East from West, culminating in the construction of the Berlin Wall in 1961.
→ The 1960 U2 crisis and the 1962 Cuban missile crisis.
→ Soviet invasions of Hungary (1956) and Czechoslovakia (1968).

Events that improved relations are fewer:

→ Khrushchev's policy of 'peaceful coexistence'.
→ The Geneva summit of 1955.
→ The abolition of Cominform in 1956.
→ The Cuban missile crisis eventually led to closer cooperation between the superpowers.

Asian developments

These included:

→ Stalin not involving the USSR in the Korean War of 1950–1953, hoping that China would weaken the USA and *vice versa*.
→ Soviet cooperation with China weakened after Khrushchev came to power in 1953. Animosity increased throughout the 1960s, although neither side was prepared to go to war.
→ The USSR attempted to increase influence in **India** and **Pakistan**, which further angered China.
→ The Soviet invasion of **Afghanistan** in 1979 once again increased the tension of the Cold War. The USSR tried to increase influence in the Middle East and protect its own borders through Afghanistan. However, strong guerrilla resistance by the *mujaheddin* and UN and US disapproval meant that the Afghanistan war was a long drawn-out problem for the USSR.

The end of the Cold War

Due to its fragile domestic position, the USSR was unable to maintain its status as a superpower, and it disintegrated in the late 1980s.

Checkpoint 3

How could events in Poland in the 1980s demonstrate a weakening in Soviet control of Eastern Europe?

"War with the West is not inevitable"

Khrushchev

Checkpoint 4

Consider the significance of the Cuban missile crisis. How can it have both increased and reduced tension?

Examiner's secrets

Make brief additional notes on the careers and characteristics of Soviet leaders from Lenin to Gorbachev. Knowledge of how individual relationships with other world leaders affected the Cold War will impress an examiner.

Exam questions   answers: pages 164–5

1 'The main aim of Soviet foreign policy has been defence.'
   Discuss. (45 min)

2 Why did Soviet foreign policy differ under the leadership of Khrushchev?
   (45 min)

US foreign policy from 1953

Action point

Study a map of the Americas. Consider the potential for communist growth in the poor countries of Central America. Why would American fears of communism in their 'backyard' introduce a new element of panic for most citizens of the USA?

"The enemy is the communist system itself – implacable, insatiable, increasing its drive for world domination"

J. F. Kennedy

Checkpoint 1

How could the Cuban crisis be viewed as a success for JFK? Was this 'victory' likely to influence further Cold War policy?

Eisenhower brought a 'new look' to US relations with the communist world. While it still involved containment, he was more reliant on the nuclear deterrent and consequently reduced conventional forces. Subsequent presidents, while they tolerated the Soviet sphere of influence in Europe, devoted massive resources to containing communism in Asia.

Latin America

The potential development of communism in the American 'backyard' was a serious concern:

→ Guatemala – the US government regarded Arbenz, the Guatemalan president elected in 1953, as a communist threat. Despite the fact that Arbenz received no aid from Moscow and was not a communist himself, the CIA actively supported a successful coup led by the pro-American Castillo Armas in 1954.

→ **Cuba – Fidel Castro's** rise to power in 1959 was a far more serious threat to the USA. His seizure of American-owned assets led to the ill-fated **Bay of Pigs** incident in 1961. This obvious statement of intent from the USA forced **Castro** closer to the USSR, and the conflict escalated with the **missile crisis** the following year. The eventual compromise settlement was kept hidden from the public for six years. However, there were significant consequences for the Cold War:

  → Both Kennedy and Khrushchev avoided an embarrassing defeat.
  → The hot line between Moscow and Washington was set up.
  → Covert opposition to communism through **Operation Mongoose** continued.

Europe

The USA continued to oppose communism in Europe, but a less threatening tone was set by the muted response to Soviet suppression of revolts in **Poland** and **Hungary** (1956) and **Czechoslovakia** (1968). America attempted to spread anti-communist information and propaganda through Radio Free Europe.

West Germany (FDR) continued to be the cause of much dispute, initially in 1955, when France opposed West German rearmament. This was achieved only after the intervention of Britain. The FDR consequently joined NATO, with French and Soviet approval, in 1955.

West Berlin caused further conflict in the early 1960s as the USA refused Soviet demands to withdraw from the last capitalist outpost in East Germany. The erection of the **Berlin Wall** in 1961 nearly led to war. However, another compromise was reached whereby both the American presence in West Berlin and the wall itself remained.

Asia and the Middle East ●●●

The need to protect the supply of oil to the West led to several attempts to contain the growth of communism in the Middle East, yet Arab attitudes to the USA were soured by US support for the creation of the state of **Israel** in 1948. The main incidents of US involvement are:

→ **Iran** – the CIA actively supported a coup in 1953 to remove the nationalist prime minister Mossadeq and replace him with a royalist. The success of the covert operation led to a belief that such methods were an effective means of opposing communism.

→ The **Baghdad Pact** of 1955 led to the formation of **CENTO**, a Middle Eastern version of NATO.

→ The **Suez crisis** led to a deterioration of relations between Britain, France and the USA. The Anglo-French invasion led to many Middle Eastern countries forging closer links with the USSR.

→ The USA again confused nationalism with communism in the Lebanon, but war was avoided when US troops were withdrawn.

In Asia, the need to contain communism was more obvious after Korea. The main crisis points were:

→ **Laos** – Kennedy opposed the communist Pathet Lao. American and **SEATO (South East Asia Treaty Organisation)** forces mobilized. However, conflict was avoided when the USSR agreed to restrict aid to communist forces in Laos. In practice, however, both sides continued to support their respective sides in secret. Laos eventually became communist in 1975.

→ **Vietnam** – the Laos situation encouraged Kennedy to act more aggressively in Vietnam, which was considered the 'cornerstone of the free world in South-east Asia'. The heavy involvement of American 'military advisers' in Vietnam was to lead to a guerrilla war that was only to conclude with American withdrawal in 1973. Vietnam and neighbouring **Cambodia** were communist by 1975.

Détente ●●●

The 1970s saw a period of more cooperation between the USA and the communist world. The breakdown of relations between China and the USSR made Nixon and Carter realize that they no longer faced a communist alliance. Nixon's visit to China in 1972 and the arms limitation talks of this decade show how the situation improved. However, the American invasion of **Grenada** and the Soviet invasion of **Afghanistan** (1979) escalated the Cold War once again.

Action point

Make your own notes on the reasons why the USA has often supported Israel.

"This is not a struggle for supremacy of arms alone. It is also a struggle for supremacy between two conflicting ideologies: freedom under God versus ruthless godless tyranny"

J. F. Kennedy

Checkpoint 2

Consider how the make-up of American society affects US relations with the countries of the Arab world.

Examiner's secrets

All questions on US foreign policy need you to balance successes against failures. However, you must do this in the context of the changing face of world communism.

Exam questions answers: page 165

1 Contrast Eisenhower's and Kennedy's policies of containment. (45 min)

2 How successful was the American policy of containment? (45 min)

The end of European empires

Action point

You should consult a world map before revising this section and try to build up a picture of the extent of European control of the world by the beginning of the 20th century and again at the end of the century. A historical atlas should help.

Checkpoint 1

How did the partition of India lead to dispute and conflict in the years after independence?

European empires had begun to decline as early as the 18th century. The chaos and financial ruin of the Great War increased the likelihood that the European powers would lose their grip on Africa and Asia, but the collapse of European control was most evident in the 20 years after the Second World War. As the indigenous resistance movements gradually helped to overthrow the wartime invaders, they were reluctant to hand control back to their former colonial masters.

Asia

The independence of Asia can be divided into the violent and the predominantly non-violent. First, the violent:

→ **Indochina** – the French colonies of Indochina, now called Cambodia, Laos and Vietnam, won their independence through the leadership of Ho Chi Minh and the military prowess of Vo Nguyen Giap. Their victory at Dien Bien Phu in 1954 led to French withdrawal. The Geneva conference created an independent Vietnam. This was short-lived, however, as the USA opposed the spread of communism in the area.

→ **Indonesia** – the former Dutch colonies quickly defeated the Dutch, who were in no position to defend their colony after five years of Nazi occupation. Indonesia was declared independent in 1947 and unified by 1950.

→ **Malaysia** – Britain supported Malayan nationalism in order to avoid communism. Malaya and Singapore were granted independence in 1957 and 1959, respectively, the former joining with Sarawak and Sabah to form Malaysia in 1963.

The non-violent handovers in Asia were as follows:

→ **Philippines** – these islands were granted independence from the USA in 1946.

→ **India** – Britain granted India independence in 1947, separating Muslim Pakistan from Hindu India. Pakistan's eastern territory eventually became Bangladesh (1971). Violence accompanied independence in India but was not directed at the British but different religious groups of Indians. Conflict still occurs over the disputed Kashmir region.

→ **Ceylon** and **Burma** were both given independence from Britain, Ceylon eventually becoming Sri Lanka.

Middle East

Once again Britain and France were forced to grant independence to their former colonies. First, the British possessions:

→ **Jordan** was granted independence in 1946.

→ **Egypt** became independent in 1955, but Nasser nationalizing the Suez Canal in 1956 led to the disastrous Anglo-French invasion.

International pressure forced them to withdraw after 6 weeks, and the canal became Egyptian property.

→ **Cyprus** became independent in 1960, although once again there were problems after independence, on this occasion between the island's Greek and Turkish populations.

→ The French had given **Syria** and the **Lebanon** independence in 1944, but the humiliation of defeat in Indochina, the discovery of oil in the Sahara in 1956 and the fact that there were a million French settlers in Algeria encouraged a more dogmatic approach in **Algeria**. The French forces fought the Algerian independence movement (FLN) between 1956 and eventual independence in 1962.

Africa

○○○

As one would expect with a continent the size of Africa, the movement towards independence has been varied. However, certain themes can be observed:

→ **Ghana**, formerly the Gold Coast, became independent in 1957 under the leadership of Kwame Nkrumah. This was the first British colony to receive its independence in Africa. It consequently set the precedent for Britain gradually to allow all colonies to follow suit.

→ Problems were to develop in **Kenya** and **Rhodesia**. Kenyan independence was achieved in 1963, but only after a bloody conflict involving both tribal and independence grievances.

→ Northern Rhodesia became the independent country of Zambia in 1963, but the territory of Southern Rhodesia, dominated by a white minority, declared unilateral independence in 1965. The following guerrilla war was not concluded until the formation of **Zimbabwe** in 1980 under the leadership of Robert Mugabe.

→ The French and Belgians learned from the disaster of Algeria and did not oppose independence for their colonies in Africa. By 1960, all French colonies were independent but were closely linked to France commercially.

→ The Belgian **Congo** was also allowed independence in 1960. However, the civil war that followed was not resolved until the formation of **Zaire** in 1965.

→ The Portuguese were the last European colonists to relinquish control of their colonies, **Angola** and **Mozambique** declaring independence in 1975.

Checkpoint 2

Why were the French determined to retain control of Algeria?

Checkpoint 3

What is meant by the term 'guerrilla war'? Why do guerrillas seem to be able to resist the might of major world powers?

> *"The wind of change is blowing through this continent"*
>
> Harold Macmillan, 1960, about Africa

Action point

You should also remember the independence of the British West Indies. This occurred gradually throughout the 1960s. In most cases this independence was peaceful.

Check the net

You can find information about the British Commonwealth at www.schools.bedfordshire.gov.uk/rcs/p6.htm

Examiner's secrets

You cannot discuss all the former European colonies in an essay, but the examiner will need you to show examples of the main areas: Africa, Asia and the Middle East.

Exam question   answer: page 166

Examine the reasons for the growth of independence among former European colonies since the Second World War. (45 min)

The recovery of Western Europe

After the defeat of Germany in May 1945, the most immediate problem facing the European nations was to repair the damage of war and restart industrial production. The **United Nations Relief Rehabilitation Administration** (UNRRA) was set up in 1944 to deal with these issues. However, the long-term future of Europe was uncertain. Integration seemed the only hope of prosperity and security, yet a consensus was difficult to achieve, especially after the conversion to communism of much of Eastern Europe.

> *"Our policy is directed against hunger, poverty, despair and chaos"*
>
> George Marshall, 1947

Checkpoint 1

How did the Marshall Plan aim to contain communism?

Check the net

You can find information on the Marshall Plan at its 50th anniversary website at lcweb.loc.gov/exhibits/marshall/m56.html

The jargon

Supranationalism was the idea that the delegates of the OEEC should reflect the interests of the whole community rather than their respective national interests. This idea was opposed by Britain, which feared the loss of national identity to a greater Europe.

> *"A step of extraordinary importance for the peace of Europe"*
>
> Adenauer's view of the ECSC

Marshall aid

The devastating winter of 1947 added to the practical problems experienced in Europe. American Secretary of State **George Marshall** developed a **European Recovery Programme** based on American aid. This **Marshall Plan** was to be offered on three conditions:

→ The aid must be requested by Europe.
→ The European states had to request this aid collectively rather than as individual states.
→ The communist bloc should be invited to join, but its refusal would not prevent the operation of the plan.

Thus the Marshall Plan, which operated for five years between 1947 and 1952, was an attempt to prevent the spread of communism as the USSR inevitably opposed the scheme, and an attempt to draw the European nations into closer cooperation with each other.

The Marshall Plan led to the creation of the **OEEC** in 1948 to administer the recovery programme. Cracks in this union began to emerge as the British and Scandinavians opposed **supranationalism**. This led, in 1948, to the British-sponsored **General Agreement on Tariffs and Trade (GATT)**.

Uniting Europe

It was certainly the belief of many Western European countries that closer union was the best hope of avoiding the problems that had led to two disastrous wars in the first half of the century.

Britain and the Scandinavian countries were opposed to these ideas and consequently did not join the **European Coal and Steel Community** in 1952. The scheme included France, West Germany, Italy and the three countries of the **Benelux Union**. The organization was taken a stage further in 1957 with the signing of the **Treaty of Rome**, formally announcing the **European Economic Community**.

Britain still opposed the idea of further integration and formed the **European Free Trade Association** in 1959 in alliance with the Scandinavian countries, Austria and Portugal. As the EEC became stronger and Britain's links with the Commonwealth proved less prosperous, Britain applied to join the EEC, but de Gaulle's veto of British inclusion postponed the event until 1973.

Political unity

As early as 1946 Churchill had urged the nations of Europe to bind together to form a stronger alliance against any external threat. He was referring to the growing danger from the communist countries of Eastern Europe. This integration occurred gradually in several stages:

→ The **Congress of Europe** met in 1948 and agreed to reconstruct Europe on a supranational basis. As a consequence of this the Council of Europe was formed to protect human rights.

→ The **Council of Europe**, significantly based in Strasbourg on the border between France and Germany, discussed matters of common concern to members but excluded defence policy.

→ The **Nordic Council** was formed in 1952 and allowed the Scandinavian countries to benefit from integration while still remaining separate from other European unions.

→ The **EEC** emerged in 1957 and became the dominant political force in Europe. While the core members have remained tied to the policy of integration, the electoral tides of various European countries, none more so than Britain, have resulted in a fluctuating approach to the concept of closer ties with Europe.

The European Economic Community has grown in size and strength since its birth in 1957. Regardless of the many advantages and disadvantages associated with the union, the original concept of unity to engender prosperity and strength has resulted in a period of relative peace and recovery.

Military unity

The expansion of military unity has been a feature of post-war Europe. The three stages of unity are as follows:

→ **Dunkirk Treaty** – signed by Britain and France in 1947, this treaty aimed to prevent the revival of German military aggression. It soon became clear that the real danger lay with the communist bloc. However, Germany was named in order to avoid offending the USSR.

→ **Brussels Treaty** – this agreement, signed in 1948, expanded the Dunkirk Treaty to include the Benelux countries.

→ **NATO** – the weakness of the countries of Western Europe meant that only with the assistance of the USA could they hope to defend themselves. The crisis in Berlin in 1948 encouraged the USA and Canada to create the North Atlantic Treaty Organisation in 1949.

Exam question   answer: page 166

Discuss the successes and failures of European cooperation since 1945. (45 min)

"We must build a kind of United States of Europe"

Winston Churchill, 1946

Action point

Make a timeline showing the agreements made between the European nations in the years after the Second World War. You could colour code this timeline blue for political agreements, red for military and so on.

Check the net

You can find lots of information about the history of the EEC at the EU site at userpage.chemie.fu-berlin.de/adressen/eu.html

Checkpoint 2

Why do you think that economic unity was easier to achieve than political unity in the Europe after the Second World War?

Examiner's secrets

Questions on this subject require the candidate to put the various European agreements into a historical perspective. You should be careful not to write an answer more suited to an Economics or Politics syllabus. Although both of these subjects are relevant, the answer must focus on the historical aspects.

The end of the Cold War

> *"When I found myself at the helm of this state, it was already clear that something was wrong . . . this country was suffocating in the shackles of the bureaucratic command system, doomed to cater to ideology"*
>
> Mikhail Gorbachev

> *"A society cannot exist without glasnost"*
>
> Mikhail Gorbachev

The last 15 years of the 20th century have seen the decline of the second great superpower. The collapse of communism in the USSR led to the end of the Cold War and the rise of nationalism in much of Eastern Europe and Central Asia. This decline has in turn resulted in new threats, instabilities and challenges to world peace.

The collapse of communism

The decline of world communism should be traced back to its roots in the USSR. The death of Chernenko in 1985 led to the rise to power of a much younger Soviet leader, Mikhail Gorbachev. He introduced three policies that were eventually to bring about the collapse of communism:

→ *Perestroika* dismantled the centrally planned state and introduced a market-led economy based on the profit motive.

→ *Glasnost* was an important part of Gorbachev's restructuring of the Soviet system. In order to obtain public support for his policy of *perestroika*, Gorbachev needed to reduce the strict Soviet censorship.

→ **Democratization** was the final strand of the reform programme. Initially, this involved genuine elections for party members but was soon expanded to include all citizens.

These reforms ultimately led to the loss of the Communist Party's monopoly of power. Consequently, the USSR split into its constituent parts and the communist bloc fragmented. Gradually, communism was overthrown in all of the former soviet republics.

The rise of nationalism

The Gorbachev reforms did not bring immediate improvement to the Soviet economy. However, where Stalinist leaders had covered up these problems through repression, propaganda and fear, the new regime had encouraged criticism through the policy of *glasnost*. This inevitably led to a loss of regional control.

From 1986–1987, Gorbachev toured the Eastern European states and publicly denounced the Brezhnev doctrine that the USSR had the right to intervene in the communist states of Europe. At the final meeting of the Warsaw Pact leaders in 1989, Gorbachev alienated the communist leaders of Eastern Europe by refusing to send Soviet troops to suppress anti-communist rebels. This marked change in Soviet foreign policy precipitated a rush to independence at the end of 1989 in the following countries:

→ Czechoslovakia

→ Hungary

→ Bulgaria

→ Romania

The most symbolic movement away from Soviet control came in November 1989 with the destruction of the **Berlin Wall**. This more than anything had been a testament to Soviet control and repression in Eastern Europe. The opportunity to reunite Germany without Soviet interference was encouraged by Gorbachev.

The many different races that made up the USSR were supposed to view the purity of socialism as more important than nationalist identity, yet Gorbachev's reforms made it obvious that these nationalist sympathies had not been removed by Stalin's policy of 'Russification'.

The independence movements began in **Kazakhstan** in 1986 and spread to the **Baltic states – Latvia**, **Lithuania** and **Estonia** declaring their independence in 1990. This was followed by the break-up of the USSR in 1991.

New threats and instabilities ●●●

The break-up of the USSR left a void in many areas of the world, notably Russia, which had little tradition or experience of government by the people. This led to the development of many competing influences, such as the rise of the extreme right and the re-emergence of communism.

On a worldwide scale, there are many other features of the 'new world order' that are of note:

→ **Nationalism**, spreading from the former communist states, challenges the existing parameters of the UN, encouraging the NATO alliance to involve itself in civil war situations such as Bosnia and Kosovo.

→ The increasing **nuclear capability** of the countries of the developing world – particularly of concern are the Arab states and Israel, Pakistan and India.

→ The persistence of communism in Asia.

→ Russian **instability**, demonstrated by Yeltsin's response to threats from within, sending tanks into Moscow in 1993.

Action point

Compare a map of the USSR with a modern map of Russia and its neighbours.

Checkpoint

Consider whether the condition of the Russian people improved during the communist period.

"In Europe we are Asiatic, while in Asia we are European"

Dostoevsky

Don't forget

Dostoevsky's comment above suggests a constant problem for Russia and the states of the former USSR. These republics do not fall into the existing alliance structures, which increases their instability.

Exam questions   answers: pages 166–7

1 Why did the Soviet Union break up in the early 1990s? (45 min)

2 'The experience of Gorbachev, attempting to retain control of the USSR, shows that such a huge area can only be controlled effectively by autocracy.' Discuss this view of the collapse of communism. (45 min)

Examiner's secrets

Most questions on this subject will focus on the collapse of communism in Russia. However, you could also bring in examples from Asia to provide a comparison.

Answers
20th-century world history

The results of the Second World War

Checkpoint

As you can see from the words of Sir Hartley Shawcross (p.139), spoken as part of the opening address of the chief prosecutor at the Nuremberg trials, the decision to try the surviving Nazi leaders as criminals was a new direction for international law. It was unusual to put on trial those charged with starting a war.

The purpose of the trials was twofold: first to rid the world of the legacy of Nazism, and second to justify the actions of the Allies in bringing Nazism to an end. This is how the Allies dealt with the moral dilemma of not punishing the USSR for invading Poland in 1939 or in fact themselves for the bombing of such cities as Dresden.

You should consider the opinion of Field Marshal Montgomery: 'Germany's crime lay in waging an unsuccessful war.'

Exam question

There are two sides to this question. The statement prompts you to analyse the development of the superpower struggle after the Second World War. In addition to this you should analyse how far the traditional European powers of Britain, France and Germany were eclipsed by the new superpowers, the USA and the USSR.

Deal first with the traditional European powers. You should explain why in each case their financial and emotional commitment to the war meant that in the years after 1945 they were unable and unwilling to play an active role in world affairs.

You should avoid becoming too narrative and quoting endless statistics about civilians and military personnel lost during the war. However, a few figures will help your analysis.

The USSR was a force in the pre-war world and does not fit with the argument that those that suffered the most heavily during the war avoided large-scale involvement in post-war diplomacy. However, you should argue that this is entirely in keeping with Stalin's view of the world that the USSR should continue to develop a world influence in order to prevent further invasion.

Finally, the major change in 20th-century world politics has been the increasing role of the USA. This is a direct consequence of its involvement in the Second World War. Once Roosevelt had persuaded Congress that isolation was impossible, the USA went on to become the major force in world politics.

You should conclude that the statement in the question has merit but is too simplistic to explain the post-war developments in international relations.

The origins of the Cold War

Checkpoints

1   The joint American and British development of the atom bomb was to have enormous consequences for world politics, and especially the Cold War.

The use of the two bombs against the Japanese cities of Hiroshima and Nagasaki in 1945 brought the war in the Pacific to a speedy conclusion, but the arrival of the nuclear age brought with it a new level of suspicion between the great powers, now called superpowers.

The American decision to keep the knowledge of the bomb from Stalin while the two nations were allies angered Stalin and increased his distrust of both Britain and the USA.

Stalin saw the American monopoly of the atomic bomb as a threat. This belief increased when Truman attempted to trade information about the bomb for Soviet concessions in Eastern Europe.

The new weapon had increased the stakes and consequently the level of distrust in post-war diplomacy.

2   Stalin differed from his predecessor Lenin in that he did not believe the world was ready for communist development. His main aim was to preserve communism in the USSR until such time as the rest of the world was ready to be educated along Marxist lines. He therefore developed his idea of 'Socialism in one country'. This meant that it was vital for the USSR to be protected against capitalist invasion. Stalin recognized the weakness of Russia's land borders and therefore attempted to develop what he referred to as a buffer zone of friendly countries between Russia and the capitalist West.

Exam questions

1   To answer this question properly you must explain the factor stated in the question but also discuss an alternative view.

A definition of the term 'cold war' would be a useful place to begin.

You should then discuss factors that could argue that the USA was responsible for the Cold War:

• American fears of communism.
• American misinterpretation of communist behaviour: most Americans believed that Stalin wanted to expand communism rather than defend his own borders. This led to the USA interpreting Soviet defensive actions as aggression.
• Failure of America to deal with Hitler in the 1930s. The American isolationism of the 1920s and 1930s encouraged Stalin to believe that the USA would be happy with Soviet destruction by Germany. This view persisted throughout the war.

The USA was also the strongest power in 1945. This, added to its recently acquired nuclear capability, gave the USSR grave cause for concern

You should also look at some of the other reasons for the outbreak of the Cold War, such as the USSR's actions in Eastern Europe at the end of the war. The failure to allow free elections seemed to suggest to the USA that its worst fears were about to be proved correct.

The situation in Asia was also out of the USA's control but increased the tension between the superpowers.

To conclude, you could argue that Soviet motives were defensive and on their own perimeter, while the USA was keen to involve itself aggressively across the globe to prevent the growth of communism.

2 The key word in this question is 'explain'. You must give reasons as well as examples for the breakdown of the wartime alliance.

The essay is really in two sections. First, you should explain why the USA and the USSR were allies in 1944; and second, explain why this alliance had broken up by 1946.

For the first part of the question, you should outline the system of wartime alliances that brought the USA and USSR together in 1941, emphasizing that there was no common ground apart from their opposition to the Axis powers.

The second part of the essay requires you to analyse the wartime conferences of Tehran, Yalta and Potsdam. You should be able to explain which promises were and which were not kept.

You should also once again refer to the American monopoly of the atom bomb and Truman's refusal to allow Stalin to share this knowledge.

A suitable conclusion should balance the very different post-war aims of the superpowers with the idea that the wartime alliance was only one of convenience

US foreign policy 1917–1953

Checkpoint

The Marshall Plan was based on the theory that communism would spread where conditions of poverty predominated, especially after the ravages of war. The American congressional decision to lend money to Europe was therefore an attempt to prevent poverty, which they hoped would prevent communism. It was also an attempt to encourage the countries of Eastern Europe to welcome American aid and therefore influence.

Exam questions

1 This question, like any that deals with the success of a particular policy, should be answered by building up an argument for success and one for failure. In this question, you can refer specifically to limited success in Europe and failure in Asia. However, you must beware of making generalizations – be precise.

In Europe, communism had been defeated in Greece and France, while conditions in Western Europe were benefiting from the Marshall Plan. The Eastern bloc's rejection of the offer of Marshall aid had led to the required difference in recovery from the war and a steady flow of refugees from East to West.

In Asia, the policy was less successful. Japan had been created as a capitalist economy and the southern half of Korea had been preserved during the Korean War, but the situation in China gave the USA grave cause for concern. The failure to prevent North Korea influencing the south was a hint of the troubles soon to erupt in Vietnam.

You should conclude this essay with a comment about why containment was more successful in Europe than in Asia. The USA devoted massive resources to Europe and thus avoided the threat of communism, while in Asia the arrival of communist revolutionary leaders with genuine national popularity such as Mao or Ho Chi Minh meant that even US dollars were of only limited effect.

2 This question falls into two categories: those occasions on which the USA was reluctant to become involved in international affairs, and those when the USA enthusiastically interfered in world diplomacy.

The first examples should take the essay from the reluctant intervention in the First World War through to the isolationism of the 1920s. This should obviously include a section explaining the USA's encouragement to create the League of Nations but its ultimate absence from it.

Once again the USA played a crucial role in the outbreak of the Second World War through its isolationism and Hitler's belief that this policy would remain so. The Japanese attack on Pearl Harbor seems to have produced the major change in American policy in the 20th century. You could include Roosevelt's quote (p.143) about abandoning the idea of isolation at this point.

From 1941 to 1953, the USA played an active role in international affairs through its involvement in the Second World War and post-war diplomacy.

The final section of this question requires you to assess whether the USA's involvement has indeed been crucial. You should explain how the major conflicts of this century and indeed the Cold War have been significantly if not decisively affected by the USA.

US domestic policy 1930–1990

Checkpoints

1 The American involvement in Vietnam obviously had many consequences for foreign policy. It signalled the end of

the aggressive policy of containment in Asia and a more rational approach to Asian communism. Kissinger's brokered peace deal of 1973 led to the final withdrawal of American troops and the conversion of South Vietnam to communism two years later. The US government came to recognise that determined, nationalistic, guerrilla warfare was almost impossible to defeat.

2 Nixon's successor, Gerald Ford, claimed his main aim was to restore public faith in the presidency. The extent to which he succeeded may be gauged from the fact that Jimmy Carter defeated Ford in the 1976 presidential campaign on the promise that he would not 'lie' to the American people.

The consequences for the presidency itself have been a more determined resistance by Congress to allowing the sort of arbitrary control demonstrated by Roosevelt.

Exam questions

1 This question requires you to cover a long period of American history, from 1930 to 1944. You will obviously need to cover a wide range of reasons for the popular support enjoyed by Roosevelt. You can divide the reasons for Roosevelt's support into three sections: economic reasons, personal reasons and his opponents.

The economic chaos caused by the Wall Street Crash of 1929 was the single biggest reason why FDR was elected for the first time in 1932. The Depression signalled the end of the American belief, fostered by the Republican presidents of the 1920s, that America had defeated poverty permanently. Roosevelt was able to benefit electorally from these false promises.

The recovery of the 1930s under FDR's New Deal was not as spectacular as many have claimed, but it did at least put the USA on the road to recovery. This increased after the outbreak of European war, when new markets for American exports were found.

Roosevelt also appealed to the ordinary American citizen, as can be seen by the landslide victories of 1932 and 1936. He seemed to offer something to the 'forgotten man'. Behind this down-to-earth approach was a political ambition that encouraged FDR to take risks and challenge the American system.

Finally, you should mention the weakness of FDR's opponents: the failure of Hoover to address the Depression led to the belief that the Republicans did not care for the ordinary Americans who were suffering from poverty. While this view has certainly been exaggerated, it convinced many people that FDR was their only hope.

You should also mention Roosevelt's fears that isolationism would lead to catastrophe; this persuaded him to stand for re-election in 1940.

This essay needs a realistic conclusion showing which of these factors was the most responsible for FDR's outstanding electoral success. While personal characteristics may have given FDR his personal popularity, economic factors were most responsible for his record four terms in office.

2 The key to this question is to recognize the different experiences of different racial groups within the USA's multi-racial society. The experiences of the black population of the southern states are obviously radically different from those of Irish-Americans.

You should begin by explaining the idea behind the 'melting pot' theory.

An analysis of American prosperity is appropriate. The question does not specify a time period, so you can afford to choose examples from a range of eras. The boom years of the 1920s and the post-war boom experienced in American industrial production lend much weight to the argument about prosperity.

You must contrast these arguments with the fact that not all areas of American society enjoyed even the boom years. Certain racial groups, notably newer immigrants and blacks, suffered throughout the boom and were the hardest hit in the Depression.

Your essay should also cover the area of the Civil Rights movement. The financial prosperity of many areas of American society does not justify the inequality experienced by the black population in the 20th century.

You should analyse the main events of the Civil Rights movement without devoting the entire essay to only one aspect of the question.

To conclude, you should argue that while American society has blended many different races together, their experiences are still to some extent dictated by their ethnic origin.

China under communism

Checkpoints

1 Karl Marx originally believed that the communist revolution would occur in an industrialized Western society, preferably Britain or Germany. Yet neither Russia nor China were predominantly industrial in 1917 and 1949, respectively. Both of these societies were still agricultural when communism took hold.

The connection between them seems to be that the existing imperial regime, foreign in the case of China, did not adapt or evolve to the changing situation, leading to their collapse in the 20th century.

2 Both China and the USSR felt they needed to increase industrial production in order to defend themselves from foreign aggression. The USSR led the way with the formation of Stalin's five-year plans in 1928. This came after Lenin had been forced to take 'a step backwards in order to move forward' by introducing the NEP In 1921.

The Chinese were initially able to benefit from the Russian experience by borrowing their technology and initiatives, Mao introducing his First Five-Year Plan in 1952.

Equally, both countries struggled to increase production naturally and were forced into repressive techniques to persuade the public to remain involved. The use of propaganda is also a similarity.

Eventually, both countries significantly increased their positions in the world economy, although it was the USSR that achieved this first.

Exam questions

1 You should begin questions such as this by dealing with the similarities:

- Both of these initiatives were Maoist attempts to increase production in both agriculture and industry.
- Both drives were accompanied by a massive wave of propaganda to persuade the ordinary citizen to play their part in the further development of the People's Republic.
- Both were prompted by Mao's belief that the new class of experts had become a capitalist style of middle class and were encouraging corruption and inequality.
- Both were attempts to pursue a more pure style of communism.

There were also a number of key differences:

- The Great Leap Forward had its roots in the desire to see China compete industrially with the West, while the Cultural Revolution was a Maoist attempt to restore his own position of supremacy after the failure of the Great Leap Forward and the hundred flowers campaign.
- The Cultural Revolution was led by the militant Red Guards, who were fervent in their propaganda-fed support for Mao. This contributed to its ultimate disastrous failure.

2 For this question, you need to remind yourself about the reasons why China became communist in 1949. You should explain that the three main reasons for communist success in 1949 were the poverty of the population, the succession of foreign invasions and civil war, and also the backward attitudes of most Chinese people, especially those in rural communities.

Your essay should analyse these problems in the light of the communist experience.

Poverty is still common in China. Although living standards have improved, there are still restrictions on personal freedoms.

Attitudes throughout rural China have slowly changed to a point where new innovations such as Western medicines are not automatically shunned.

Finally, China has managed to avoid foreign intervention and invasion since communist rule.

You should conclude that while communism has not solved the practical problems of poverty and a lack of education, it is slowly improving these areas, while China has at least become self-governed.

Chinese foreign policy

Checkpoints

1 Mao's statement (p.149) encourages a union of all people's democracies throughout the world. This kind of alliance was precisely what the USA and other Western nations feared would lead to the worldwide growth of communism and potentially the end of capitalism.

Clearly, the USA was relieved when Mao fell out with Khrushchev after 1953.

2 The domino theory is the name given to the idea that communism would spread rapidly throughout Asia from one country to its neighbours like a row of dominoes toppling over when the first is pushed.

The USA believed that it was vital to prevent any of the countries of South-east Asia 'falling' to communism if they were to prevent the whole Asian continent from becoming communist. This is why the USA was so eager to spend vast amounts of money defending South Korea and Vietnam.

Exam questions

1 This question is spread over a long period of time, between 1949 and the 1990s. You should focus on the main trends in Chinese–Soviet relations, i.e. cooperation before 1953 and conflict afterwards.

First, you should discuss the support for China from Stalinist Russia, for example the collaboration over the first Chinese five-year plan in 1952, and the presence of many Russian advisers to assist the development of Chinese industrial production.

Your next section should explain the reasons for the breakdown in relations between the two countries, such as the personal animosity between Mao and Khrushchev, Mao's belief that Khrushchev was betraying the legacy of Lenin by his policy of peaceful coexistence, and Khrushchev's belief that Mao's China should be junior partner to the USSR.

You should then mention some of the outbreaks of hostility between the two countries, such as the Ussuri River incident in 1969 or the removal of Russian advisers during the Great Leap Forward.

You should conclude that the variable relationship between the world's two great communist powers has led to a reduction in tension between the capitalist powers and the communists. The détente of the 1970s occurred because neither the USSR nor China wanted to be isolated.

2 In this question, you must examine the merits of the statement you have been given and then provide an alternative theory.

The statement rests on the Chinese experience before communism. It is therefore relevant for you to discuss this area briefly; you should stress how the history of foreign intervention and oppression had created a culture of mistrust of all foreigners, especially Western imperialists.

You should avoid the temptation to write an essay about pre-communist history.

It would then be appropriate to summarize the main communist foreign policy principles, explaining how the relationship between the USA and Chiang Kai-shek soured Chinese relations with the USA even further.

Your essay should then give examples of Chinese attempts to protect or extend its territory (Tibet, Korea and Vietnam). China felt threatened by foreign powers intervening in Asia and therefore attempted to prevent this.

Chinese foreign policy has only differed from the principle of self-reliance since the 1970s when relations with the West improved in the Nixon era, although you could argue that this is partly because China felt less threatened after the USA withdrew from Vietnam.

Relations with the USSR seem to challenge the statement in the question. However, you should point out that positive relations were developed only because of the common bond of communism, and were brief, 1949–1960.

Conclusion – you should reassert the merits of the statement in the question with the caveat of relations with the USSR and the détente with the West since the 1970s.

Soviet foreign policy

Checkpoints

1 Unlike his predecessor Lenin, Stalin believed that all other goals should be sacrificed in order to achieve Russian protection. As you can see from the quote (p.150), his aim was to develop Russian heavy industry to such an extent that the USSR could compete militarily with the West.

2 The wartime alliance between Stalin and the West was one of convenience. In the 1930s he had been convinced that Britain, France and the USA would gladly see Hitler invade the USSR and attempt to destroy communism. To prevent this, Stalin authorised the Molotov–Ribbentrop Pact in 1939. This in turn made it clear to the Western allies where Stalin's main priority lay, in other words the protection of the USSR. There was therefore an underlying mistrust between East and West before the Cold War.

3 The emergence of Lech Walesa's independent trade union Solidarity in the early 1980s was a vital breakthrough for the West. It showed to the world, and most importantly the communist bloc, that the communist party did not represent the workers.

Although Solidarity was banned, Walesa put under house arrest and martial law imposed under Jaruzelski, with hindsight it shows that soviet control of Eastern Europe was beginning to weaken.

4 The Cuban crisis was an important moment for the USSR. It meant that it finally had a direct threat to the US mainland, from its bases on Cuba. This increased the already heightened tension of the Cold War.

The eventual back-down led to improved relations between the superpowers and the development of the 'hot line' link between the Kremlin and the White House.

Exam questions

1 The statement makes a bold claim about Russian foreign policy. You should be able to present a case that both challenges the statement and agrees with it.

It is easier to deal with the challenge to the statement. You should be able to build up a case that shows continued Soviet aggression in Eastern Europe, beginning with the territory they gained in Poland at the end of the First World War. This can be followed through to the 1939 Nazi–Soviet Pact, again increasing Soviet claims in Poland.

The post-war settlement and the ruthless way in which pro-communist governments were set up in the countries of Eastern Europe should also be explained as Soviet aggression.

Similarly, you can argue that Soviet influence in Asia as late as the invasion of Afghanistan in 1979 shows that the USSR was still attempting to extend the influence of communism, and Russian communism in particular, throughout the globe. In this argument you should draw a line of continuity through the various Soviet leaders, Lenin, Stalin, Khrushchev and so on, all of whom have extended communism further, for either practical or ideological reasons.

The opposite argument should also be explained thoroughly. In this argument, you should take the brief period of Lenin's pursuit of 'world communism' and contrast it with Stalin's pragmatic belief of 'socialism in one country'.

To argue that Soviet foreign policy has been defensive in character you should explain that all areas of Soviet concern, with the exception of Cuba, have been on the perimeter of the USSR, therefore expansionism has had the purpose of protection.

The Cuban crisis is the obvious exception to this rule, yet you should be able to explain that by the 1960s it was important for the USSR to threaten the USA in the same way as the USA threatened the USSR from its numerous bases in West Germany.

The change in leadership is again relevant: only Lenin believed in extending communism directly, and this period lasts for only five years. You should trace this line of development through Stalin's beliefs to Khrushchev's 'peaceful coexistence' and the period of détente in the 1970s.

Examiner's secrets

The examiner will expect you to have a broad overview of Soviet foreign policy but be able to refer to specific examples clearly.

2 To answer this question you should first question how different the foreign policies of Khrushchev and Stalin actually were.

You should use examples such as Cuba, Hungary and the Berlin Wall to point out that the USSR continued to maintain its position in Eastern Europe and indeed threaten the USA in the case of Cuba.

You should then explain why Khrushchev was able to follow a policy of 'peaceful coexistence' with the West:

First, Khrushchev was not as obsessed with the idea of Russian security as his predecessor, but this may be because of the improvements in heavy industry and military hardware under Stalin.

Second, the USSR felt more stable by 1953. The victory against Nazism in 1945 was a morale-boosting win for the USSR and enabled Khrushchev to follow a more rational approach to foreign policy.

Conclusion – argue that Khrushchev's policy was still to present a firm stance against Western aggression, but without the rhetoric of Stalinist days.

US foreign policy from 1953

Checkpoints

1 The significance of Cuba for Kennedy was twofold: first, he was able to claim publicly that he had stood up to the USSR when it threatened US citizens for the first time. This was obviously a propaganda success.

Second, relations between the superpowers were improved by the development of the 'hot line' between the two leaders.

2 Successive US presidents have struggled to maintain the balance of Middle East politics. The large and powerful American Jewish community has meant that the USA has always strongly supported the state of Israel, but this has often soured relations between the USA and the vital oil-producing Arab world.

Exam questions

1 The key word in this question is 'contrast'. You must consider Eisenhower's containment in relation to Kennedy's.

Therefore you should point out the similarities and the differences.

You should compare the aims of both presidents, which were largely similar, to accept the existence of the communist countries in Eastern Europe while aggressively pursuing containment in Asia.

The methods of new look (Eisenhower) and flexible response (Kennedy) should now be explained, as this is where the key difference lies. While the new look scaled down conventional forces in the front line, Kennedy's flexible response used nuclear, conventional and covert methods of intimidation to suppress communism.

You should conclude by summarizing the differences and similarities of the two presidents' attempts to prevent the growth of communism, and suggest reasons why these differences occurred.

2 There is a similar question to this on the section 'US foreign policy 1917–1953'. You should approach this essay in a similar way but focus on the period from Eisenhower to Ford.

The essay breaks down into geographical areas: Latin America, Asia and Europe. You should take each of these areas in turn and state the level of success of containment:

- The situation in Latin America saw the rise of Castro's communist Cuba. Here there is evidence to suggest that US policies drove Castro closer to the USSR when he would otherwise have remained neutral. The propaganda success of the missile crisis should not detract you from the persistence of communism in Cuba.
- Similarly, the disastrous intervention in Vietnam has not prevented the spread of communism in Asia. The reasons why should also be briefly explored: guerrilla warfare and passionate support for inspirational local leaders.
- You should also mention the situation in the Middle East, where US attempts to prevent nationalism were successful in Iran but failed in the Lebanon. In both of these cases the US government confused nationalism with communism.
- The European situation has been more of a propaganda war than military conflict. This is also the area where the USA has enjoyed the most success. You should explain the stand-off achieved in Europe in the 1960s after the Berlin Wall's erection and the gradual increase in anti-communist protest throughout the 1970s and 1980s.

You should conclude that ultimately containment has succeeded as communism has not spread beyond its limits after the Vietnam War concluded in the 1970s. The modern collapse of Russian communism suggests that the policy has worked. However, you should be able to draw the examiner's attention to the many failures along the way and the connection between a less aggressive stance and the collapse of communism.

The end of European empires

Checkpoints

1 The partition of India in 1947 led to a series of religious conflicts between the mainly Muslim north and the predominantly Hindu south. These regional characteristics are only generalizations, as the population of India is genuinely mixed. The formation of Muslim Pakistan and eventually Bangladesh calmed the situation eventually but led to a series of brutal crises between religious refugees. Conflict still exists over the disputed Kashmir territory on the border between India and Pakistan.

2 The dogged French approach to Algeria was really the result of the humiliation of Nazi occupation between 1940 and 1945 and the loss of French Indochina. The French felt that Algeria was where they were determined to make a stand. This had disastrous results.

3 Guerrilla warfare differs from conventional warfare in that it involves hit and run tactics rather than open fighting, although this often occurs. The American experience in Vietnam and the French conflict in Algeria demonstrate the impotence of conventional forces to wipe out determined guerrillas. The enemy is usually invisible and made up of the local population. Thus reprisals are the only way of attempting to prevent further terrorism. This has the effect of alienating the local population and increasing their sympathies for the guerrillas.

Exam question

This is a straightforward question that requires you to explain the many reasons for the growth of aspirations for independence throughout the colonies:

- The culture of rebellion was present as early as the 1776 American War of Independence.
- The Russo-Japanese war of 1904–1905 shattered the myth that Europeans were invincible.
- The Great War lost the European powers the respect of their colonies, and weakened them financially. The European powers actively encouraged their enemies' colonies to revolt during the war.
- The Great War also led to the independence of 'white' colonies such as Canada and Australia – the only justification for maintaining other colonies seemed to be racism.
- The colonies themselves were able to campaign vociferously, often with the benefit of European education. This led to independence organizations such as the India Congress or the Pan-African Congress.
- The Second World War finally led to the decline of most colonies, the example of Asia is a good one where the nationalist resistance groups fought against Japanese invasion and gained popularity.

Finally, you should emphasize the post-war situation, which encouraged independence as the European nations were in no position financially to defend their possessions, and the new superpowers vehemently opposed colonialism. This is the most important section and deserves a detailed argument.

The recovery of Western Europe

Checkpoints

1 The principle behind the Marshall Plan was that communism would thrive where poverty predominated. Thus the financial restoration of wartorn Europe was vital if communism was to be contained.

2 Economic unity could be achieved through the intervention of banks and business organizations. It was also possible to show how mutual prosperity could be achieved in the aftermath of the war.

Political unity, on the other hand, was a much more serious engagement as countries, notably Britain and Denmark, feared the loss of national identity that would result from supranationalism.

Exam question

This question can easily fall into a personal or judgemental view of European politics. You should avoid this and concentrate on the many agreements between the European nations.

First, NATO and the various military agreements should be considered as a success, on the basis that war has been avoided between European nations since 1945. However, it is also worth pointing out that although Europe has been a secure military entity since the arrival of NATO, the threat of invasion has been minimal.

You should also consider the successes of the ECSC in that it was intended to form a union between the 'enemies' of the Second World War. To this end it should be considered a success; however, the opposition of countries such as Britain and the Scandinavian nations meant that its economic value was negated.

Thus the EEC or EU, in its current form, can also fall into both camps: in many eyes it is a huge success, fostering cultural, economic and political links. However, its many critics argue that supranationalist views mean the loss of national independence. These criticisms are just as popular now as in the 1960s.

The various attempts at political unity such as the Council of Europe or the Nordic Council have also had many critics. You should attempt to argue the case for both success and failure of these institutions.

You should conclude by questioning what the aims of this European unity were. If they were simply to present a strong barrier to potential enemies then the case for success or failure is very different than if economic and political union are considered the main aims.

The end of the Cold War

Checkpoint

The original slogan of the Bolshevik Party in 1917 in the midst of the Great War was 'peace, bread and land'. As nationalist conflicts broke out in the late 1980s these sentiments were once again echoed in Moscow.

Communism failed to deliver lasting peace, the command economy did not work to the best interests of the ordinary citizen, and all land was owned by the state. To many Russians, this was no better than exploitation under the tsarist system.

Exam questions

1 When answering this question you should be careful not to answer a question on the collapse of communism in

Russia. While this is relevant, the main focus of this question is the loss of control over the regions of the USSR.

A brief account of the collapse of communism with an explanation of Gorbachev's key reforms of *perestroika* and *glasnost* is essential. You should then explain the link between the third strand of Gorbachev's reforms, demo-cratization, and the loss of control over the regions.

The regions had witnessed the reluctance of the Soviet leader to send troops to help Honecker's communist regime in the DDR, which gave them the confidence to elect non-communist leaders in their regional assemblies. This was facilitated by Gorbachev.

Finally, you should explain that the main reason for the break-up of the USSR was that the Communist Party had never possessed a mandate from the majority of the citizens of the USSR. The attempts to forge national unity were impossible in such a diverse territory, and the regions had never been as convinced of the merits of communism as Russia itself, where communism was also beginning to fall.

Examiner's secrets

You can use a question such as this to bring in some very current themes, such as the position of Yeltsin and Putin or the continuing struggle of nationalist groups in Russia. But beware: these issues quickly become out of date.

2 This question is one of a number of variations on a similar theme, i.e. the collapse of communism. You should attempt to adjust the structure of your essay to suit this precise question.

You should begin by giving a brief explanation of the size and diversity of the territory of the USSR, pointing out that there are no common bonds of language, climate, culture, history or even religion.

The diversity of the USSR's population made it impossible to appeal to a common ideal.

You should then discuss the practical problems experienced by Soviet leaders in maintaining discipline over Soviet territory, and from 1945 to 1989 this could include the Eastern bloc countries.

The fragile balance was preserved by the use of terror, propaganda and intimidation.

Gorbachev's policies of *perestroika*, *glasnost* and democratization actively encouraged what previous hard-line leaders had tried to avoid.

You could conclude that the experience of Russia before communism suggests that a lack of experience of democratic government may mean that autocracy was indeed the best method of controlling such a diverse territory.

To be an effective student of A- or AS-level History you need to develop your skills in historical reasoning and critical analysis of primary and secondary evidence, and learn to construct well-supported historical arguments. Examiners want to see that you can take a body of facts and ideas and apply them to a specific historical question to come to a reasoned conclusion. This section focuses on these key skills. It is designed to be used with any syllabus content. Just adapt the examples for the topics that you are studying.

Exam boards

In order to organize your notes and revision you will need a copy of your exam board's syllabus specification. You can obtain a copy by writing to the board or by downloading the syllabus from the board's website.

→ **AQA** (Assessment and Qualifications Alliance)
  Publications Department, Stag Hill House, Guildford, Surrey
  GU2 5XJ – **www.aqa.org.uk**

→ **EDEXCEL**
  Stewart House, 32 Russell Square, London WC1B 5DN –
  www.edexcel.org.uk

→ **OCR** (Oxford, Cambridge and Royal Society of Arts)
  1 Hills Road, Cambridge CB2 1GG – **www.ocr.org.uk**

→ **WJEC** (Welsh Joint Education Committee)
  245 Western Avenue, Cardiff CF5 2YX – **www.wjec.co.uk**

→ **NICCEA** (Northern Ireland Council for Curriculum,
  Examinations and Assessment)
  Clarendon Dock, 29 Clarendon Road, Belfast BT1 3BG –
  www.ccea.org.uk

Topic checklist

○ AS ● A2

	AQA	EDEXCEL	OCR	WJEC
Reading and note taking	○●	○●	○●	○●
Interpreting historical writing	○●	○●	○●	○●
Questioning documents	○●	○●	○●	○●
Answering document questions	○●	○●	○●	○●
Direct answers to essay questions	○●	○●	○●	○●
Essay writing	○●	○●	○●	○●
Structured questions	○	○	○	○
Personal Study and synoptic writing	●	●	●	●
Effective revision in history	○●	○●	○●	○●

Reading and note taking

The amount of reading and note taking you will be expected to do may seem daunting. It is important to be selective in your reading and to make your notes as concise and purposeful as you can.

Reading with a purpose

How can you cope with the vast quantity of reading material available? First, select what you read carefully. Then read and make notes with a clear purpose in mind.

Types of reading material

→ **A-level texts** – specifically written for A-level, usually with study questions to guide you through the book.
→ **General histories** – written for academic study at many levels, these are by renowned historians and tend to cover large periods or themes.
→ **Historical monographs** – written by the specialist historian for specialist study. These will tend to have important and even controversial conclusions and be the result of original historical research. They are useful for in-depth study.
→ **Historical journals** – some are written for the general historian; others are more specialized. A journal article may be an excellent introduction to a current historical debate.

As a rule, start with the general and work up to the specific. If in doubt, check with your teacher what you should be reading.

Selective reading

Before you begin your reading you have to ask yourself what you want to achieve. Do you need to find a specific set of facts? Are you looking for information about a particular person or issue? Are you just reading generally to increase your understanding of a period and are on the look-out for ideas you had not encountered before?

You do not always have to read every word, let alone every chapter, of a book. Start by looking carefully at the book's subject matter. Chapter headings and a quick scan through the introduction will help you to work out which parts are relevant.

→ **Skim-reading** – this is quickly looking through a page or chapter to find out the basic subject matter and whether it is relevant for you to look at it more closely. If irrelevant, move on.
→ **Searching for particular information** – reading more slowly but with a very distinct purpose in mind. If you are trying to construct a timeline then look out for dates or other indications ('the following year', etc.).
→ **In-depth study** – careful reading of a passage to examine a historian's evaluation of a situation. It is normal to have to read some passages more than once in order to understand the full meaning.

Note taking

Note taking performs two functions:

→ Recording useful information for essays and exam revision.
→ Organizing your ideas and selecting the key points of a situation.

Developing your note-taking style

There are many different ways of taking notes. Practise to develop your own style.

→ Notes should be brief and to the point – cut out unnecessary content.
→ Notes do not need to be grammatical – use abbreviations and symbols.
→ Try arranging your notes in patterns and diagrams with arrows linking key events and concepts. Use numbering and bullet points. This will be particularly helpful if you have a visual memory.
→ One useful tactic is to draw a very wide margin along the right-hand side of your paper. Write your notes in the left-hand column, leaving the right-hand column to add information from later reading and research.
→ Keep a record of your sources of information. Put specific book and page references in the margin so that you can return to your sources. If a passage is particularly good, do not write it out, just make a reference.
→ Rewrite your notes. This should be part of your ongoing revision process.
→ When taking notes in lessons, listen closely to the teacher's tone of voice and learn to distinguish when something important is being stressed. Teachers often repeat key points.

An exercise in reading and note taking

Follow the instructions opposite as an exercise in putting all this into practice. As you go, note down and look up unfamiliar words.

> By the eighteen-sixties the population of England and Wales had been boosted by a further five million since the accession of Queen Victoria. Again the large towns showed a disproportionate increase, reflected most dramatically in the Irish migrations into Liverpool in the forties. The dilatory and flimsy schemes elaborated by the early Victorians did little more than hold their own with the widening nature of the problems it was hoped they would solve. In a word, pauperdom, the death rate and the level of crime were little better in 1865 than in 1835. As if to underline this fact with harrowing and graphic poignancy, the cotton famine shook Lancashire profoundly in the eighteen-sixties. The adverse effects of the American Civil War created extensive unemployment in the cotton areas, and attendant upon it came near-starvation, an epidemic of typhus or 'famine fever', as it was aptly called, and then, to cap it all, the scourge of cholera once more in 1866.

Eric C. Midwinter (1968) *Victorian Social Reform*, Longman

Interpreting historical writing

Historians tend to disagree with each other. This is the nature of the subject. Your task is to approach historical writing critically and somehow form your own conclusions about which is the most appropriate interpretation.

Why do historians disagree?

The first step is understanding the reasons behind disagreement.

Different access to evidence

If historians are working with different evidence in the first place then there are bound to be differences of interpretation. A good historian will seek out all the evidence available, but this will depend on the place and time in which they are writing. Most official government papers will be kept confidential for a set time period. In Britain the 30-year rule generally applies, but some particularly sensitive documents may be withheld from public view for much longer. The private papers of individuals may be held back by their families until after their deaths. Other documents may only come to light many years later by accident. Furthermore, changing political situations can affect the access to documentary evidence. A classic example is the way in which the collapse of the Soviet empire has allowed Western historians access to previously hidden Soviet archives. This has led to a reappraisal of many aspects of Russian and Soviet history.

Different historical perspectives

Consider the historian's purpose. They may have a particular ideo-logical standpoint, which conditions the perspective they have on the past. For example, historians influenced by Marxist theories of history will tend to focus on the economic relationship between classes rather than the importance of individuals. Other historians, who believe in the importance of individual action, will tend to look upon the same events with different eyes. Historians who are attempting a balanced survey of a particular period will write in a different way from historians who are trying to put forward a radical new interpretation of that period.

Writing at different times

The present in which we live affects our view of the past. In other words, we know what happened next but not what will happen. Historians are conditioned by the present in which they live. British historians of the late nineteenth century (nicknamed the 'Whig historians') were writing at a time when the British Empire covered a third of the world's population, British industry dominated the world's trade routes, and the British system of government seemed to offer a sense of security and peace, unlike its revolution-torn European neighbours. They saw British history as an irreversible line of progress stretching from the Magna Carta to the present day and wrote history that reflected this, feeling that somehow the British had 'got it right'.

The jargon

Karl Marx was one of the most influential thinkers of the nineteenth century. As well as being the 'father' of communism, Marx developed an important theory of history that explained historical developments by looking at the changing economic relationships between different groups in societies.

Historiography is the study of how history is written and how successive generations of historians reinterpret the past.

Fifty years later, after a world war had left Britain struggling both imperially and economically, historians' views of Britain's past were different. Similarly, American views in the 1950s of the Soviet Union were heavily conditioned by the fanatical anti-communism that gripped American society in the McCarthy era. Russian views of their own history are now influenced by the knowledge that communism collapsed in the early 1990s.

Interpreting these differences

How can you begin to make sense of all these differences?

Know the historian

Find out about the historian you are reading. When were they writing? Who are they? Where do they come from? Where did they find their evidence? Are they promoting a particular ideological viewpoint?

Read their writing critically

Do not assume that just because an historian is, for example, an American writing about the Cold War, they will be prejudiced against the Soviet Union. People are more complex than this. If this is what you think, look for evidence of this in the writing. Test their interpretation against what you already know. If you find no evidence of prejudice then do not make it up just to fit your theory. On the other hand, no matter how respected the historian you are reading, you should always try to think of an alternative interpretation or argument.

An exercise in interpreting historical writing

Read through the passages below about Disraeli and the 1867 Second Reform Act and then answer the questions opposite.

A: from P. Adelman (1970) *Gladstone, Disraeli and Later Victorian Politics,* Longman.
It is now clear that Disraeli's attitude during the Reform crisis was purely opportunistic. He neither sought to 'educate his party', nor displayed firmness or consistency of purpose in his support for 'democracy'. Indeed, during these months Disraeli had only one major aim: to destroy Gladstone's leadership over a united Liberal Party, and, by seizing the initiative in reform himself and promoting a Reform Bill, to consolidate his own leadership of the Conservative Party.

B: from John K. Walton (1990) *Disraeli,* Routledge.
The Second Reform Act provides a further illustration of Disraeli's concern to use a necessary measure of reform to sustain the threatened power and fortunes of the landed interest. It was expressly intended to make the world a more congenial place for Conservatives . . . the important thing for Disraeli . . . was to sustain and strengthen the influence of landed Conservatism of the counties and boroughs.

"There is no final end to the study of history"

G. R. Elton, *The Practice of History*

The jargon

Objectivity is trying to explain exactly what happened. *Subjectivity* is when the writer's personal viewpoint colours their interpretation of the facts. Most historians would argue that complete objectivity in history is impossible.

The jargon

A *judgement* is an opinion, well supported by the factual evidence.

Test yourself

Even if this is not a topic you are studying, try these questions about Disraeli's motives:
1 How do historians agree and disagree about Disraeli's motives?
2 Why might this be the case?

Answers:
They do agree about what Disraeli did not want but put different emphases on what he did want. Blake emphasizes that Disraeli wanted to destroy Gladstone and become leader of the Conservatives, Walton argues that he was more interested in strengthening the Conservative vote. These views are not incompatible, they are just different stresses and probably reflect their different interpretations of the evidence available.

Questioning documents

Documents are the raw material for a historian. The key to answering document questions successfully is to learn to ask questions of the documents in front of you.

Three basic questions

When reading a document, three basic questions should be running through your mind:

1 **Who?** – who wrote/created the document you are studying? Do you know anything about them? Are they *contemporary* or a historian?
2 **When?** – when was the document first written? How first-hand is the content? Was the author present at the events being described, or was it written long after?
3 **Why?** – what was the author's purpose? Was it just to record events privately? Is it a public speech written to persuade an audience? Is it written by a historian trying to explain/understand the past?

You need to be thinking of these questions as you first read through a document, before you look at the questions the examiner actually wants you to answer.

Types of documentary evidence

You will be asked to look at extracts from a range of sources. The three basic questions remain, but different types of source raise particular issues.

Official papers

These are documents drafted by government ministers and civil servants. Do not assume that they are purely factual but think about the purpose of the author. Is anything being concealed? Is the author overstating the case in order to persuade a minister to introduce a new policy?

Private papers and diaries

Think carefully about who was meant to see these. This will affect how accurate the author is in stating their real feelings and thoughts. Also, be aware that they may offer a very personal view of events and be highly subjective.

Public speeches and debates

Again think of the audience and the purpose of this speech. Keep in mind that it is meant to be heard, not read. Listen to the document – in what tone of voice would it have been delivered? What message does the speaker want to get across? Is the message being simplified for a mass audience? What is being left unsaid?

Newspapers and political journals

Be aware of the political outlook of the newspaper or journal from which the extract is taken. It may be obvious from the content. Is this an on-the-spot article or a considered piece of journalism? If it is strongly opinionated keep in mind that the readership would not necessarily agree with the opinions being expressed. Have you any evidence that the report would have been officially censored or been subject to *self-censorship*?

Autobiographies and memoirs

Look very carefully at the authorship. What evidence is there that they had first-hand knowledge of the events they are describing? Think about the purpose of the author in writing their autobiography or memoir. Authors may be wishing to justify actions they took earlier in their careers or may even be exaggerating their own importance. On the other hand, they may be able to look back at events with a degree of impartiality and hindsight.

Statistical evidence

Do not take statistics at face value just because they are numbers. Think about who collected the statistics and their purpose. Was it purely to see what the state of things was or was there an ulterior motive such as trying to prove the success of a particular policy? Think about what has been left out while you are looking at what has been included.

Political cartoons

Sometimes you may get a political cartoon. These will have been published originally in a newspaper or journal, and while they may have been designed to make the readership chuckle they will contain a serious comment on a contemporary situation. Your first task will be to unravel the meaning of the cartoon to discover the point that is being made. Look at the details of the cartoon to get the depth of the cartoonist's meaning. Think about how a contemporary audience would react to the message of the cartoon – what sorts of people would agree with the cartoonist, and who would disagree?

Historians

Particularly at A2, you may be asked to evaluate historians' comments on a historical situation. The three questions are still relevant. Who is the historian? Do you know anything about them and the assumptions they bring to their historical study? When did they write? What evidence was available to them and how did the situation they were in affect their judgement of a historical situation? Why were they writing? Did they have a particular argument they wished to put across? Read the section 'Interpreting historical writing' (p.172) for more details about how to tackle the work of historians.

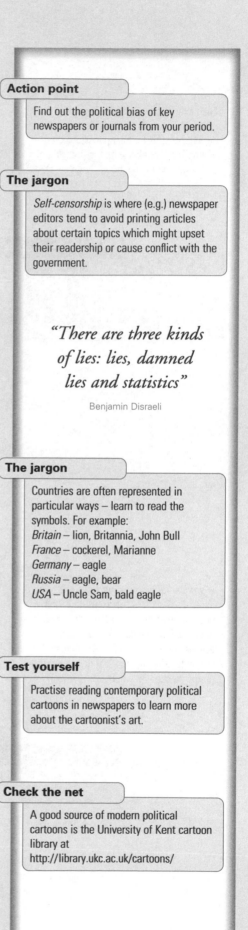

Action point

Find out the political bias of key newspapers or journals from your period.

The jargon

Self-censorship is where (e.g.) newspaper editors tend to avoid printing articles about certain topics which might upset their readership or cause conflict with the government.

"There are three kinds of lies: lies, damned lies and statistics"

Benjamin Disraeli

The jargon

Countries are often represented in particular ways – learn to read the symbols. For example:
Britain – lion, Britannia, John Bull
France – cockerel, Marianne
Germany – eagle
Russia – eagle, bear
USA – Uncle Sam, bald eagle

Test yourself

Practise reading contemporary political cartoons in newspapers to learn more about the cartoonist's art.

Check the net

A good source of modern political cartoons is the University of Kent cartoon library at
http://library.ukc.ac.uk/cartoons/

Answering document questions

Examiners expect you to be able to read and understand the documents in front of you. Questions are designed to test your ability to analyse and form judgements about documentary evidence.

Styles of document questions

Document questions are subdivided to test a range of historical skills. Common styles of question are:

Explaining references

Phrases such as, 'In the context of the documents, explain the significance of . . .' or 'Explain briefly the following references' are asking you to identify a particular phrase and its significance for the issue being discussed. Look at the marks to see how much detail you need to go into and to what extent you are expected to bring in your background knowledge. Do not be afraid to state the obvious – it may only be obvious to you because you know the answer.

Selecting content

Questions such as 'What does Document X reveal about . . .' or 'To what extent does Document Y support the view that . . .' are asking you to select information from the document for a particular task. Do not be tempted to write out the whole document on the principle that the right answer will be in there somewhere. You are being judged on your ability to select appropriate evidence.

Judging reliability

Phrases such as 'How reliable is Document X to historians studying . . .' ask you directly to consider the 'trustworthiness' of the evidence in front of you. All your basic questions come into play here, but remember that any points you make must be supported by precise evidence from the document itself. Vague points about the author being biased with no explanation will not score you any marks. Consider the authenticity of the document – does it 'ring true' with what you already know? If not, then either what you thought you knew, or the document, needs to be reappraised.

Judging usefulness

This is slightly different from judging reliability and requires you to think about the usefulness of a document for a particular task. The three questions (Who?/What?/Why?) and evaluations of reliability are part of judging a document's usefulness. So is the actual content.

Comparison questions

Usually in conjunction with one of the skills above, these ask you to directly compare one or more documents. Avoid dealing with one and then the other – try to make direct comparisons throughout your answer.

Mini-essay

Questions carrying a substantial number of marks such as 'Using the evidence of all the documents and your background knowledge . . .' are basically mini-essays. You will not get more than half marks if you use only the documents *or* your knowledge. The key is to make a mini-plan of the answer, as you would for any structured question, and to weave the evidence in as support. Do not forget to create an argument – look at both sides of the debate.

Combination questions

Some questions will be asking you to combine different skills. Do not panic. Just unpick the wording of the question and make sure you deal with all the parts.

Key tips

Do

→ Examine the document carefully before looking at the question.
→ Read the wording of the question carefully.
→ Approach documents critically – question them.
→ 'Listen' to the document – in what tone of voice would you read it? Look out for subtle sarcasm and irony.
→ Support your judgements with direct reference to the content of the document.
→ Keep quotes from the document short – a simple phrase or word is enough.
→ Check the content of the document against what you already know.
→ Spend time thinking about and planning your answer so that your answer is concise and precise.
→ Use the names of the authors when discussing a document.
→ Match the length of your answer to the marks allocated for the question.

Don't

→ Copy out the content of the document – either word for word or in paraphrase.
→ Use the words 'bias', 'primary evidence' or 'secondary evidence' – they are too often used simplistically. Think of another way to say what you mean.
→ Make vague judgements about the document based on simple facts about the author, e.g. 'The author is American, so he is bound to . . .'
→ Make up judgements that seem plausible but are not substantiated by the wording of the document.

Test yourself

Think of words to use instead of 'bias'; for example, exaggerated; prejudiced; subjective, etc.

Direct answers to essay questions

In an exam, you do not have time to waste. Irrelevance, waffle and repetition all represent wasted opportunities to show an examiner what you really can do. The key is to plan your essay so that you *directly* answer the question.

Types of essay question

Essay titles tend to fall into one of two categories:

→ **Explanatory** – which explain why or how something happened, for example 'Why did the Liberal Party decline after the First World War?'
→ **Interpretative** – in which you make judgements about a particular interpretation of events, for example 'To what extent would you agree that the First World War was responsible for the decline of the Liberal Party?'

At first glance both of these essay titles might look identical, but they actually require answering in different ways. This is true of all essay titles. Each title is unique and needs a response crafted to its particular wording. There are some general procedures that you should follow to help you to achieve this.

Unpicking the title

Analyze the title in the following ways:

→ First select the **instructive words**. These tell you what you are supposed to do. It is no use giving a detailed description of *how* the 1832 Great Reform Act was passed if the essay question asks you *why* it was passed.
→ Next look for the **main topic** of the question. What is it about? This might seem obvious, but it is vital to check what you are supposed to be writing about and what you are *not* supposed to be writing about. Dates are also crucial. They are not selected randomly by examiners but because they are significant. Ask yourself why they have been chosen. If a question is asking you about Britain and Ireland between 1868 and 1874 you need to cover the period specified but not go on to discuss events in the 1880s.
→ Lastly, look for **key words**. These tell you which aspect of the main topic you need to focus on. Look for words that need specific definition, such as 'successful' – what criteria would you use to judge success?

The jargon

Instructive words include:
How far . . .
To what extent . . .
Discuss . . .
Why . . .
Examine the role of . . .

Test yourself

Try unpicking the following questions:
1 What part was played by economic depression in stimulating radical politics in England in the period 1815–1820?
2 With what success did Bismarck deal with the problems facing Germany between 1871 and 1890?
3 Examine the view that fear of the socialists was the main factor behind Mussolini's rise to power.

To illustrate, the two questions we started with have been unpicked as follows, with the instruction words in *italics*, the main topic in **bold** and the key words <u>underlined</u>. This brings out their differences.

1 *Why* did the **Liberal Party** <u>decline</u> after the First World War?
2 *To what extent* was <u>the First World War responsible for</u> the **decline of the Liberal Party**?

Developing your argument

There are three main elements:

→ **The core response** – at A-level you are expected to create an argument to answer the question set directly. Start by imagining that you have to answer it in one basic sentence. For example, to the first question on the decline of the Liberal Party you might decide on *one* of the following responses:
  → the First World War was the key factor.
  → the decline was due to the long-term changing socio-economic situation and pre-dates 1914.
  → it was mainly due to a failure of leadership in the 1920s, and so on.
     This is your core response and will provide the main theme of your argument.

→ **Supporting evidence** – next consider the key points you need to make to support your core argument.

→ **The other side to the debate** – now look at the alternative arguments you could have made. Even if you know what your core response is gong to be you need to discuss alternative responses, and to show why you consider them less important.

The skeleton plan

Now you need to create a skeleton plan. It might help to think of each paragraph having a central idea (the 'bones'), which is then 'fleshed' out with explanation and evidence. Your skeleton plan should just consist of these 'bones'. For example, taking the second essay title on the decline of the Liberal Party, the skeleton plan might be:

1. Intro: outline core response.
2. To some extent the First World War was responsible.
3. Also role of political infighting in the 1920s, BUT
4. The decline dates back to pre-1914, when Liberals were losing touch.
5. This was because of socio-economic change and rise of Labour Party.
6. Conclusion.

Further tips on how to actually write the essay are on pp.180–1.

Tips for the exam

You might think that you have not got time to do all this in an exam. However, time spent creating a *short* plan is not wasted.

→ Practise planning in timed situations so that you get used to following the steps outlined here automatically.
→ If half-way through a plan you realize you have chosen the 'wrong' question, you still have time to change.
→ Keep referring back to the plan to check you are still on course.
→ Beware trying to change the focus of an essay to fit a topic area you would rather be discussing or a question you did previously. Stick to the question. Irrelevancies will not gain and may lose you marks.

Test yourself

Select some essay titles relevant to your course and go through the basic planning procedure. Remember the steps:
1. Unpick the question
2. Core response
3. Skeleton plan

Essay writing

Now you need to actually write the essay. You will probably develop your own essay style as you progress through the course, but here are some key pointers.

The introduction

The introduction should be short and to the point. Aim for four–six sentences. You want to cover the following three areas:

→ *Explain the question* – this involves defining the key terms in the question and explaining what you see the question as being about. The significance of dates used in the question should be commented upon.
→ *State your argument* – now state your core argument.
→ *Outline other key themes* you wish to consider and link to the first paragraph.

Key tips
These include:

→ Avoid lengthy descriptions written in the first person of how you are going to answer the title, on the lines of 'First I will look at the arguments which show that economic factors were responsible, then I will look at the arguments which show that economic factors were not responsible and then I will come to a conclusion'. This does not tell the examiner anything they are not already expecting.
→ Do not be tempted to go into long factual descriptions of the topic covered by the essay title. Impressive though your knowledge may be, you are not actually answering the question.
→ Do not use the introduction to change the wording or purpose of the question. The examiner phrased the question for a reason.

The main body of the essay

As another rule of thumb, aim for around six distinct paragraphs in your essay. Each paragraph should tackle a key theme related to your core argument. The first sentence should outline what point you are making in the paragraph. The last sentence should link to the theme of the next paragraph.

Analytical writing
Analytical writing is writing that makes judgements but uses the facts in a supporting role. Narrative writing relates the facts as a 'story' and requires the reader to come to their own analytical conclusions about why and how events came to happen. You want to aim for analytical rather than narrative writing. This will ensure that you explicitly tackle the question you have been asked and do not waste time reeling out paragraphs of accurate, fascinating but in essence useless information.

Test yourself

Practise writing introductions to key essay titles.

Test yourself

Take a photocopy of one of your old essays. Take two coloured pens and underline all the analytical sentences in one colour and all the narrative sentences in the other. You will now see clearly if you have the narrative/ analytical balance right and whether you need to reassess your essay writing. Try rewriting paragraphs in a purely analytical style.

Grammar and vocabulary

The ability to communicate clearly is one of the historian's key skills. Examiners expect you to be able to write grammatically correct English and your spelling to be accurate. You are also expected to use appropriate academic vocabulary. Mistakes will be seen as a sign that you do not take care with your work.

Especially avoid:

➜ Slang.
➜ Misspelt proper names – particularly of key historical figures.
➜ Long sentences that ramble on and on without a break.
➜ Abbreviations such as 'govt' and 'PM'. Commonplace abbreviations used in textbooks such as the names of political parties and organizations (NSDAP, WSPU) are acceptable. If in doubt do not abbreviate, or at least write it out in full first time with the abbreviation in brackets afterwards.
➜ Writing in the first person – always write in the third person.
➜ Common grammatical errors such as misplaced apostrophes.
   If you are in doubt, go and learn the correct grammatical rules.

Quotations

Quotations are a useful way to give weight to your arguments and to show evidence of your reading. Quotations can come from primary sources or from historians. There are a few key rules:

➜ Do not quote just for the sake of it. Many successful essays have no quotations at all. A poor quote is worse than no quote.
➜ Choose a quotation from a historian because it says something that you can then go on to discuss. Quotations should not be left on their own. Instead, explain the importance of the content and how it links to the argument.
➜ Quotations need not be long. Short phrases that express an idea or clever metaphors are ideal candidates for quoting.
➜ Always state the author of a quotation. Try to incorporate the author's name in to the sentence: 'Fotherinton-Smythe has argued that . . .' If you cannot do this, at least put the author's name in brackets after the quotation.
➜ You can paraphrase a historian's argument if you cannot remember it word for word.
➜ Do not try to invent quotations.

The conclusion

The conclusion rounds the essay off. Your core argument should be obvious by now, but use the conclusion to state it very firmly and to relate it back to the essay title. Some tips:

➜ The conclusion should not introduce new concepts or arguments.
➜ Avoid phrases such as 'in summary' or 'thus it can be seen' – they sound vague.
➜ Keep it short and to the point.

Examiner's secrets

'Many candidates need to improve the quality and accuracy of their use of English . . . the widespread use of 'definately', 'could of', and the equally widespread misspelling of well-known proper names represents not haste or lack of ability but sloppy preparation and bad habits.'
AEB Examiners' Reports, 1995

Test yourself

Correct this passage (answers at the foot of the page).
The nazi's spent alot of time on propaganda. The minister for propaganda goebels, could of used obvious images but prefered films that were masked as pure entertainment. Such as Historical dramas etc.

Examiner's secrets

'. . . where quotations were used excessively, irrelevantly and frequently inaccurately, there was no credit gained.'
AEB Examiners' Reports, 1998

Test yourself – answer

Parts that have been corrected are in italics.
The *Nazis* spent *a lot* (or *considerable amount*) of time on propaganda. The Minister for Propaganda, *Goebbels*, could *have* used obvious images but *preferred* films that were masked as pure entertainment, *such as* historical dramas.

Structured questions

AS exams may take the form of structured questions. These look similar to the type of question you will have encountered at GCSE, but they require more sophisticated A-level skills of evaluation and interpretation.

Types of question

Look first at the 'instruction part' of the question to see which historical skills are being examined.

Explanation questions

→ These start with words such as 'Explain how . . .', 'Explain the effects of . . .', 'Account for . . .', 'Discuss the part played by . . .', 'Examine the role of . . .'
→ These questions test your *knowledge* and *understanding* of the events you have studied.
→ You may be tempted just to write out a detailed factual account, but description, no matter how accurate, will not be enough to score the higher marks. Focus on explaining *why* the factors chosen are important.

Evaluation and assessment

→ Look for phrases such as 'Compare the importance of . . .', 'Assess the influence of . . .', 'Evaluate the role of . . .'
→ Your answer must definitely focus on explanation, not narrative.
→ Longer answers will need:
  → an introduction, giving your core response to the question;
  → a developed argument, divided into paragraphs and dealing with all the aspects of the question;
  → a conclusion, which is your more sophisticated response to the question.

Keywords

Every question has one or more keywords.

→ Look for the keywords in the question title. One of the most common failings in an examination is lack of relevance. You must ensure that you are dealing with all the aspects of the questions. Look carefully at the scope of your question – are any dates specified? How many factors must you consider? Is it about causes or consequences?
→ The following example is a question about the First World War. A list of factors has been given and this question asked. Keywords have been underlined:

Compare the importance of at least <u>three</u> of these factors in <u>affecting the lives</u> of the <u>civilian population</u> <u>during</u> the <u>First World War</u>.

Writing your answers

Length and timing

The allocated marks will indicate to you how much time and therefore how long the answer to a question should be. In timed situations it is crucial to keep an eye on the clock and be aware when you need to move on to the next questions. Keep in mind that the second or third parts of a structured question tend to be worth more than the first.

Developing an analytical approach

Compare the following two statements:

A: In 1914 the British government passed the Defence of the Realm Act, which gave it extra powers in wartime.

B: During the war the government interfered with people's daily lives in a manner that would have been unthinkable before 1914.

Statement A is a piece of description. Statement B is analytical because it makes a judgement about the novelty of government action during the First World War. Make your argument *explicit* by starting with an analytical statement and then supporting it with descriptive evidence. This is better than leaving your argument implicit by 'telling the story' and leaving the reader to make their own conclusions.

Relevance

It is crucial that you stick to the question at all times. Keep looking back at the wording to make sure that you are still on track.

Good grammar and spelling

Historians are expected to communicate in accurate and clear English. Grammatical errors and simple spelling mistakes are seen by examiners as signs of carelessness and sloppy thinking. See 'Grammar and vocabulary' in the 'Essay writing' section on p.181.

Quotations

You may want to support your judgements with those of other, more professional, historians. This can be very effective as long as your quotation is brief, accurate and explained. Again, look at the section on 'Essay writing' for more advice about using quotations.

Conclusions

Do not forget to end your answer with a brief conclusion. This should summarize your main answer and you can refer directly to the keywords to ensure that you have stuck to the focus of the question. A conclusion, though, should not be used to introduce a completely new idea or focus.

Text yourself

Look at a typical structured question for your board. Work out how much time you would have to write each part in an examination and roughly how long each answer would be in your handwriting.

The jargon

Descriptive writing is factual writing that tells the story.
Analytical writing makes judgements about historical events and developments.

Examiner's secrets

Never put in quotations just for the sake of it. If you are going to use a quotation (and you certainly do not have to) ask yourself if it is really relevant to your answer.

183

Personal Study and synoptic writing

At A2 you may have the opportunity to complete a 'course essay' or 'personal study' on a theme of your choice instead of doing an examination.

Choosing your subject

The topic must be an area in which you are interested. Course essays are very time-consuming, and you must spend considerable time on them. Choose a topic for which you have access to appropriate information. Then narrow it down to a *specific question*. Course essays are intended to be an investigation, usually with a synoptic theme (see below). If you want to look at a historical figure, for example, you need to focus the study on a line of enquiry such as 'How important was X to the events he/she was involved in?' The most successful course essays are usually those that are specific and focused. A broad or unusual topic on which it is difficult to find information will be very difficult to write. Do not worry if in the course of your research you narrow down your enquiry. Most historians work in this way.

Doing the research

Get plenty of advice on this from your teachers and anyone else who can help. Libraries are common sources of information, but be prepared to order in specific books. The internet can be a very useful research tool, but subject the material to the questions you would ask of any evidence. Look particularly carefully at the authorship and origin of the website. Some topics lend themselves to original documentary research. Evaluate evidence carefully and note any problems of interpretation or reliability to include in your study. Lastly, you may get information by writing to an appropriate museum or organization. Be polite and ask for specific information.

Recording your research

Log your research carefully. Note down the full publishing details of any books you have used for your bibliography. Keep your notes carefully and in an organized fashion in a notebook or on record cards. Some boards ask you to keep an official log or diary of your research – use this to note down problems you encounter with sources and further lines of enquiry you think about.

Writing up

This is like an extended essay. Use subheadings and read the advice in 'Essay writing' (p.181) on grammar and quotations. A high standard of presentation is expected. Stick to your word limit. Do not let yourself wander off your main line of enquiry into long descriptions. Do not forget the bibliography and any footnotes (specific references to reading and general points not part of the main enquiry). Come to a clear conclusion.

Watch out!

Check the guidelines for your particular board carefully and listen to the advice from your teacher about whether an enquiry you have chosen is really suitable.

Examiner's secrets

'The success of the study is usually dependent on the candidate selecting a manageable, challenging problem.'
AEB Examiners' Reports, 1998

The jargon

Footnoting conventions are that publishers' details. They usually follow the same format – (1) Author (2) Title (3) volume or series number, date (4) page reference.
e.g. Asa Briggs: *The Age of Improvement 1783–1867* (1979), p.147.

Synoptic writing

Within the A2 exam there will be *synoptic* writing. This involves the drawing together of your knowledge and skills to demonstrate your overall historical understanding by making connections between different parts of your course.

Examples of synoptic writing

These include:

→ Assessing the contribution of individuals to the social, political, cultural and/or economic developments of their age, for example, the role of the philanthropists in bringing about social reform in industrializing Britain.

→ Assessing the importance of an idea or philosophy to developments, e.g. the importance of imperialism in foreign policy.

→ Evaluating contemporary perspectives of a key historical event or development, for example comparing the attitudes of the social classes to industrial change in nineteenth-century Britain.

→ Looking at the process of change across the full breadth of the period studied, for example, the role played by women.

→ Comparing the similarities and differences between two leaders and/or their methods of government, for example, the ways in which Hitler and Stalin achieved dictatorial power.

→ Linking different historical perspectives on an event or development, for example, 'Explore the link between economic and political change'.

→ Comparing contemporary accounts of a key historical event, for example, the media reporting of the origins of the Cold War in the late 1940s.

Answering synoptic questions

Synoptic questions will often be phrased in a broad way. For example, you may have a question, 'How important has war been as an agent of progress in any period you have studied?' Your task is to select the appropriate area(s) you have studied to use as examples.

→ Look carefully at the restrictions placed on your answers. The question may ask you to refer to one period, or a period of at least 50 years, or at least two countries, and so on. Do not ignore this.

→ Use the 'Essay writing' advice. Plan your answer properly, be analytical, look at alternative arguments, come to a conclusion.

→ One of the biggest problems is that you may know too much. Select a few examples that you can explore in depth rather than lots of vague comments and pieces of information.

→ Use the examples you have selected to make broader judgements about the issue.

The jargon

Synoptic means 'taking or affording a comprehensive view' (*Concise Oxford Dictionary*).

Test yourself

Practise writing synoptic questions that link together different aspects of your course. Try to write at least one to cover each of the categories opposite.

Examiner's secrets

Carefully check the way in which synoptic questions are phrased for your examination board. Look at past and sample papers and practise deciding which examples you would use for each of the questions.

Effective revision in history

It is a myth that revision is something you do just before an exam. In fact, regular revision should be an essential part of your course. You are revising every time you look over your notes, rewrite them or review past topics. The key to successful revision lies in being active. This means *doing* something, such as creating new notes as you revise, rather than just reading it all through hoping that, as if by magic, all that information will somehow become permanently lodged in your long-term memory.

Long- and short-term revision

Long-term revision is mostly concerned with extending and consolidating your knowledge and understanding of topics. This involves:

→ Rewriting class notes (preferably that day) and checking that you understand it all (see section on note taking on p.171).
→ Using textbooks to go over topics covered in lessons, particularly areas you do not understand.
→ Making lists of questions you have that you can ask your teacher.

Short-term revision is the learning of key dates, numbers, detailed facts and quotations for an actual test or exam. Some strategies for this are covered below.

How your memory works

Psychologists say that everything you have ever learned is sitting somewhere in your brain. The difficult thing is trying to unlock all this knowledge when it is needed. Think about what sorts of things you tend to remember easily. They will probably display one of the following aspects:

→ **Immediacy** – you will tend to remember what you ate for lunch yesterday more vividly than what you ate for lunch on this date last year. It is important to review factual information soon after first learning it. This links to:
→ **Repetition** – you easily remember something you have been told often. Revision is a process, not a once-only exercise. You will need to revisit topics, especially those you find difficult, many times.
→ **Patterns** – facts that link to each other are easier to recall than isolated pieces of information. Try to create patterns and links you remember. This links to:
→ **Unusualness** – you will remember a fact or idea that sticks out.
→ **Visual** – many people remember things as pictures or because of their position on the page. Putting information into diagrams or setting it out using colours and pictures may help.

Test yourself

Read the following list of words slowly, without pausing or going back. When you have finished, close the book and write out all you remember. Then check the original list with your list. What part did each of the aspects listed opposite play in determining what you remembered?

fish
back
spinning
smile
Sleeping Beauty
hope
needle
wheel
it
master
great
social
mistress
street
smart
fast
smile

Some revision strategies

The key to success is to create a variety of revision notes rather than just to read through your notes and textbooks. Anything that makes your revision more interesting and memorable is worthwhile. The actual process of creating notes in a new way, for example on record cards, is what matters. As a prompt to your own ideas, a few strategies are listed below. Try them out!

Who's who

Make your own 'who's who' of all the personalities of each period. You do not need their whole life history, but key dates and the events with which they were involved. Include any particularly memorable quirks that, while not necessarily relevant in an exam question, will help you to remember the more crucial points.

Timeframes

These are a version of an extended timeline. For example, if you are studying 19th-century European history you will have generally looked at it a country at a time, yet it makes sense to see the whole picture. Take a large sheet of paper (stick two pieces of A4 together) and put the dates in the margin. Divide the page into columns, each headed with a different country, and then fill in the key events and trends for each country, one at a time. Not only do you have to look through your notes for these key events but you will also build up a broader picture of European history and be able to see events in context.

Mind maps

These are diagrams that show all the features of a period and the connections between them. Not only are you revising by creating them, but they may also help you to visualize key connections and ideas. Below, for example, is a mind map created to explain the passage of the Great Reform Act of 1832.

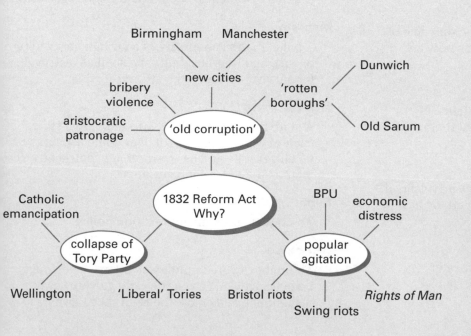

Speed learning

Use **mnemonics** to learn lists and orders of events. A mnemonic is created when you associate a fact (in this case historical) with something else you already know. Take a 'mental walk', for example along your route to school or college. Associate each of the items you wish to remember (such as the 19th-century legislation on working conditions) with different locations along your 'walk'. To remember the items you have to replay your 'walk' in your mind. Reaching the appropriate place, such as the bus stop, should trigger off the information stored there, such as the 1842 Mines Act. Try it!

Test yourself

Create your own mind maps. Start with the topic and then brainstorm ideas around it, using lines to show connections. Practise with the same topic a few times and with different topics.

Glossary

The following list contains some of the terms you should be familiar with. The list is not exhaustive – keep your own glossary of other concepts you encounter.

abdication

When a monarch voluntarily gives up his/her throne.

anarchy

When there is no government; it has come to mean a state of disorder. Anarchists campaign for a revolution that would abolish all government.

autarky

Economic self-sufficiency.

autocracy

A form of absolute government where the (hereditary) ruler has total power.

bourgeoisie

Loosely the middle classes. More strictly, the owners of the means of production.

capitalism

(Belief in) an economic system dominated by private business and the principle of production for profit.

civil rights

The rights of a citizen, especially rights to free speech, fair trial, equal treatment by the government, etc.

coalition

When two or more political parties join together in government.

communism

According to Karl Marx, the extreme outcome of socialism in which all members of society are economically equal.

conservatism

A belief that emphasizes the importance of maintaining existing institutions and that rapid change is not good.

constitutional government

Government according to a set of clearly defined rules that even those doing the governing have to obey, e.g. in a liberal democracy.

coup d'état

Where a government of a state is speedily replaced, by force, by another government.

de facto

In actual fact – especially when this is not according to the official law (opposite of **de jure**).

de jure

According to the law (opposite of **de facto**).

demagogue

A public speaker who has the ability to arouse great emotion in a crowd through a simplistic message.

democracy

A political system whereby the leaders are chosen by the people.

deploy

To make ready for use.

devolution

Delegating political power down to local or regional administration.

disarmament

Reduction in the level of arms.

Dissenter

Another word for **Nonconformist**.

elite

Those with power and influence in society.

empirical

Based on facts.

executive

The part of government responsible for day-to-day governance and carrying out decisions made by the other branches. See **judiciary** and **legislature**.

fascism

A belief in the superiority of a certain nationality or race and that life should be seen as a struggle for survival in which the strongest wins.

federal state

A state that is subdivided into individual states, each of which has control over some aspects of its citizens' lives. The overarching central government is the federal government.

fiscal

To do with government taxation policy.

franchise

The right to vote in public elections. One could be enfranchised (given the right to vote) or disenfranchised (have the right taken away).

free trade

Where there are no tariffs or other barriers to trade between countries. See **protectionism**.

hegemony

Influence and control over, as in 'US hegemony over Western Europe after 1945'.

impeach

To accuse a government minister of failing to abide by the principles and rules of their office.

imperialism

A belief in the right of one nation to take over the government of another nation.

industrialization

The process of transforming an economy into one based on the wealth created by industry and commerce.

inflation

Rises in the general level of prices.

judiciary

The part of a political system with responsibility for ensuring that the laws are maintained through the courts. See **executive** and **legislature**.

legislature

The law-making body in a political system, e.g. a parliament. See **judiciary** and **executive**.

liberalism

A belief in the importance of the freedom of the individual from unnecessary government interference.

mercantilism

The economic theory that improvements in one country's trade can only be achieved at the expense of another country.

monopoly

Sole control (usually in economic terms).

nationalism

A belief in the independence of and importance of one's nation-state.

Nonconformist

Literally, someone who does not conform. In Britain, it means a member of one of the non-Anglican Protestant Churches.

oratory

Public-speaking ability.

patronage

Using money or influence to advance the career of someone in a lower position.

petite bourgeoisie, petty bourgeoisie

The lower-middle classes.

philanthropist

Someone who seeks to use money and influence to help those less fortunate than themselves.

plebiscite

A vote on an issue put to the people. Otherwise known as a referendum.

proletariat

The working/labouring classes.

protectionism

The protection of domestically produced goods from foreign imports, usually by import tariffs.

radical

Literally, extreme, as when describing change. Radicals in the 19th century were people who demanded extreme political and social reform.

reactionary

Someone who looks back to a 'golden age' in the past to which they would like to return.

republic

A political system in which the head of state is elected.

retrenchment

Cutting back – saving money.

revolution

A complete change in the power structure of a country – can be political, social or economic.

socialism

A set of political theories that argue that the wealth of society should be shared out equally by the state.

social revolution

A revolution that seeks to alter the relationship between different classes in society and the ways in which people spend their lives.

syndicalism

Originally, a movement among French industrial workers to transfer the means of production and distribution to the workers. It has taken on different meanings, notably in fascist Italy.

universal suffrage

Every person (often this has just been restricted to men) has the right to vote.

veto

The power to block decisions or legislation.

Index

Abnormal Importations
  Act 63
Abolition of Slavery Act 1833 13
Abyssinia 64, 117, 124
Acerbo Law 117
Addison's Housing Act 1919 61
Afghanistan 40, 45, 151, 153
aggressive nationalism 64
Aix-la-Chapelle 79
Alabama case 39
Anglo-German naval
  agreement 64
Anglo-Japanese alliance 1902
  49, 56
Anti-Corn Law League 15
appeasement 65, 124, 150
aristocratic settlement 43
Army reforms 1870–1874 38–9
Artisans Dwellings Act 1875 43
Ashley, Lord 23
Asquith 53, 57, 60
Attlee, Clement 66
Attwood, Thomas 16
austerity 66
Austria 64–5, 85, 88, 90
autarky 121
authoritarian empire 86

Baldwin 62, 125
Balfour 53
Balkan crisis 1886 49
Ballot Act 1872 38–9, 46
Banquet movement 83
Bay of Pigs 152
Beaconsfieldism 40
Belgian independence 1830 25
Benthamites 12
Berlin airlift 67, 143, 151
Berlin Wall 152, 159
Bessemer converter 18
Bevan 66–7
Beveridge Report 66–7
Bevin 66
Bismarck 40, 44, 48, 85, 90–1,
  94–5, 96–7, 108
Bismarck's foreign policy 96–7
board schools 38
Boer War 41, 49
Bolsheviks 114–15
Bonar Law 60, 62
Booth 52
Boulanger affair 93
Bourbon restoration 82, 92
Bright 15
British Broadcasting
  Corporation 62
British history 1783–1868
  3–36

British history 1868–1951 37–65
'Bulgarian Atrocities' 44

Canning 8, 9, 24
Carson 51
Castlereagh 8, 24, 78
Cat and Mouse Act 55
Catholic emancipation 9
Cato Street conspiracy 7
Causes of First World War 108–9
Cavour 88
Cawdor–Fisher naval reforms 56
Central Electricity Board 62
Chadwick, Edwin 12, 22–3
Chamberlain, Joseph 40, 41, 43, 48
Chamberlain, Neville 65, 125
Chamberlain's Housing Act 62
Chartists 16–17, 20
Children's Act 1908 52
China 146–7, 148–9
cholera 22
Cholera Act 1832 23
Churchill, Winston 52, 66, 157
Civil Rights movement 145
Civil service reform 1870 38–9
Clause 4 of Labour Party
  Constitution 66
Cleveland message 49, 56
Climbing Boys Act 1875 43
Coal Mines Act 1908 52
coalition 60
Cobbett, William 6
Cobden, Richard 15
Cold War 140–1, 144, 151,
  158–9
collectivization 122
Collectivism 38
Combination Acts 9, 20
communism 140, 143, 146–9,
  150, 152, 158–9
Companies Act 1844 15
Concert of Europe 79
Congress of Berlin 1878 44
Congress of Vienna 1815 24
congress system 24
congresses 79
Conservative Party 42–3, 48–9,
  59, 62–3, 66
Consolidated Fund 4
Contagious Diseases Act 1864 23
Corn Laws 1815 6
Corn Laws, repeal of 15, 42
Corrupt Practices Act 1883
coup d'état 86
Crimean War 25, 87
Criminal Law Amendment
  Act 1873 38–9
Cripps 66

Crompton's mule 18
Cross, Richard 43
Cuba 152
Curragh mutiny 51
Czechoslovakia 65

Dardenelles campaign 60
Dawes plan 1924 64
death rate 22
Decembrist revolt 80
denazification 139
Derby, Lord 42
Derbyshire rising 7
disease 22
disestablishment 38, 50
Disraeli, Benjamin 15, 38, 40–1,
  42–5
Dissenters 13
divine right 80
domestic system 18
Dreikaiserbund 1881 96–7
Dreyfus case 93

Eastern question 24, 44
Education Act 1870 38–9, 54
Education Act 1876 43
Employer and Workman
  Act 1876 43
Enabling Act (Germany) 1933 120
entente 57
Entente cordiale 108
European history 1815–1894 77–
  106
European history 1895–1945 107
European unity 156–7
Evangelicals 12, 21

Factory Act 1844 15
Factory Act 1878 43
Factory Acts 13, 15, 21, 43
Fashoda incident 1898 49, 56
Fawcett, Millicent 54
Fenian outrages 50
Ferdinand, Archduke Franz 109
feudalism 84
First World War 108–9, 110–11
forcible feeding 55
foreign policy 1815–1865 24–5
foreign policy 1902–1914 56
foreign policy in the 1930s 64–5
Forster's Education Act 1870 38–9
Fox, Charles 4
France 1815–1848 82
Frankfurt parliament 1849 84
free trade 8, 14, 19
French revolutions 5, 82–3, 84–5
French Third Republic 92–3
Fry, Elizabeth 9

Garibaldi 89
General Strike 63
Genoa Conference 1922 64
genocide 121, 127
German unification 90–1
Gladstone, William 19, 38–41, 46
Gordon, General 41
government of national unity 60
Great Exhibition 1851 18
Great Reform Act 1832 10–11, 16
Grey, Earl 10–11
gunboat diplomacy 25

habeas corpus 7
Hardenburg 78
Hardie, Keir 58
Henderson 59, 60
Hitler 64–5, 111, 119, 120, 126–7
Hodgkinson's amendment 46
Hohenzollern candidature 87, 91
Holy Alliance 79
home rule (Irish) 41, 50–1
Home Rule Bill 1886 50
Home Rule Bill 1893 50
Home Rule Bill 1912 51
House of Lords, conflict with
    Liberals 53
Housing 22, 61, 62, 67
Housing Act 1919 61
Housing Act 1949 67
Howard, John 9
Hungry Forties 14
Hunt, Henry 'Orator' 7
Huskisson 8, 9, 19
Hyndman, H. M. 58

Import Duties Act 1932 63
income tax, introduction of 5
independence of former
    colonies 154–55
Independent Labour Party 58
industrialization 18
Ireland, and Pitt 5
Irish Free State 51
Irish home rule 41
Irish Land Act 1870 38–9, 50
Irish Land Act 1881 41, 50
Irish potato famine 15
Italy 87, 88–9, 116–17

Jameson raid 56
Junkers 94

Kadets 114
Kellogg–Briand Pact 64, 150
Kemal 111
Kenney, Annie 55
Khartoum 41
Kilmainham Treaty 41, 50

knife-and-fork issue 16
Korean War 143, 148, 151
Kornilov affair 114
Kossuth 85
Kruger telegram 56
kulaks 122
Kulturkampf 95

Labour Party 58–9, 66–7
Labour Representation
    Committee 58
laissez–faire 6, 20–2
Land Purchase Act 1891 51
League of Nations 111, 142, 150
Lebensraum 126
legitimacy 78
Lend-Lease 140, 143
liberal empire 86
Liberal Party 38–41, 52–3, 54, 59,
    60–1
liberalism 78, 84, 116
Licensing Act 1872 38–9
Liverpool, Lord 6–9
Lloyd George, David 47, 51,
    52–3, 55, 60–1
Lloyd George Fund 61
Local Government Act 1929
local government reform 1888 48
Locarno Treaties 1925 64
London Working Men's
    Association 16
Long Knives, Night of the 120
Lovett, William 16
Lowe, Robert 46
Luddism 6–7, 18, 20
Lytton, Lord 45

MacDonald, Ramsay 58–9, 63
Manchester School 14
Manchuria 64
Mansion House speech 57
Marriage Act 1836 13
Married Women's Property
    Act 1882 54
Marshall aid 66, 143, 151, 156
Maynooth grant 15, 42
Mazzini 85, 89
Mediterranean agreements 1887
    49, 97
Merchant Shipping Act 1876 43
Merchant Shipping Act 1906 52
Metternich 78, 85
Mexico 87
Midlothian campaign 40, 45
Mines Act 1842 15, 21
Mitteleuropa 126
Molotov–Ribbentrop Pact 1939
    127, 150

Money Bills 53
Monroe doctrine 24, 49
moral-force Chartists 16
Munich agreement 1938 125
Munich Conference 65
Municipal Corporations
    Act 1835 13
municipalization 58
Mussolini 116–17

Napoleon, Louis 86–7
National Assistance Act 1948 67
national debt 4
National Government 1931–
    1939 63
National Insurance Act 1911 52, 67
National Insurance Act 1946 67
national revival 4
nationalization 66
nationalism 78, 84
NATO 67
Naysmith steam hammer 18
New Deal 144
New Liberalism 52
New Towns Act 1946 67
new unions 58
Newport rising 17
Nonconformists 13, 38

Oastler, Richard 21
O'Connell, Daniel 9
O'Connor, Feargus 16
Opium War 25
Orleanist house 92
Osbourne judgement 1909
O'Shea divorce case 41

pacifism 64
Palmerston 24–5, 46
Pankhurst, Christabel 55
Pankhurst, Emmeline 54
Paris Commune 92
Parliament Act 1911 47, 53
Parliamentary reform 1867–1918
    46–7
Parnell 41, 50
Peel, Robert 8–9, 10, 14–15, 42
People's Budget 1909 53
People's Charter 1837 16
Peterloo massacre 7
Phoenix Park murders 41
physical-force Chartists 16
Piedmont 88
Pitt the Younger 4–5, 19
plebiscite 86
Plombières agreement 88
plug plot 17
pocket boroughs 10

Poland 65
Poor Law Amendment Act 1834 12
Poor Law Commission 23
poor relief 12
Potsdam 67
proletariat 112
proportional representation (PR) 116, 118
protectionism 94
Prussia 90, 94
public health 22–3
Public Health Act 1875 43

Quadruple Alliance 79

radicals 6, 38
Railway Act 1844 19
railway mania 19
railways 18
Red Guards 147
Redistribution of Seats Act 1885 47
Reform Act 1867 46
Reform Act 1884 47, 48
Reform Bill 1844 40
regency crisis 5
Reinsurance Treaty 1887 97
Representation of the People Act 1918 47, 55
Rhineland 64
Rhodes, Cecil 48
Risorgimento 88
Roosevelt, F. D. 142–3, 144–5
rotten boroughs 10
Rowntree 52
Royal Titles Act 1876 45
Russell, Lord John 46
Russia 1815–1894 80
Russia 1917–1924 114–15, 150
Russian Civil War 61, 114–15, 150
Russo-Japanese War 112

Sale of Food and Drugs Act 1875 43
Salisbury, Lord 40, 47, 48–9
Samuels Commission 63
Sandon's Education Act 1876 43
Sanitary Act 1866
Schlieffen Plan 57
second Balkan crisis 1912–1913 109
Second World War 138–9

Seditious Meetings Act 1817 7
Self-determination 110
sensation mongering 54
Shaftesbury, Lord 13, 21
Shaw, G. B. 58
show trials 123
Sicily 85
Sinn Fein 51
Six Acts 1819 7
slavery 5, 13
Smith, Adam 19
Snowden 59, 63
South Africa 41, 45
Spa Field riot 7
Spanish Civil War 64
Spanish marriages 25
Special Areas Act 1934 63
Speenhamland system 12
splendid isolation 48–9, 56
Stalin 122–3, 141, 150, 151
steam engine 18
Stephenson, George 18
Stolypin 113
Stresemann 110
study skills 169–89
Sudan 41, 48
Sudetenland 65
Suez Canal 41, 44
suffrage 54
suffragettes 54
suffragists 54
superpowers 141

Taff Vale case 58
Taiwan 148
Talleyrand 78
Tamworth manifesto 14
tariff reform 62
tariffs 8, 62
Three Emperors' League 1881 96
Three Fs 41
Trade Union Act 1871 38–9
Trade Union Act 1913 59
trade unions 8–9, 38, 58–9
Trades Disputes Act 63
Trades Union Congress 58, 63
Treaty of Frankfurt 92
Treaty of Versailles 61, 64, 110–11, 119, 124
Treaty of Vienna 1815 78, 87
Treaty of Villafranca 88
Triple Alliance 1882 96
Triple Entente 108

Truman doctrine 143, 151
Tsar Alexander I 78, 80
Tsar Alexander II 81
Tsar Alexander III 81
Tsar Nicholas I 80
Tsar Nicholas II 112–13
Turkey 111
twin evils 78
two nations 20
two-power standard 49

Ulster 51
Ultras 9
Ultras (French) 82
Unemployment Act 1934 63
Unemployment Insurance Act 1927 62
University Tests Act 1871 38–9
US foreign policy 152–3
USA 140–1, 142–3, 144–5, 149, 152–3
USSR 122–3, 140–1, 144, 146, 148, 150–1

Vaccination Act 1840 23
Verona 79
Vienna settlement 1815 78–9, 87, 88
Vietnam War 145, 148–9, 153
Votes for women 54–5

Wall Street crash 59
wars of German unification 87, 91
Washington agreements 1921 64
water supply 22
Watergate 145
Weimar Republic 110, 118–19
Wellington 9
Whig reforms 1833–1841 12–13
Whigs 10–14, 38
White terror 82
Widows, Orphans and Old Age Pensions Act 1925 62
Wilberforce, William 13
Witte 113
workhouse relief 20
workhouses 12, 20

Young England 15, 42

Zinoviev letter 59, 123
Zollverein 90